Everyday
to
Entertaining

Everyday to Entertaining

to

Entertaining

200 sensational recipes
that transform from casual to elegant

Meredith Deeds & Carla Snyder

Robert
ROSE

For complete cataloguing information, see page 384.

Disclaimer

The recipes in this book have been carefully tested by our kitchen and our tasters. To the best of our knowledge, they are safe and nutritious for ordinary use and users. For those people with food or other allergies, or who have special food requirements or health issues, please read the suggested contents of each recipe carefully and determine whether or not they may create a problem for you. All recipes are used at the risk of the consumer.

We cannot be responsible for any hazards, loss or damage that may occur as a result of any recipe use.

For those with special needs, allergies, requirements or health problems, in the event of any doubt, please contact your medical adviser prior to the use of any recipe.

Design & Production: Kevin Cockburn/PageWave Graphics Inc.
Editor: Carol Sherman
Copy Editor: Sheila Wawanash
Recipe Editor: Jennifer MacKenzie

Cover & Recipe Photography
Photographer: Colin Erricson
Associate Photographer: Matt Johannsson
Food Styling: Lasha Andrushko (pages 27, 43, 51, 73, 89, 113, 121, 137, 153, 169, 185, 201, 209, 225, 241, 257, 273, 285, 293, 301, 317, 331, 339, 355) and Kathryn Robertson (cover and pages 2, 6)
Prop Styling: Charlene Erricson

Additional Photography

pages 8–9: ©iStockphoto.com/Stephanie Connell; pages 10–11: ©iStockphoto.com/Lisa Thornberg; pages 12–13: ©iStockphoto.com/Lisa Thornberg, page 14: ©iStockphoto.com/Robyn Mackenzie; page 19: (top left) ©iStockphoto.com/Oleg Karpenko, (top right) ©iStockphoto.com/Daniela Jovanovska-Hristovska, (bottom left) ©iStockphoto.com/Alistair Cotton, (bottom right) ©iStockphoto.com/Svetlana Kolpakova; page 21: ©iStockphoto.com/Barbara Dudzinska; page 24: ©iStockphoto.com/Joe Gough; page 29: ©iStockphoto.com/sf_foodphoto; page 32: ©iStockphoto.com/Matt Boone; page 35: (top left) ©iStockphoto.com/Lauri Patterson, (top right) ©iStockphoto.com/Klaus Sailer, (bottom left) ©iStockphoto.com/Tom Tomczyk, (bottom right) ©iStockphoto.com/Blackbeck; page 37: ©iStockphoto.com/Jorge Gonzalez; page 41: ©iStockphoto.com/Zack Smith; page 45: ©iStockphoto.com/Creativeye99; page 59: (top left) ©iStockphoto.com/George Jurasek, (top right) ©iStockphoto.com/John Solie, (bottom left) ©iStockphoto.com/Jean-Francois Schmit, (bottom right) ©iStockphoto.com/Mark Gillow; page 60: ©iStockphoto.com/kimeveruss; page 65: (top left) ©iStockphoto.com/Tom Foxall, (top right) ©iStockphoto.com/Robyn Mackenzie, (bottom left) ©iStockphoto.com/Simon Jeacle, (bottom right) ©iStockphoto.com/Julie Nicholas; page 67: ©iStockphoto.com/Kelly Cline; page 75: ©iStockphoto.com/Ben Phillips; page 77: ©iStockphoto.com/Floortje; page 79: ©iStockphoto.com/Robert Lopshire; page 81: (top left) ©iStockphoto.com/zkruger, (top right) ©iStockphoto.com/Emilie Duchesne, (bottom right) ©iStockphoto.com/Bronxgebiet, (bottom left) ©iStockphoto.com/jerrydeutsch; page 83: ©iStockphoto.com/Eric Hood; page 97: (top left) ©iStockphoto.com/Joan Vicent Cantó Roig, (top right) ©iStockphoto.com/Gabor Izso, (bottom left) ©iStockphoto.com/Tanya_F, (bottom right) ©iStockphoto.com/YinYang; page 102: ©iStockphoto.com/John Goldstein; page 105: (top left) ©iStockphoto.com/Eric Hood, (top right) ©iStockphoto.com/Emilie Duchesne, (bottom left) ©iStockphoto.com/Alejandro Rivera, (bottom right) ©iStockphoto.com/Gary Cookson; page 107: ©iStockphoto.com/akaplummer; page 115: ©iStockphoto.com/Dean Birinyi; page 117: ©iStockphoto.com/Melissa Woods; page 123: ©iStockphoto.com/Vladimir Vladimirov; page 125: ©iStockphoto.com/YinYang; page 127: ©iStockphoto.com/Ben Phillips; page 129: (top right) ©iStockphoto.com/Srdjan Stefanovic, (top right) ©iStockphoto.com/Joan Vicent Cantó Roig, (bottom left) ©iStockphoto.com/Ivan Bajic, (bottom right) ©iStockphoto.com/Kelly Cline; page 131: ©iStockphoto.com/Sandra O'Claire; page 138: ©iStockphoto.com/Jill Fromer; page 142: ©iStockphoto.com/Magdalena Kucova; page 144: ©iStockphoto.com/stuartbur; page 147: ©iStockphoto.com/Graham Klotz; page 151: ©iStockphoto.com/Joan Vicent Cantó Roig; page 155: ©iStockphoto.com/Kjell Brynildsen; page 157: ©iStockphoto.com/Judith Winn; page 161: (top left) ©iStockphoto.com/Kelly Cline, (top right) ©iStockphoto.com/Jill Chen, (bottom left) ©iStockphoto.com/Robert Linton, (bottom right) ©iStockphoto.com/Gabrielle Morehead; page 163: ©iStockphoto.com/eyewave; page 171: ©iStockphoto.com/Chris Elwell; page 176: ©iStockphoto.com/Stephanie Connell; page 181: ©iStockphoto.com/Amanda Kerr; page 187: ©iStockphoto.com/picamaniac; page 193: ©iStockphoto.com/Oliver Hamalainen, (top right) ©iStockphoto.com/urric, (bottom left) ©iStockphoto.com/Robert Glas, (bottom right) ©iStockphoto.com/Melissa Woods; page 195: ©iStockphoto.com/Paweł Burgiel; page 197: ©iStockphoto.com/Imagesbybarbara; page 199: ©iStockphoto.com/tedestudio; page 205: ©iStockphoto.com/Paul Turner; page 213: ©iStockphoto.com/Lew Robertson; page 215: ©iStockphoto.com/Andreas Kaspar; page 216: ©iStockphoto.com/Svetl; page 219: ©iStockphoto.com/Nadezda Verbenko; page 221: ©iStockphoto.com/Lehner; page 223: ©iStockphoto.com/Doug Berry; page 227: ©iStockphoto.com/Nolwenn Daniel; page 229: ©iStockphoto.com/Joan Vicent Cantó Roig; page 233: (top left) ©iStockphoto.com/akaplummer, (top right) ©iStockphoto.com/John Shepherd, (bottom left) ©iStockphoto.com/Emilie Duchesne, (bottom right) ©iStockphoto.com/roelofse; page 235: ©iStockphoto.com/Sue Riseley; page 237: ©iStockphoto.com/Kelly Cline; page 247: ©iStockphoto.com/Jason Poole; page 248: ©iStockphoto.com/Robyn Mackenzie; page 251: ©iStockphoto.com/Elena Elisseeva; page 253: ©iStockphoto.com/YinYang; page 255: ©iStockphoto.com/vikif; page 259: ©iStockphoto.com/Adrienne Miller; page 261: ©iStockphoto.com/travellinglight; page 265: (top left) ©iStockphoto.com/Eva Serrabassa, (top right) ©iStockphoto.com/Jim Jurica, (bottom left) ©iStockphoto.com/Nick M. Do, (bottom right) ©iStockphoto.com/Liv Friis-Larsen; page 269: ©iStockphoto.com/VMJones; page 275: ©iStockphoto.com/RawFile; page 276: ©iStockphoto.com/Andrew Rich; page 293: (top left) ©iStockphoto.com/Tomas Bercic, (top right) ©iStockphoto.com/Maris Zemgalietis, (bottom left) ©iStockphoto.com/Mark Wragg, (bottom right) ©iStockphoto.com/Jeff Giniewiczl; page 295: ©iStockphoto.com/inaquim; page 297: ©iStockphoto.com/Tanya_F; page 309: (top left) ©iStockphoto.com/kkgas, (top bottom) ©iStockphoto.com/matka_Wariatka, (bottom left) ©iStockphoto.com/Kristen Johansen, (bottom right) ©iStockphoto.com/jerrydeutsch; page 311: ©iStockphoto.com/Mark Fairey; page 319: ©iStockphoto.com/Tatyana Nyshko; page 322: ©iStockphoto.com/Svetl; page 325: ©iStockphoto.com/Kelly Cline; page 341: ©iStockphoto.com/gaffera; page 343: ©iStockphoto.com/YinYang; page 347: (top left) ©iStockphoto.com/ac_bnphotos, (top right) ©iStockphoto.com/NightAndDayImages, (bottom left) ©iStockphoto.com/Kelly Cline, (bottom right) ©iStockphoto.com/Kelly Cline; page 351: ©iStockphoto.com/house_red; page 353: ©iStockphoto.com/Andreas Kaspar; page 361: ©iStockphoto.com/Richard Vandenberg; page 363: (top left) ©iStockphoto.com/matka_Wariatka, (top right) ©iStockphoto.com/Magdalena Kucova, (bottom left) ©iStockphoto.com/crolique, (bottom right) ©iStockphoto.com/Joan Vicent Cantó Roig; page 365: ©iStockphoto.com/FotografiaBasica; page 371: ©iStockphoto.com/Ha Huynh.

Cover and page 2: Beef Fajitas (page 196)
Cover and page 6: Lime and Tequila–Marinated Flank Steak with Sweet-and-Sour Chipotle Sauce (page 198)

We acknowledge the financial support of the Government of Canada through the Book Publishing Industry Development Program (BPIDP) for our publishing activities.

Published by Robert Rose Inc.
120 Eglinton Avenue East, Suite 800, Toronto, Ontario, Canada M4P 1E2
Tel: (416) 322-6552 Fax: (416) 322-6936
www.robertrose.ca

Printed and bound in Canada

1 2 3 4 5 6 7 8 9 TCP 19 18 17 16 15 14 13 12 11

To cookbook authors everywhere,
who understand the agony and the ecstasy
of the creative process.

Contents

Acknowledgments

Many thanks to our testers, friends, students and family all: Julie Neri, Ann Norvell, Barbara Tatum, Greg Griffith, Beth Balzarini, Camerin Winovich, Anne Jenkins, Sarah McNally, Lisa Simpson, Linda DeCioccio, Anne Pitkin, Alicia Ravens, Barb Snow, Mary Lohman, Dave McIlvaine, Mary Ann Mooney, Beth Anne Sharkey, Julie Gehling, Auddie Gundling, Anne Haynam, Jennifer Wolfe Webb, Jamie Stevens, Nancy Studebaker, Brigitte Gottfried, Patti Hermsen, Elsa de Cardenas, Rose Reedy, Judy Jaffray, Betsy Spak, Judy Meyers, Jan Redman, Rosemary McDonald and Theresa and Bob Delphus. Their willingness to break out the pots and pans and give us their honest evaluation is appreciated beyond words.

Introduction

Everyday to Entertaining is full of multipurpose recipes that any home cook can accomplish with ease and panache. We start out with the "basic" version of a dish and with a few changes also offer a more sophisticated version of the recipe.

Gazpacho is a perfect example; it's mouth-watering and easily accomplished, but it's also versatile. When yellow tomatoes are exchanged for the usual red and the resulting yellow tomato gazpacho is topped with crab salad instead of croutons, the dish is transformed into something completely different and unexpected. But the real beauty of this transformation is that once the cook has learned the technique required to make "everyday" gazpacho, they can confidently ladle the "entertaining" yellow tomato version into the same dinner guests' bowls without feeling as though they've served the same dish twice.

This cookbook features delectable basic recipes ranging from the straightforward White Wine Braised Chicken to Grilled Thai Shrimp. Then each is presented in a more stylized or dressed-up version. Sometimes these variations can be as simple as adding a few additional ingredients. Using this technique, we transform the simple White Wine Braised Chicken into Coq au Vin with Mushrooms, Bacon and Pearl Onions. Sometimes, though, as in the case of the Grilled Thai Shrimp, the change is more complete. In the dressed-up version here, we use the shrimp as the foundation for an extraordinary Vietnamese Grilled Shrimp Summer Roll with Peanut Dipping Sauce.

Chapters include everything from appetizers to meat and poultry, fish and seafood, sides and, finally, the finishing touch — desserts.

Most recipes include a section titled The Dish that features an important ingredient, technique or entertaining tip.

And *Everyday to Entertaining* is filled with confidence-building tips drawn from our years of teaching experience. These tips help the reader execute the dish with ease and, of course, style. In addition, for the time-pressed, we include hands-on and start to finish times and make-ahead notes.

Ingredient Essentials

The ingredients in this book make some assumptions about what is standard when it comes to basic ingredients. For the best results, follow the recipe and use the recommended ingredient, unless other options are indicated in a tip or variation. Here is a list of what is assumed:

- All eggs used are large eggs.

- Whole milk and yogurt unless otherwise specified.

- Butter is unsalted unless otherwise specified.

- Fresh vegetables and fruits are medium size unless otherwise indicated. Any inedible peels, skins, seeds and cores are removed unless otherwise indicated. Wash and dry all produce before using.

- "Onions" means regular cooking onions unless otherwise indicated.

- "Mushrooms" means white button mushrooms unless otherwise indicated.

- With canned tomatoes and tomato products, the juice is also used unless the recipe instructs you to drain it.

- When broth (chicken, beef or vegetable) is called for, homemade is the ideal, but low-sodium store-brought broth is a close second. If you can only find canned broth, do not dilute.

- Chopped or minced garlic is freshly chopped or minced, not purchased already minced and preserved.

- When greasing barbecue grill, rub the grate with an oiled paper towel before you turn it on.

First Impressions
Appetizers

Everyday		to	Entertaining	
Tapenade	16	▶	Sun-Dried Tomato Tapenade and Mascarpone Phyllo Bites	17
Smoked Salmon Platter	18	▶	Smoked Salmon Mousse with Caper Caviar on Endive Spears	20
Fresh Tomato and Basil Bruschettas	22	▶	Roasted Tomato, Mozzarella and Pesto Bruschettas	23
Grilled Prosciutto-Wrapped Scallop Skewers	26	▶	Prosciutto-Grilled Scallops with South Seas Salsa	28
Basic Sliders	30	▶	Trio of Uptown Sliders	31
Mini Grilled Caramelized Onion and Brie Sandwiches	34	▶	Brie Strudel with Red Onion and Mango Chutney	36
Pico de Gallo	38	▶	Black Bean and Corn Salsa Mini Tostadas with Chipotle Sour Cream	39
Shrimp Cocktail Shooters with Pickled Vegetables	40	▶	Tequila Bloody Mary Shrimp Cocktails	42
Crab Dip with Artichokes and Jalapeño	44	▶	Crab and Goat Cheese Bouchées	47
White Bean Salsa	48	▶	Bruschetta with Tuscan White Beans, Kalamata Olives and Roasted Red Peppers	50
Rustic Cheese Tart with Sun-Dried Tomatoes	52	▶	Pissaladière with Leek, Olive and Sun-Dried Tomatoes	53
Tartine with Figs, Prosciutto and Ricotta	54	▶	Tartine with Roasted Figs, Prosciutto and Gorgonzola	55
Wild Mushroom and Thyme Spread	56	▶	Wild Mushroom Turnovers	58

Tapenade

We love this briny, garlicky, olive-based spread because its uses are endless. How can we transform a simple vinaigrette into something special? Whisk in some tapenade. How can we get an appetizer to the table in less than 2 minutes? Slice up a baguette and serve it with a bowl of tapenade. Want to make those mashed potatoes sing? You got it — fold in some tapenade. Have we made our point yet? The best thing is that you can make it days ahead of time and have it ready in the fridge, just waiting for its next assignment.

Makes about 2 cups (500 mL)

Hands-on time
20 minutes

Start to finish
20 minutes

Make Ahead
Tapenade can be made up to 1 week ahead and kept covered and refrigerated.

- **Food processor**

1½ cups	kalamata olives, pitted	375 mL
2	cloves garlic, minced	2
3	anchovy fillets	3
3 tbsp	capers (preferably packed in salt), rinsed	45 mL
	Zest of 1 lemon	
1 tbsp	freshly squeezed lemon juice	15 mL
¼ cup	chopped flat-leaf parsley	60 mL
2 tsp	chopped fresh thyme	10 mL
	Freshly ground black pepper	
¼ cup	extra virgin olive oil	60 mL
	Toasted baguette slices	
	Thinly sliced Granny Smith apple	

1. In a food processor, process olives, garlic, anchovies, capers, lemon zest, lemon juice, parsley, thyme, black pepper to taste and olive oil until ingredients are combined, but still slightly chunky. Transfer to a serving bowl and serve with toasted baguette slices and thin slices of Granny Smith apple.

THE DISH **Pitted Olives.** If you've ever spent quality time pitting olives, this one will be self-explanatory. Pitted olives are a common sight at grocery stores everywhere these days. That said, even if you buy pitted olives, look through them to make sure a stray pit hasn't found its way into the batch.

If by chance you feel the need to pit olives yourself, the easiest method is to lay an unsuspecting subject on a cutting board and whack it or squish it, if you prefer, with the broad side of a chef's knife. Then the pit can be separated from the olive easily.

Sun-Dried Tomato Tapenade and Mascarpone Phyllo Bites

Sun-dried tomatoes, even with their intense flavor, still manage to have a calming effect on the inherent brininess of tapenade. Here we're using the combination to top off purchased mini phyllo cups filled with creamy, herb- and lemon-scented mascarpone cheese. The contrast between the brightness of the sun-dried tapenade and the richness of the cheese makes this a wonderful little bite.

Makes 30 bites

Hands-on time
35 minutes

Start to finish
35 minutes

Make Ahead

The sun-dried tomato tapenade can be made up to 4 days ahead and kept covered and refrigerated. The mascarpone cheese filling can be made the day before. Assemble no more than 1 hour before serving.

- **Piping bag with round tip**

½	recipe Tapenade (page 16)	½
½ cup	finely chopped sun-dried tomatoes in oil	125 mL
1 cup	mascarpone cheese, softened	250 mL
1½ tsp	finely chopped fresh thyme	7 mL
2 tbsp	freshly squeezed lemon juice	30 mL
Pinch	salt	Pinch
	Freshly ground black pepper	
30	mini phyllo shells	30
30	whole flat-leaf parsley leaves	30

1. In a medium bowl, combine tapenade and sun-dried tomatoes. Set aside.

2. In another bowl, combine mascarpone cheese, thyme, lemon juice, salt, and pepper to taste.

3. Place phyllo shells on a serving platter and spoon or pipe, using a piping bag and round tip, about 1½ tsp (7 mL) of the mascarpone cheese into each shell. Carefully spoon about ½ tsp (2 mL) of the tapenade on top of cheese (save remaining tapenade for other uses. See page 16 for suggestions). Top each with a parsley leaf. Serve.

Fashion Plate

These lovely little bites would be wonderful served on the deck as you're grilling Grilled Herbed Pork Tenderloin (page 212) with Grilled Summer Vegetable Salad on Sourdough Croutons (page 82). Top it all off with Oranges and Pink Grapefruit with Cardamom and Ginger (page 373) and you've just experienced the perfect summer evening.

Smoked Salmon Platter

During the holidays, when entertaining becomes more a probability than a possibility, the clever host will keep the makings for this delicious and elegant dish on hand at all times. You can throw together this colorful platter of smoked salmon, capers, red onion and dilled sour cream in a matter of minutes, making it one of the best options for spontaneous partying.

Serves 8 to 10

Hands-on time
15 minutes

Start to finish
15 minutes

Make Ahead

The platter can be assembled up to 4 hours ahead and kept covered and refrigerated.

½ cup	sour cream	125 mL
1 tbsp	chopped fresh dill	15 mL
1 tsp	grated lemon zest	5 mL
Pinch	salt	Pinch
12 oz	thinly sliced smoked salmon	375 g
½ cup	chopped red onion	125 mL
3 tbsp	drained capers, rinsed	45 mL
	Crackers or toast points	

1. In a small bowl, combine sour cream, dill, lemon zest and salt.

2. Arrange salmon slices on large platter. Place red onion and capers separately into small ramekins. Arrange ramekins and sour cream mixture on platter with salmon. Serve with crackers or toast points on the side.

THE DISH **A Cool Serving Platter.** Whenever you're dishing out something simple, make sure the dish it sits on is something to talk about. Find a lovely piece that reflects your personality. Do you tend toward the modern and contemporary? Or are you more traditional? Whatever you are, you can find a plate that screams, "Look at me! And while you're looking, feel free to nosh on some delicious smoked salmon."

Fashion Plate

For some reason we tend to reserve smoked salmon for appetizer parties, setting it out on a table with an array of other tasty bites. Try this with Mini Grilled Caramelized Onion and Brie Sandwiches (page 34), Wild Mushroom and Thyme Spread (page 56) and a colorful crudités tray.

Smoked Salmon Mousse with Caper Caviar on Endive Spears

We love it when a plan comes together, and in the case of this dish, it really came together. We wanted to take all the flavor elements of a simple, elegant smoked salmon platter and transform them into something even more sophisticated, and this light, mouth-watering, tuxedo-worthy appetizer is the result. The smoked salmon is whipped into a mousse, which rests like a cloud on a spear of crisp endive. Capers, onions and dill are turned into a relish, or "caviar," and spooned delicately on top of the mousse. If there was ever a reason to polish your silver platter, this dish is it.

Serves 6 to 8

Hands-on time
30 minutes

Start to finish
1 hour 30 minutes

Make Ahead

The mousse and caper relish may be made 1 day in advance and kept covered and refrigerated. The endive spears may be assembled up to 4 hours ahead and kept covered and refrigerated.

- **Food processor**

1 tsp	unflavored gelatin	5 mL
4 oz	sliced smoked salmon	125 g
¼ cup	sour cream	60 mL
1 tbsp	freshly squeezed lemon juice	15 mL
	Salt	
½ cup	heavy or whipping (35%) cream	125 mL
3 tbsp	drained capers, rinsed	45 mL
¼ cup	finely chopped red onion	60 mL
1 tbsp	freshly squeezed lemon juice	15 mL
1 tbsp	olive oil	15 mL
2 tsp	finely chopped fresh dill	10 mL
3	heads white and/or red Belgian endive, separated into spears	3

1. In a very small saucepan, sprinkle gelatin over 2 tbsp (30 mL) water and let soften for 1 minute. Heat mixture over medium-low heat, stirring, just until gelatin is dissolved (do not let boil). Let cool to room temperature.

2. In a food processor, purée salmon, sour cream, lemon juice, ½ tsp (2 mL) salt and gelatin mixture until smooth. Transfer to a medium bowl.

3. In a bowl, using an electric mixer, beat whipping cream until it just holds stiff peaks. Fold into salmon purée and season with salt to taste until combined well. Refrigerate mousse, covered, for 1 hour or until slightly firm.

4. Meanwhile, in a small bowl, combine capers, red onion, lemon juice, olive oil and dill. Cover and refrigerate until you're ready to assemble.

5. To assemble, arrange endive spears on a platter. Spoon or pipe, using a piping bag with a star tip, 1 tbsp (15 mL) of mousse onto end of each spear. Spoon $\frac{1}{2}$ tsp (2 mL) of caper caviar on top of salmon mousse.

THE DISH **An Academy Award Party.** OK, we have to admit that we've never had this particular party, but this appetizer screams, "And the winner is . . ." Sometimes it's all right for the tail to wag the dog, and there's no reason to be embarrassed to throw a bash just to show off a great dish or have a martini — whatever works.

Fashion Plate

Pull out all the stops for this one and serve it with a few other sophisticated bites like Tartine with Figs, Prosciutto and Ricotta (page 54), Sun-Dried Tomato Tapenade and Mascarpone Phyllo Bites (page 17) and Bruschetta with Tuscan White Beans, Kalamata Olives and Roasted Red Peppers (page 50).

Fresh Tomato and Basil Bruschettas

Tomato and basil are the dynamic duo of bruschetta. Certainly the combo most people think of for this popular Italian appetizer, it's also one of the simplest. Fresh ripe tomatoes, a hint of garlic and a generous helping of fragrant basil make this appetizer the epitome of summer. These are really best made right before serving.

Makes 36 bruschettas

Hands-on time
25 minutes

Start to finish
30 minutes

● **Preheat broiler**

1	large baguette, cut into 36 ½-inch (1 cm) slices	1
½ cup	olive oil	125 mL
2	large cloves garlic, cut in half	2
4	medium ripe tomatoes, cut into small dice	4
¼ cup	chopped fresh basil	60 mL
1 tbsp	balsamic vinegar	15 mL
	Salt and freshly ground black pepper	
	Extra virgin olive oil	

1. Brush bread slices lightly on both sides with olive oil. Place bread on a pan and broil until lightly browned on both sides. Let cool. When cool enough to handle, rub one side of each bread slice with cut side of a garlic clove. Set bread slices aside.

2. In a medium bowl, stir together tomatoes, basil and vinegar. Season with salt and pepper to taste.

3. Spoon some of the topping onto each slice of bread and drizzle with a little bit of olive oil. Place on a serving plate and serve immediately.

THE DISH **Ripe Red Tomatoes.** To make this dish with out-of-season tomatoes — James Beard described them accurately as tasting like "pink flannel" — just makes no sense. If you can't find great tomatoes, try using the cherry tomatoes referred to as grape tomatoes. They are usually good any time of year. Although you'll have to spend some time quartering them, it's worth the effort.

Roasted Tomato, Mozzarella and Pesto Bruschettas

Borrowing from the fabulous flavors of the Fresh Tomato and Basil Bruschettas, here we've taken them one step further, roasting grape tomatoes and drizzling them with basil pesto for an intense hit of summer even when summer is long gone. Small cubes of creamy fresh mozzarella are added to the mix, adding lovely flavor and color to these delightful bites.

Makes 36 bruschettas

Hands-on time
20 minutes

Start to finish
50 minutes

Make Ahead

The tomatoes can be roasted up to 2 days ahead and kept covered and refrigerated. The bread can be toasted up to 8 hours ahead and kept at room temperature. Add mozzarella and assemble just before serving.

- **Preheat oven to 425°F (220°C)**
- **Rimmed baking sheet**

2 cups	grape tomatoes	500 mL
2 tbsp plus ¾ cup	extra virgin olive oil, divided	200 mL
	Salt and freshly ground black pepper	
1	large baguette, cut into 36 ½-inch (1 cm) slices	1
2	large cloves garlic, cut in half	2
12 oz	fresh mozzarella, cut into small dice	375 g
¼ cup	Pesto (page 25) or store-bought	60 mL

1. In a bowl, toss together tomatoes, 2 tbsp (30 mL) of the oil and salt and pepper to taste. Arrange tomatoes on baking sheet. Bake in preheated oven for about 30 minutes or until tomatoes are wrinkled and slightly browned in spots. Let cool.

2. Preheat broiler. Brush bread slices lightly on both sides with ½ cup (125 mL) of olive oil. Place bread on a pan and broil for about 2 minutes per side or until lightly browned on both sides. Let cool. When cool enough to handle, rub one side of each bread slice with cut side of a garlic clove. Set bread slices aside.

3. In a medium bowl, stir together tomatoes and mozzarella. Season with salt and pepper to taste.

4. In a small bowl, whisk together pesto with ¼ cup (60 mL) of olive oil. Spoon some of the tomato topping onto each slice of bread and drizzle with a little bit of pesto oil. Place on a serving plate and serve immediately.

Continued on next page

Real Bread. What's real bread, you ask? Isn't any bread real? Well . . . not so much. Bread is an ingredient we take seriously, and not all breads are created equal. For instance, the soft white bread that kids love to roll into what we used to call "bread balls" and either eat or throw at their siblings is not real bread. Real bread has a crust and cannot be crushed without considerable crackling and spraying of crust dust. Its inside is flavorful and tender but sturdy — nothing like the cotton candy texture of some "French baguettes" sold at your local grocery store. Do yourself a favor and find a good baker. Trust us, it will be worth it.

Fashion Plate

We love to serve these tasty morsels outside on the deck when we're grilling something for dinner. We often throw the bread on the grill to toast while we're waiting for the main event and pile the luscious tomato mixture on them while they're still warm. OMG is that good. Serve with Grilled Veal Rolls with Arugula, Currants and Pine Nuts (page 190) and Limoncello Shortcakes with Berries and Vanilla Gelato (page 352).

Pesto

Buying small expensive jars of pesto will be a thing of the past once you realize how easy it is to do at home. It freezes beautifully as well.

Makes about 1 cup (250 mL)

Hands-on time
10 minutes

Start to finish
10 minutes

Make Ahead

If not using immediately, store in an airtight container with a thin coating of olive oil on top to keep the sauce from turning dark. Pesto keeps well in the refrigerator for up to 1 week or frozen for up to 2 months.

- **Food processor**

2 cups	packed fresh basil leaves	500 mL
1/2 cup	extra virgin olive oil	125 mL
2	cloves garlic, chopped	2
2 tbsp	pine nuts	30 mL
1/3 cup	freshly grated Parmesan cheese	75 mL
2 tbsp	grated Pecorino Romano	30 mL
1 tsp	salt	5 mL
	Freshly ground black pepper	

1. In a food processor, pulse basil, olive oil, garlic, pine nuts, Parmesan and Romano cheeses until finely chopped but not completely puréed. Stop from time to time and scrape down side of bowl, if necessary. Taste for seasoning and add more salt or black pepper, if desired.

Grilled Prosciutto-Wrapped Scallop Skewers

Wrapping delicate, sweet, lemony scallops in prosciutto is a wonderful way to add flavor and keep in moisture. We use this technique time and time again with all kinds of seafood and shellfish, because it's impressive and easy. Just breeze into the kitchen, spend just a few minutes cooking, and make sure you spritz yourself with water on the way out so people think you really worked hard. These are best if made just before serving.

Makes 6 skewers
Serves 6 as an appetizer

Hands-on time
20 minutes

Start to finish
40 minutes

- **Six 12-inch (30 cm) bamboo skewers, soaked in water for 30 minutes**
- **Preheat greased barbecue grill to medium-high**

1	clove garlic, minced	1
	Olive oil	
2 tbsp	freshly squeezed lemon juice	30 mL
½ tsp	salt	2 mL
12	large sea scallops	12
6	thin slices prosciutto, sliced in half lengthwise	6

1. In a medium bowl, combine garlic, 3 tbsp (45 mL) oil, lemon juice and salt. Add scallops and toss to coat.

2. Wrap each scallop with 1 strip of prosciutto. Thread 2 scallops on each skewer and brush with additional oil. Grill scallops about 5 inches (12.5 cm) above heat for 3 to 4 minutes per side or until just cooked through and prosciutto is slightly crispy.

3. Alternatively, lightly brush scallops with additional oil and grill in a hot well-seasoned ridged grill pan, covered, over medium-high heat, 3 to 4 minutes per side or until cooked through and prosciutto is slightly crispy.

THE DISH **Dry or Dry-Packed Scallops.** Sometimes scallops and other seafood are soaked in a chemical called phosphate, which helps them retain their moisture. Too much phosphate can also cause them to soak up additional water, adding to the buyer's cost and ruining their lovely sweet flavor. Savvy scallop shoppers buy scallops labeled "dry" or "dry-packed" that have not been soaked in chemicals and are generally considered to be of higher quality.

Prosciutto-Grilled Scallops with South Seas Salsa

South Seas Salsa, South Seas Salsa, South Seas Salsa. Try saying that five times fast! It's definitely a mouthful in more ways than one. This sunny combination of mango, pineapple, mint and cilantro turn our simple Grilled Prosciutto-Wrapped Scallops into a dish that will make you want to put your Mai Tai down, brush the sand off your feet and wander into the dining room. These are best if made just before serving.

Makes 6 skewers
Serves 6 as an appetizer

Hands-on time
20 minutes

Start to finish
40 minutes

- **Six 12-inch (30 cm) bamboo skewers, soaked in water for 30 minutes**
- **Preheat greased barbecue grill to medium-high**

1	clove garlic, minced	1
	Olive oil	
2 tbsp	freshly squeezed lemon juice	30 mL
12	large sea scallops	12
1	mango, cut into small dice	1
1 cup	fresh pineapple, cut into small dice	250 mL
½ cup	finely chopped red onion	125 mL
2 tbsp	finely chopped fresh mint	30 mL
2 tbsp	finely chopped fresh cilantro	30 mL
1	serrano chile pepper, seeded and finely chopped	1
2 tbsp	freshly squeezed lime juice	30 mL
1 tbsp	liquid honey	15 mL
Pinch	salt	Pinch
6	thin slices prosciutto, sliced in half lengthwise	6

1. In a medium bowl, combine garlic, 3 tbsp (45 mL) oil and lemon juice. Add scallops and toss to coat. Marinate in refrigerator for 10 minutes.

2. Meanwhile, in a medium bowl, combine mango, pineapple, red onion, mint, cilantro, chile, lime juice, honey and salt. Set aside.

3. Wrap each scallop with 1 strip of prosciutto. Thread 2 scallops on each skewer and brush lightly with additional oil. Grill scallops about 5 inches (12.5 cm) above heat for 3 to 4 minutes per side or until just cooked through.

4. Alternatively, brush scallops with additional oil and grill in a hot well-seasoned ridged grill pan, covered, over medium-high heat, 3 to 4 minutes per side or until cooked through.

5. Serve scallops with salsa on the side.

THE DISH **A Ripe Mango.** An unripe mango is a sad thing. It's hard and more sour than sweet. When shopping for mangos, look for fruit that has orange-reddish skin, gives slightly when pressed and smells like, well — like a mango. Remember that mangos will continue to ripen until you eat them. To slow this process, store them in the refrigerator until needed.

Fashion Plate

We like to serve this dish as a prelude to Tequila-Marinated Chicken Breasts with Mango Citrus Salsa (page 234) and finish the meal with Vanilla Gelato with Summer Berries and Limoncello (page 350).

Basic Sliders

Is it just us, or have burgers gotten bigger? It seems like restaurants have stopped making quarter pounders and have now upped the ante, and the scale, to three-quarter pounders. Well, we're sorry, but it's hard to look good trying to wrap your mouth around a burger that's as big as your purse. That must be why the slider was invented. It's perfect for anyone who craves a juicy, beefy burger but can't commit to eating the whole cow. These adorable and tasty little numbers will satisfy the urge to be bad while still looking good.

Makes 12

Hands-on time
20 minutes

Start to finish
35 minutes

Tip

Along with the standard mayo, mustard and ketchup, try offering a variety of different cheeses, bacon, sautéed mushrooms, barbecue sauce, etc.

Make Ahead

The patties can be assembled up to 1 day ahead and kept covered and refrigerated. They can also be frozen for up to 4 weeks. Thaw in refrigerator before cooking.

● **Preheat broiler**

12 oz	ground chuck	375 g
12 oz	ground sirloin	375 g
1 tsp	salt	5 mL
½ tsp	freshly ground black pepper	2 mL
12	dinner rolls, cut in half crosswise (see The Dish, page 33)	12
2 tbsp	unsalted butter, melted	30 mL

1. In a large bowl, combine ground chunk and sirloin with salt and pepper. Form into 12 patties, about 3 inches (7.5 cm) wide.

2. Brush both cut sides of rolls lightly with butter. Place, cut side up, on a baking sheet. Toast rolls under preheated broiler.

3. Grill or pan-fry patties over medium heat for about 2½ minutes per side for medium-well or until cooked through. Place patties on the toasted rolls and garnish as desired.

THE DISH **The Proper Cuts of Beef.** It may seem like a good idea to use 99% lean beef for these burgers. Unfortunately, the result will be a burger as dry and tough as a hockey puck. Using a combination of ground chuck and sirloin gives just the right amount of fat, flavor and tenderness.

Fashion Plate

These can be served with a variety of other appetizers for a cocktail party. Or you can make them the main course by making lots and setting up a condiment bar for your guests to concoct their own slider creations.

Trio of Uptown Sliders

Sophisticated sliders have become the darling of the upscale bar menu. More and more, you can find all kinds of creative combinations sandwiched in a baby bun. We've seen everything from foie gras to tuna tartar sliders, and people seem to universally love them. With that in mind, we thought it would be fun to create our own little ménage à trois, in slider terms of course.

Makes 12

Hands-on time
1 hour

Start to finish
1 hour 20 minutes

Make Ahead

The flavored mayonnaises can be made up to 2 days ahead and kept covered and refrigerated. The balsamic onions can be made 2 days ahead and kept covered and refrigerated. The onions can be rewarmed in the microwave on High for 30 seconds or until warm. Sliders should be cooked and assembled just before serving.

Southwest Sliders

Chipotle Mayo

½ cup	mayonnaise	125 mL
2 tbsp	minced chipotle chile peppers in adobo sauce	30 mL
2 tsp	freshly squeezed lime juice	10 mL

Sliders

1	recipe Basic Sliders (page 30)	1
1 cup plus 2 tbsp	shredded Monterey Jack cheese	280 mL
12	dinner rolls, cut in half crosswise, toasted	12
12	slices bacon, cooked	12
1	ripe avocado, cut into 12 slices	1

1. *Chipotle Mayo:* In a small bowl, mix together mayo, chipotle and lime juice. Set aside.

2. When you are cooking the meat patties for the basic sliders, just after you have turned patties over to second side, add 1½ tbsp (22 mL) Monterey Jack cheese on top and continue cooking until cheese is melted and patties are cooked through.

3. Slather toasted dinner rolls with Chipotle Mayo and garnish with a slice of crispy bacon and avocado. Serve warm.

Continued on next page

Gorgonzola and Balsamic Onion Sliders

Gorgonzola Mayo

½ cup	mayonnaise	125 mL
4 oz	Gorgonzola cheese, crumbled	125 mL
½ tsp	freshly ground black pepper	2 mL

Sliders

1 tbsp	olive oil	15 mL
2	onions, thinly sliced	2
1 tbsp	balsamic vinegar	15 mL
	Salt and freshly ground black pepper	
1	recipe Basic Sliders (page 30)	1
12	dinner rolls, cut in half crosswise, toasted	12

1. *Gorgonzola Mayo:* In a small bowl, combine mayonnaise, Gorgonzola and pepper. Set aside.

2. In a medium skillet, heat oil over medium heat. Sauté onions for about 15 minutes or until walnut brown. Remove from heat and add balsamic vinegar. Season with salt and pepper to taste.

3. Cook meat patties for basic sliders. Slather toasted dinner rolls with Gorgonzola Mayo. Add meat patties and garnish with a dollop of caramelized onions. Serve warm.

Slider Italiano

Pesto Mayo

1/2 cup	mayonnaise	125 mL
1/4 cup	Pesto (page 25) or store-bought	60 mL

Sliders

1	recipe Basic Sliders (page 30)	1
1 cup plus 2 tbsp	shredded fontina cheese	280 mL
12	dinner rolls, cut in half crosswise, toasted	12
2	tomatoes, cut into 6 slices each	2
1 1/2 cups	arugula leaves, stems trimmed	375 mL

1. *Pesto Mayo:* In a small bowl, combine mayonnaise and pesto. Set aside.

2. When you are cooking meat patties for basic sliders, just after you have turned patties over, add 1 1/2 tbsp (22 mL) fontina cheese on top and continue cooking until cheese is melted and patties are cooked through. Slather toasted dinner rolls with Pesto Mayo. Add meat patties and garnish with a slice of tomato and a few arugula leaves. Serve warm.

THE DISH **Good Buns.** In this case we're talking about the rolls you use to frame your sliders. We have found that a good-quality dinner roll works perfectly. Look for rolls (and buns) that are firm but not dry. You don't want crusty rolls that will disintegrate with the first bite.

Fashion Plate

These are great fun for a poker night, served with kettle-style potato chips and Coffee Cookie Tower with Espresso Hot Fudge Sauce (page 370). We're all in!!

Mini Grilled Caramelized Onion and Brie Sandwiches

If you're a closet ooey gooey grilled cheese sandwich lover, it's time to come out. But before you do, make sure you kick off your bunny slippers and grab a pair of high heels, because our version is meant to be eaten in style. With slowly cooked onions and a rich slice of Brie cheese, these tiny temptations are then grilled in a skillet until they're toasty brown and absolutely irresistible.

Makes 20 mini grilled cheeses

Hands-on time
50 minutes

Start to finish
50 minutes

Make Ahead

The onions can be caramelized up to 3 days ahead and kept covered and refrigerated. The sandwiches can be assembled up to 1 day ahead and kept covered and refrigerated. Heat sandwiches on medium-high just before serving.

2 tbsp	unsalted butter	30 mL
1½ lbs	onions (about 2 large), thinly sliced	750 g
1 tsp	granulated sugar	5 mL
1 tsp	salt	5 mL
1 tsp	minced fresh thyme	5 mL
¼ tsp	freshly ground black pepper	1 mL
¼ cup	balsamic vinegar	60 mL
1½	baguettes, sliced into about 40 slices	1½
½ cup	unsalted butter, softened	125 mL
8 oz	thinly sliced Brie cheese, rind removed	250 g

1. Melt butter in a large skillet over medium-low heat. Sauté onions, sugar, salt, thyme and pepper for 15 to 20 minutes or until onions are walnut brown. Add balsamic vinegar and continue to cook for about 1 minute or until vinegar has evaporated. Set aside.

2. Butter baguette slices and lay them, buttered side down, on a work surface. Spread a scant tbsp (15 mL) of the caramelized onion on unbuttered side of half the baguettes. Top with a slice of Brie. Top cheese with a baguette slice, buttered side up.

3. Heat a large nonstick skillet over medium heat. Cook 4 or 5 mini sandwiches for 1 to 2 minutes per side or until golden brown. Arrange grilled cheese sandwiches on a platter and serve hot or at room temperature.

THE DISH **Patience.** It takes more than a few minutes to properly caramelize onions, but it's worth the wait. Don't be tempted to jack up the heat to get the job done quickly. You're likely to burn them instead of slowly caramelizing the onions' natural sugars. Trust us, there is a small but very important distinction between caramelized and burnt. You'll know it when you taste it, though!

Brie Strudel with Red Onion and Mango Chutney

Phyllo is one of those things that looks good without really trying. No wonder we love it. Here, we've taken the spirit of the delicious but more casual Mini Grilled Caramelized Onion and Brie Sandwich and transformed it into a sophisticated appetizer by adding mango, ginger and hot pepper flakes to the onion, making it essentially a chutney, and wrapping it all in phyllo.

Makes 26 pieces

Hands-on time
1 hour

Start to finish
1 hour 30 minutes

Make Ahead

The unbaked strudels can be frozen. Keep them on the baking sheet and cover them and the sheet with plastic wrap and foil. Bake frozen, adding 5 more minutes to baking time.

- **Baking sheet, lined with parchment paper**

2 tbsp	unsalted butter	30 mL
1 lb	red onions (about 2 medium), chopped	500 g
2	mangos (about 1½ lbs/750 g total), cut into ¼-inch (0.5 cm) cubes	2
1 tbsp	finely minced gingerroot	15 mL
¼ cup	packed light brown sugar	60 mL
½ tsp	hot pepper flakes	2 mL
½ tsp	salt	2 mL
¼ tsp	freshly ground black pepper	1 mL
¼ cup	apple cider vinegar	60 mL
6	sheets phyllo pastry	6
¼ cup	melted butter	60 mL
8 oz	thinly sliced Brie cheese, rind removed	250 g

1. Melt butter in a large skillet over medium-low heat. Sauté red onions for 15 to 20 minutes or until walnut brown. Add mangos, ginger, brown sugar, hot pepper flakes, salt, black pepper and cider vinegar. Sauté for 10 minutes, until mangos are just cooked but not yet broken down. Set aside and let cool.

2. Preheat oven to 400°F (200°C). Cut each phyllo sheet in half, making two 13- by 7½-inch (33 by 19 cm) rectangles. Cover phyllo with a damp paper towel to prevent drying. Place 1 piece on a work surface and brush lightly with butter. Lay another piece on top and brush again lightly with butter. Repeat with 4 more layers, brushing with butter each time. There should be 6 layers in total. Spread half of the chutney down middle of phyllo lengthwise and top with half of the Brie slices. Starting with one of the long ends, roll phyllo up into a log. Repeat with remaining phyllo and ingredients.

3. Place strudels on prepared baking sheet and brush tops with butter. Using a serrated knife, score dough crosswise in 1-inch (2.5 cm) intervals. This will make it easier to slice once baked.

4. Bake in preheated oven for 20 minutes or until golden brown on top. Let cool for 10 minutes before slicing. Carefully slice along scored lines. Transfer slices to a serving platter. Serve warm or at room temperature.

THE DISH **Silicone Pastry Brush.** If you've ever had to pluck stray pastry brush hairs out of your food, you're going to appreciate these durable little wonders. Crafted from heat-resistant silicone, these soft-bristled brushes won't tear your pastry, and certainly won't shed in your food.

Fashion Plate

This dish is the perfect opener for Glazed Pork Loin Stuffed with Apricots and Figs (page 210) and a side of Potato Haystacks with Gruyère (page 283). Finish the meal with Chocolate Mousse–Filled Profiteroles (page 340).

Pico de Gallo

Just the name puts us in the mood for Mexican food. Pico de Gallo is a delightfully simple, uncooked salsa made of ripe tomatoes, onion, cilantro and chiles. Its bright flavor comes from a liberal splash of freshly squeezed lime juice. Of course, tortilla chips are the obvious accompaniment to this zesty condiment, but there are a million different uses. We love it on scrambled eggs or on a salad with tortilla chip croutons or as a topping to a south-of-the-border bruschetta. Oh yeah, it's great on tacos, too!

Makes about 2 cups (500 mL)

Hands-on time
20 minutes

Start to finish
50 minutes

Make Ahead

This can be made up to 4 hours ahead and kept covered and refrigerated.

1 lb	ripe tomatoes, seeded and chopped	500 g
½ cup	finely chopped red onion	125 mL
¼ cup	finely chopped fresh cilantro	60 mL
2 tbsp	freshly squeezed lime juice	30 mL
1	small clove garlic, minced	1
1 to 2 tbsp	minced jalapeño or serrano chile peppers	15 to 30 mL
	Salt	

1. In a medium bowl, combine tomatoes, red onion, cilantro, lime juice, garlic and jalapeño, using as much or as little minced chiles to taste. Toss to blend well. Season with salt to taste. Let stand at room temperature for at least 30 minutes to allow the flavors to develop.

THE DISH   **A Sharp Knife.** There are two types of Pico de Gallo. One is the colorful, salad-like salsa where the ingredients have all been finely diced by hand with a sharp knife and then gently combined. The other is a uniformly pinkish mixture where all the ingredients have been tossed into a food processor and pulsed into an indiscernible mass. Hmm. Which one sounds more appetizing?

Fashion Plate

Pico de Gallo is a wonderful starter to a meal where bold flavors follow. Try it with Beef Fajitas (page 196) or Baja Grilled Fish Tacos (page 270) and serve extra on the side!

Black Bean and Corn Salsa Mini Tostadas with Chipotle Sour Cream

Once you've made Pico de Gallo, these lovely little smoky tostadas are just a hop, skip and a margarita away. We simply add corn, black beans and avocado to our basic salsa, spoon it onto a tortilla chip (we especially like to use the ones shaped like little scoops) and drizzle with a chipotle- and lime-flavored sour cream. Any leftover salsa makes a great filling for a veggie burrito.

Makes about 50 tiny tostadas

Hands-on time
35 minutes

Start to finish
1 hour 25 minutes

Make Ahead

The corn and black bean salsa can be made 2 hours ahead. The chipotle sour cream can be made up to 1 day ahead. The tostadas should be assembled just before serving.

1	recipe Pico de Gallo (page 38)	1
1	can (14 to 19 oz/398 to 540 mL) black beans, drained and rinsed	1
1½ cups	frozen corn kernels, thawed	375 mL
1	avocado, cut into small dice	1
1 cup	sour cream	250 mL
1 tbsp	finely minced chipotle chile pepper in adobo sauce	15 mL
1 tbsp	freshly squeezed lime juice	15 mL
2 tbsp	milk, plus more if necessary	30 mL
¼ tsp	salt	1 mL
	Tortilla chips (preferably scoop-style)	

1. In a large bowl, combine Pico de Gallo, black beans, corn and avocado. Taste and season with more salt, if necessary. Set aside.

2. In a medium bowl, combine sour cream, chipotle with sauce, lime juice, milk and salt. The mixture should be the consistency of whipping cream. Add more milk if too thick.

3. Place several tortilla chips onto a serving plate. Place a spoonful of black bean and corn salsa onto each tortilla chip. Drizzle chipotle cream over top of each tostada. Serve.

THE DISH **Good Canned Black Beans.** We love canned beans. They're easy and convenient, and let's face it, it's not always in the cards to stand over a simmering pot for 2 hours. But it is important to find good-quality canned beans. It's frustrating to open a can of beans and have them come out in a solid mass of mush.

Shrimp Cocktail Shooters with Pickled Vegetables

Using store-bought, already cooked and peeled shrimp makes this the easiest appetizer to pull off. We've reformed this old guard favorite into a playful soup shot with the shrimp and pickled vegetables skewered across the top of little 2-oz (60 g) shot glasses. Raid your mom and dad's vintage barware for the glasses or find them in your local thrift shop. A kitschy variety of glasses from around the world make for interesting conversation and party buzz while you reign supreme as the hostess with the mostess.

Makes about 2¼ cups (550 mL)
Makes about 18 shots

Hands-on time
30 minutes

Chilling time
2 hours

Start to finish
2 hours 30 minutes

Make Ahead

The sauce can be made 24 hours in advance and kept covered and refrigerated.

- **Food processor or blender**
- **Eighteen 2-oz (60 g) shot glasses**

1	can (14 oz/398 g) diced tomatoes	1
2	green onions, white and green parts, chopped	2
¼ cup	finely diced celery	60 mL
½ cup	Beef Stock (page 132) or ready-to-use broth	125 mL
2 tbsp	freshly squeezed lime juice	30 mL
2 tbsp	tequila	30 mL
1 tbsp	Worcestershire sauce	15 mL
1 tbsp	prepared horseradish	15 mL
1 tbsp	liquid honey	15 mL
1 tsp	hot pepper sauce or more to taste	5 mL
½ tsp	salt	2 mL
¼ tsp	freshly ground black pepper	1 mL
	Juice of 1 lime	
3 tbsp	kosher salt	45 mL
1 lb	cooked medium shrimp (28 to 30), thawed if frozen	500 g
	Assortment of pickled vegetables, such as carrots or green beans	
	Green olives	
2 tbsp	minced fresh cilantro	30 mL

1. In a food processor or blender, process tomatoes, green onions, celery, stock, 2 tbsp (30 mL) lime juice, tequila, Worcestershire, horseradish, honey, hot pepper sauce, salt and pepper until smooth. Taste for seasoning and adjust with more salt, pepper, hot sauce or lime juice, if necessary. Refrigerate sauce for at least 2 hours for mixture to chill and flavors to blend.

2. When ready to serve, squeeze 1 lime on a small plate and spread kosher salt on another. Dip rim of each shot glass into lime juice and then into salt to create a salted rim. Skewer a shrimp, pickled vegetable and olive on wooden toothpicks. Divide Bloody Mary among glasses and lay skewers over top of each glass. Sprinkle with cilantro.

THE DISH **Pickled Vegetables.** The skewers of pickled carrot, olive and shrimp are a great accompaniment to the delicious, tequila-spiked Bloody Mary. Whether we dip the skewered tidbits into the drink or not, we can't get enough of those salty, tangy vegetables paired with succulent shrimp.

Fashion Plate

We love to serve this unique starter with Sun-Dried Tomato Tapenade and Mascarpone Phyllo Bites (page 17) and Mini Grilled Caramelized Onion and Brie Sandwiches (page 34).

Tequila Bloody Mary Shrimp Cocktails

We've taken everyone's favorite morning after drink and adapted it to that perennial but bourgeois darling of steak houses and country clubs, the shrimp cocktail. The fashion police will definitely approve of the vessel in which it is served, the always chic martini glass, making it a simple task to quaff down the tequila-spiked thirst quencher within.

Serves 6

Hands-on time
30 minutes

Chilling time
2 hours

Start to finish
2 hours 30 minutes

Make Ahead

The sauce can be made 24 hours in advance and kept covered and refrigerated. Add the shrimp 2 hours before serving.

- **Food processor or blender**
- **6 martini glasses**

1	recipe Shrimp Cocktail Shooters, omitting pickled vegetables (page 40)	1
	Juice of 1 lime	
3 tbsp	kosher salt	45 mL
2 tbsp	minced fresh cilantro	30 mL
	Celery branches with leaves attached, cut into 4-inch (10 cm) lengths	

1. Follow the Shrimp Cocktail Shooters recipe through Step 2, adding the shrimp to the tomato cocktail sauce. Refrigerate for at least 2 hours for sauce to chill and flavors to blend.

2. When ready to serve, squeeze 1 lime on a small plate and spread salt on another. Dip rim of each martini glass into lime juice and then into salt to create a salted rim. Divide shrimp and chilled sauce among glasses. Garnish with cilantro and celery branches.

THE DISH **Good Canned Tomatoes.** It may seem like a small thing, but all tomatoes are not the same. We try to use San Marzano tomatoes, imported from Italy. The taste is surprisingly better than most domestic brands. You definitely owe it to yourself to discover the difference.

Fashion Plate

For a great start to a celebratory dinner, follow this appetizer with Steak with Red Wine Sauce and Mushrooms (page 183) and Pommes Anna (page 294).

Crab Dip with Artichokes and Jalapeño

In our experience, crab dishes really add razzle-dazzle to a cocktail party, especially when combined with goat cheese, artichoke hearts and nutty Parmesan. When served in a chafing dish (so it stays hot), this retro crabby dip reaches back through time to the '50s and '60s, when neighbors dressed up and met for hors d'oeuvres and cocktails before dinner. Remember the party scene in the movie Breakfast at Tiffany's? *If only Holly Golightly had had the sense to make this little nosh for her guests to nibble, her little party might not have gotten so out of hand.*

Makes about 3 cups (750 mL)

Hands-on time
30 minutes

Start to finish
1 hour

Tip

When fresh crabmeat isn't available, look for the pasteurized tubs in the chilled seafood section of your grocery store. This is a much better, fresher-tasting alternative to the canned crab.

Make Ahead

The dip can be assembled 24 hours in advance and kept covered and refrigerated. If baking the dip directly from the refrigerator, add 10 minutes to the warming time.

- **Preheat oven to 350°F (180°C)**
- **4-cup (1 L) ovenproof dish**

2 tbsp	vegetable oil	30 mL
1/4 cup	minced red bell pepper	60 mL
2	green onions, white and green parts, minced	2
1	stalk celery, minced	1
1	clove garlic, minced	1
5 oz	goat cheese, crumbled	150 g
1 tbsp	drained pickled jalapeños	15 mL
1	can (14 oz/400 g) artichoke hearts, drained and chopped	1
1/3 cup	freshly grated Parmesan cheese	75 mL
3 tbsp	mayonnaise	45 mL
1 tbsp	Worcestershire sauce	15 mL
1 tsp	freshly squeezed lemon juice	5 mL
8 oz	fresh or pasteurized crabmeat, drained (see Tip, left)	125 mL
1/4 cup	minced flat-leaf parsley	60 mL
1/4 tsp	salt	1 mL
1/4 tsp	freshly ground black pepper	1 mL
1/4 cup	toasted almond slices	60 mL
	Pita Chips (page 46)	

1. In a medium sauté pan, heat oil over medium heat. Sauté red pepper, green onions and celery for about 6 minutes or until vegetables are tender. Add garlic and sauté for 1 minute. Transfer to a large bowl. Add goat cheese and let heat from vegetables melt it.

2. Add jalapeños, artichoke hearts, Parmesan, mayonnaise, Worcestershire, lemon juice, crab, parsley, salt and pepper and stir to combine. Transfer to ovenproof dish and top with almond slices. Bake in preheated oven for 30 minutes or until dip is hot all the way through. Serve hot with pita chips as an accompaniment.

THE DISH **Chafing Dish.** Savvy partygivers love chafing dishes because they keep hot foods hot and require minimal attention during the party. We prefer chafing dishes with a Pyrex liner dish and Sterno heat source. That way, you can fill the Pyrex dish with the crab dip and heat it in the oven, then transfer it to the chafing dish and essentially forget about it for the night.

Fashion Plate

Partner this dish with something light, like Fresh Tomato and Basil Bruschettas (page 22) and Tapenade (page 16). For a dinner pairing, we'd love to follow this starter with the Arugula Salad with Grape Tomatoes and Shallot Vinaigrette (page 86), Grilled Herbed Pork Tenderloin (page 212) and Creamy White Winter Gratin with Caramelized Onions (page 310).

Pita Chips

Pita chips are tasty, homemade crispy breads that taste so much better than anything you can buy readymade.

Make Ahead

Pita chips can be made 1 day ahead and kept at room temperature.

- **Preheat oven to 400°F (200°C)**

8	6-inch (15 cm) or small pita rounds, cut into 6 wedges and separated	8
⅓ cup	olive oil or unsalted butter, melted	75 mL
	Kosher salt	

1. Brush inside of each pita wedge with olive oil and arrange on a baking sheet. Sprinkle with salt and bake in preheated oven for about 8 minutes or until chips are crisp. Let cool on pan. Store in an airtight container at room temperature for up to 1 day.

Crab and Goat Cheese Bouchées

You'll love this vogue version of sinful crab dip. Bouchée is French for "mouthful," and this divine dish of rich crab wrapped in crispy pastry is sure to be everyone's favorite at your next soirée.

Makes 30

Hands-on time
30 minutes

Start to finish
1 hour

Make Ahead

The filling can be assembled 24 hours in advance and kept covered and refrigerated. The shells can be filled up to 4 hours ahead and kept, covered and refrigerated, for up to 4 hours.

- **Preheat oven to 350°F (180°C)**
- **Baking sheet, lined with parchment paper**

1	recipe Crab Dip with Artichokes and Jalapeño (page 44)	1
30	small readymade frozen puff pastry shells, thawed	30
¼ cup	toasted almond slices	60 mL

1. Assemble crab dip and arrange puff pastry shells on prepared baking sheet. Fill shells with crab filling and top with almonds. Bake in preheated oven for 15 to 20 minutes or until shells are crispy and filling is hot.

THE DISH **A Beautiful Presentation.** Make these bites even more tantalizing by lining a plain white platter with the colorful leaves of kale, chard or even beet greens. It's an old caterer's trick that always keeps the serving table looking fresh and up to date. Keep another lined platter waiting in the refrigerator for when the next batch of nibbles comes out of the oven. That way, the platter remains crisp and ready for its next close-up with your guests.

Fashion Plate

Serve these tidbits with Winter Salad with Orange Vinaigrette (page 98) and Fast and Fresh Vegetable Soup (page 140).

White Bean Salsa

This brilliant, out of the pantry appetizer is the equivalent of that extra pair of sheer black stockings you have tucked in the back of your lingerie drawer — a kind of insurance policy, if you will. Guests will lap up this lemony, garlicky salsa, so be sure to keep a few extra cans of white beans in the pantry at all times.

Makes about 24 crostini

Hands-on time
20 minutes

Start to finish
20 minutes

Variation

Transfer the salsa to a decorative bowl, sprinkle on the remaining parsley and serve with pita chips. Or add a finely chopped tomato or avocado for even more visual and textural interest.

Make Ahead

The salsa can be made and kept at room temperature for up to 3 hours or refrigerated for up to 8 hours. Let come to room temperature before continuing with the recipe.

White Bean Salsa

1	can (14 to 19 oz/398 to 540 mL) cannellini or navy beans, drained and rinsed	1
1	green onion, white and green parts, minced	1
¼ cup	extra virgin olive oil, divided	60 mL
1 tsp	grated lemon zest	5 mL
1½ tbsp	freshly squeezed lemon juice	22 mL
1	clove garlic, minced	1
¼ tsp	salt	1 mL
⅛ tsp	cayenne pepper	0.5 mL
	Freshly ground black pepper	
3 tbsp	minced flat-leaf parsley, divided	45 mL
	Crostini (page 49) or Pita Chips (page 46)	
¼ cup	goat cheese, softened, optional	60 mL

1. In a large bowl, combine beans, green onions, 2 tbsp (30 mL) of the olive oil, lemon zest, lemon juice, garlic, salt, cayenne, black pepper and 2 tbsp (30 mL) of the parsley. Taste for seasoning and add more salt, pepper or lemon juice, if necessary.

2. Just before serving, spread toasted bread with goat cheese, if using, and top with a heaping tbsp (15 mL) of the salsa. Sprinkle over remaining parsley.

THE DISH **Canned White Beans.** The darlings of our pantry, canned beans wait patiently in the wings to come to our rescue whenever we need delicious food fast. Canned white beans provide a blank palette on which to paint your favorite tastes and textures. Explore other spicy add-ins such as cumin or coriander and fresh herbs such as thyme, basil or cilantro.

Crostini

These small, crispy bread slices make a great foundation for an infinite number of toppings.

**Makes about
36 crostini**

Hands-on time
10 minutes

Start to finish
20 minutes

Tip

It's best to use an Italian or French loaf that is about 3 inches (7.5 cm) in diameter for this recipe.

• **Preheat broiler**

1	loaf Italian or French bread, cut into ½-inch (1 cm) thick slices (see Tip, left)	1
¼ cup	olive oil	60 mL

1. Brush bread slices lightly on both sides with olive oil. Arrange on a baking sheet. Broil on highest rack, turning once, for 3 to 4 minutes total or until lightly browned. Let cool. The bread slices can be toasted several hours in advance and kept at room temperature in an airtight container.

Bruschetta with Tuscan White Beans, Kalamata Olives and Roasted Red Peppers

We've morphed the previous salsa recipe from day to evening with this enticing spread served on toasted baguette slices. The salty olives and sweet roasted pepper make a savory topper and elevate the previous humble dish to haute couture status. Only you (and us, of course) will know how easy it is to pull together. Don't worry . . . we can keep a secret.

Serves 6
Makes about
25 pieces

Hands-on time
30 minutes

Start to finish
40 minutes

Variation

For a nutritious yet elegant version, serve the spread in a bowl with carrots and celery sticks arranged in a wheel-spoke pattern around it.

Make Ahead

The toasts can be made up to 3 hours ahead and the spread can be made up to 24 hours ahead. Let spread come to room temperature before continuing with the recipe. Assemble the bruschetta just before serving.

1	recipe White Bean Salsa (page 48)	1
1	recipe Crostini (page 49)	1
¼ cup	goat cheese, softened, optional	60 mL
½ cup	halved kalamata olives, or quartered if large	125 mL
½ cup	roasted red peppers, cut into thin strips	125 mL
3 tbsp	minced flat-leaf parsley	45 mL

1. Make White Bean Salsa but don't include the parsley at this stage. Mash with a potato masher or a fork. Taste and adjust seasoning with more salt, pepper or lemon juice, if necessary.

2. Top crostini with goat cheese, if using, 1 tbsp (15 mL) of the salsa and lay an olive and a strip of red pepper decoratively across the top. Sprinkle parsley over all.

THE DISH **Toasted Baguette Slices.** Toasting the bread is an extra step, but we think it is worth the effort for a few reasons. First, it makes the bread more firm and stable so that it is easier to eat. And secondly, toasted bread just tastes better. Especially when drizzled with olive oil and rubbed with garlic.

It just makes sense that any dish is better when all the components can stand alone. We prefer thinner baguettes (no more than 3 inches/7.5 cm in diameter) because they can be eaten in two bites. Have the bakery slice the baguette for you. It will save you time and a lot of crumbs on your countertop.

Rustic Cheese Tart with Sun-Dried Tomatoes

Puff pastry, creamy rich cheese and succulent sun-dried tomatoes form a trifecta-winning blend of flavors. This bewitching tart is destined to be your new best (friend) appetizer for toting to potlucks. We guarantee that the hungry hordes will descend and pick the platter clean in no time flat. Pity the poor soul who brought that barely touched little tray of celery and carrots with the low-fat dip. It probably seemed like a good idea at the time.

Makes 2 tarts
Serves 8 as a luncheon dish or 32 pieces as an appetizer

Hands-on time
25 minutes

Start to finish
1 hour

Make Ahead

The tarts can be assembled prior to baking and frozen, unfilled, for up to 4 weeks. Thaw at room temperature for 1 hour, then bake, fill and bake as directed. The filling can be mixed together up to 3 days ahead and kept covered and refrigerated.

- **Preheat oven to 425°F (220°C)**
- **Baking sheet, lined with parchment paper**

1	package frozen puff pastry (2 sheets)	1
2	large egg yolks, beaten	2
5 oz	Boursin or other herbed soft cheese, softened	150 g
4 oz	goat cheese, softened	125 g
1 tsp	freshly squeezed lemon juice	5 mL
	Freshly ground black pepper	
½ cup	sun-dried tomatoes in oil, julienned	125 mL

1. On a lightly floured work space, roll out 1 piece of pastry into a 14- by 11-inch (35 by 28 cm) rectangle. Transfer pastry to prepared baking sheet and cut 1-inch (2.5 cm) strips from each side. Brush edges of rectangle with water and position cut strips on top of the edges, creating a border. Poke holes in bottom of pastry with a fork. Repeat with remaining pastry. Bake in preheated oven for about 10 minutes or until puffy and brown. Remove from oven and poke again with a fork. Push pastry down, as it will be puffy and raised, and return to oven to cook for 5 minutes more. Let cool on a wire rack.

2. Reduce the heat to 350°F (180°C). In a medium bowl, combine egg yolks, Boursin, goat cheese, lemon juice and pepper to taste. Spread mixture over cooled pastries. Top with sun-dried tomatoes.

3. Return tarts to oven and bake for about 20 minutes or until cheese is set. Let cool on a wire rack. Cut into squares and serve warm or at room temperature.

THE DISH **Boursin Cheese.** Boursin is one of the most seductive of cheeses.

Pissaladière with Leek, Olive and Sun-Dried Tomatoes

A pissaladière is kind of like a little French pizza. It summons visions of the sunshine-kissed but hearty flavors of the fragrant wild herbs that grow on the hillsides there. If that isn't reason enough to make this dish, flick on that Edith Piaf CD, slip into a pair of kitten heels and channel the French Riviera's Brigitte Bardot. Maybe add a saucy little apron to the mix. You (and it!) will be delicious.

Makes 2 tarts
Serves 8

Hands-on time
35 minutes

Start to finish
1 hour 10 minutes

Make Ahead

The tarts can be assembled prior to baking and frozen, unfilled, for up to 4 weeks. Thaw at room temperature for 1 hour, then fill and bake as directed in Step 2. The filling and leek mixture can be made up to 3 days ahead and kept covered and refrigerated.

2 tbsp	olive oil	30 mL
2	leeks, white part only, thinly sliced	2
Pinch	salt	Pinch
1	recipe Rustic Cheese Tart with Sun-Dried Tomatoes (page 52)	1
1 cup	kalamata or niçoise olives, pitted	250 mL
½ cup	sun-dried tomatoes in oil, julienned	125 mL

1. In a medium skillet, heat oil over medium-high heat. Sauté leeks and salt for about 6 minutes or until leeks begin to soften. Reduce heat to medium-low and cook for 10 minutes or until leeks are meltingly tender. Let cool.

2. Assemble tart as in previous recipe, topping cheese layer with a scattering of cooked leek, olives and sun-dried tomatoes, and bake as directed. Cut into squares and serve warm or at room temperature.

THE DISH — **Leeks.** A bona fide member of the onion family, leeks are the onion's cultured, urbane city cousin. If the onion is the hearty, hard-working farmer's wife with a big laugh, the leek is the elegantly dressed sophisticate who speaks several languages fluently — but quietly. In a pinch, you could substitute thinly sliced red onion, but try the leeks for a more subtle oniony flavor.

Fashion Plate

Couple this starter with the Sautéed Chicken Breasts with Lemon Sauce (page 226) and Roasted Asparagus (page 290).

Tartine with Figs, Prosciutto and Ricotta

If a tartine is nothing more than an open-faced sandwich, maybe even those tuna melts from your childhood could be dressed up by calling them a tuna tartine. The name "tartine" does confer a bit more chic, and who couldn't use more chic? We've provided a very saucy little tartine here, which, though simple, tantalizes with the flavors of salty ham, sweet figs and tangy cheese.

Serves 6

Hands-on time
30 minutes

Start to finish
30 minutes

Tip

If you want to cut each tartine into smaller, finger-shaped slices, this appetizer can serve many.

Make Ahead

The recipe can be completed through Step 3 up to 4 hours before assembling and serving.

- **Preheat oven to 375°F (190°C)**

18	dried figs, stemmed and quartered	18
½ cup	port wine	125 mL
2 tbsp	extra virgin olive oil	30 mL
6	slices country-style bread	6
½ cup	ricotta cheese	125 mL
2 tbsp	chopped fresh basil	30 mL
¼ tsp	salt	1 mL
Pinch	freshly ground black pepper	Pinch
Pinch	freshly grated nutmeg	Pinch
⅓ cup	chopped walnuts, toasted	75 mL
6	slices prosciutto	6

1. In a small saucepan over medium heat, combine figs and port. Bring to a simmer. Remove from heat and let stand for 15 minutes to rehydrate.

2. Meanwhile, drizzle olive oil over bread slices. Bake in preheated oven for about 15 minutes or until crispy. Let cool on a wire rack.

3. In a small bowl, combine cheese, basil, salt, pepper and nutmeg. Taste for seasoning and adjust with more salt, pepper or nutmeg, if necessary.

4. Spread cheese mixture over bread and top with a sprinkling of walnuts, a slice of prosciutto and figs. Cut into serving-size pieces and serve immediately.

THE DISH **Country-Style Bread.** It should come as no surprise that when making bread-based dishes, the quality of the bread is très important.

Tartine with Roasted Figs, Prosciutto and Gorgonzola

Roasting these succulent fresh figs really concentrates their flavor, making them even sweeter and more complex. It is an easy step to make and just gives this tartine a bit more finesse. The Gorgonzola adds an extra savory note that we find irresistible and plays beautifully off the nutty tannins of the walnuts. It all comes together to make a simple dish that really sizzles.

Serves 6

Hands-on time
30 minutes

Start to finish
40 minutes

Make Ahead

The recipe can be completed through Step 3 up to 4 hours before assembling and serving.

- **Preheat oven to 375°F (190°C)**

12	fresh figs, stemmed and quartered	12
1 tbsp	balsamic vinegar	15 mL
3 tbsp	extra virgin olive oil, divided	45 mL
6	slices country-style bread	6
½ cup	ricotta cheese	125 mL
¼ cup	Gorgonzola cheese, crumbled	60 mL
2 tbsp	chopped fresh basil	30 mL
¼ tsp	salt	1 mL
Pinch	freshly ground black pepper	Pinch
Pinch	freshly grated nutmeg	Pinch
⅓ cup	chopped walnuts, toasted	75 mL
6	slices prosciutto	6

1. On a baking sheet, toss together figs, vinegar and 1 tbsp (15 mL) of the olive oil. Bake in preheated oven for about 15 minutes or until figs have dried and caramelized slightly. Let stand at room temperature for up to 4 hours.

2. Drizzle remaining olive oil over bread slices. Bake in preheated oven for about 15 minutes or until crispy. Let cool on rack.

3. In a small bowl, combine ricotta cheese, Gorgonzola, basil, salt, pepper and nutmeg. Taste for seasoning and adjust with more salt, pepper or nutmeg, if necessary.

4. Spread cheese mixture over bread and top with a sprinkling of walnuts, a slice of prosciutto and roasted figs. Cut into serving-size pieces and serve immediately.

THE DISH **Fresh Figs.** Depending on where you live, figs can be in season for a very short time (late summer to early fall), so when you see figs, dash home and make this dish.

Wild Mushroom and Thyme Spread

Guests will swoon over this rich goat cheese and earthy mushroom spread with hints of lemon and thyme. It makes the perfect nibble between lunch and dinner and has even been known to appear atop eggs at breakfast. Because it keeps for days, you will be sure to use up every last delectable drop by adding it to the top of a grilled steak or chicken breast or as a filling in a simple omelet.

Makes about 2 cups

Hands-on time
30 minutes

Start to finish
30 minutes

Make Ahead

The spread can be made up to 24 hours ahead of time and will keep, refrigerated, for up to 3 days.

• **Food processor**

3 tbsp	unsalted butter	45 mL
4	green onions, white and green parts, thinly sliced	4
Pinch	salt	Pinch
12 oz	oyster, shiitake or cremini mushrooms or a blend, chopped	375 g
2	cloves garlic, minced	2
¼ cup	dry white wine	60 mL
1 tbsp	soy sauce	15 mL
10 oz	goat cheese, softened	300 g
½ cup	walnuts, toasted	125 mL
2 tbsp	chopped flat-leaf parsley	30 mL
2 tsp	chopped fresh thyme	10 mL
1 tsp	grated lemon zest	5 mL
Pinch	cayenne pepper	Pinch
	Salt and freshly ground black pepper	
	Sprigs of thyme	
	Crostini (page 49) or bagel rounds	
	Minced parsley, optional	

1. In a large sauté pan, heat butter over medium heat. When butter sizzles, sauté green onions and salt for about 2 minutes or until onions begin to look translucent. Add mushrooms and sauté for 3 to 4 minutes or until they begin to give off some liquid. Add garlic and sauté for about 4 minutes or until mushrooms are dry.

2. Add wine and soy sauce and cook for about 2 minutes or until pan is dry.

3. Transfer mushrooms, goat cheese, walnuts, parsley, thyme, lemon zest and cayenne to a food processor. Process in 4 or 5 short bursts to coarsely chop and mix ingredients. Don't overprocess. Leave it a little bit chunky. Taste and adjust seasoning with more salt and pepper, as desired.

4. Transfer spread to a decorative bowl and refrigerate if not using right away. Before serving, let come to room temperature, garnish with sprigs of thyme and serve with crostini or bagel rounds. Or spread onto toasted bread and garnish each with a sprinkling of minced parsley.

THE DISH

Wild Mushrooms. From the now familiar cremini, oyster and shiitake to the more exotic trumpet, chanterelle and morel, there has never been a better time to discover wild mushrooms. Their meaty goodness will add allure to all manner of vegetarian dishes, not to mention using them as a vegetable side dish.

Most wild mushrooms found in your grocer's produce section aren't technically wild but are farmed much like the familiar white button mushroom. If you love mushrooms, try searching your regional farmers' market in the spring and fall for local varieties. They will be much fresher than the trucked-in mushrooms at the big grocery chains, and you will be rewarded with enormous mushroom flavor. Avoid purchasing mushrooms packaged in plastic, as they become slimy and off-smelling. Try to select mushrooms from bins, avoiding any that are shriveled and wrinkled. Once home, keep them refrigerated in paper bags for up to 2 days.

Fashion Plate

Take advantage of the fact that the mushrooms mimic a meaty taste and serve this rich vegetarian spread with Winter Salad with Orange Vinaigrette (page 98) and Tuscan Bean and Barley Soup with Crispy Pancetta (page 135).

Wild Mushroom Turnovers

Because they are so easy make and bake from frozen, wild mushroom turnovers figure prominently as a The Dish appetizer waiting in the freezer to be enjoyed by friends and family at a moment's notice. You'll be the only one who knows that it didn't take days of slave labor to produce these crispy, buttery treats.

**Makes
36 turnovers**

Hands-on time
45 minutes

Start to finish
1 hour

Tip

When working with puff pastry, it is important that it stay cold, so if you are slow to assemble these wondrous bites and the pastry becomes difficult to handle, pop the dough in the refrigerator for a few minutes to rechill before continuing.

Make Ahead

The mushroom mixture may be made the day before and kept in the refrigerator until ready to use. The turnovers can be assembled and frozen on a baking sheet, lined with parchment paper. Once frozen, transfer them to resealable freezer bags and freeze for up to 2 months. They can be baked directly from the freezer. Just add a few extra minutes to the baking time.

- **Preheat oven to 425°F (220°C)**
- **Baking sheet, lined with parchment paper**

1	recipe Wild Mushroom and Thyme Spread, cooled (page 56)	1
2	packages frozen puff pastry sheets (4 sheets), thawed	2
1	egg yolk	1
1 tbsp	heavy or whipping (35%) cream	15 mL

1. On a floured work surface, roll out pastry sheets to make them a little larger, about 12 inches (30 cm) square. (Keep pastry you aren't working with at the moment in the refrigerator.) Cut each sheet of pastry into 9 squares (36 total). In a small bowl, beat together egg yolk and cream. Brush egg around outer edges of pastry squares.

2. Spoon 1 tbsp (15 mL) of the mushroom mixture slightly off-center onto one of the pastry squares. Fold over to enclose filling and make a triangle. Seal edges by pressing with tines of a fork. Brush egg over top of turnover. Repeat with remaining pastry squares and filling. Place turnovers on prepared baking sheet. Pop in refrigerator to chill for 10 minutes. Bake in preheated oven for about 12 minutes or until golden brown and crisp. Serve warm or at room temperature.

THE DISH **Frozen Puff Pastry.** Puff pastry is an ingredient we turn to time and time again. There is no end to the many fillings and flavorings that can be wrapped in this buttery package. Whether you make your own or buy a good-quality frozen puff pastry such as Dufour, your guests will wait impatiently by the oven for the next round of these luscious, buttery turnovers to appear.

Lettuce Eat
Salads

Baby Greens Salad with Goat Cheese and Balsamic Vinaigrette

The beauty of a green salad is that it can be the essence of simplicity and the height of complexity all at the same time. Its clean flavors are the perfect palate cleansers. Its color always adds interest to a meal, and it can be accessorized in so many ways, making it the perfect recipe. Our version uses a balsamic vinaigrette and a sprinkling of goat cheese to lend interest, but even without the cheese this salad is a standout.

Serves 6

Hands-on time
10 minutes

Start to finish
10 minutes

Make Ahead

The vinaigrette can be made up to 3 days ahead and kept covered and refrigerated. Dress the salad just before serving.

- **Chilled serving plates**

Balsamic Vinaigrette

2 tbsp	balsamic vinegar	30 mL
2 tsp	Dijon mustard	10 mL
1	clove garlic, minced	1
¼ cup	extra virgin olive oil	60 mL
	Salt and freshly ground black pepper	
8 cups	baby greens	2 L
4 oz	goat cheese, crumbled	125 g

1. *Balsamic Vinaigrette:* In a small bowl, combine vinegar, mustard and garlic. Add oil in a slow steady stream, whisking constantly. Season with salt and pepper to taste.

2. In a large bowl, gently toss greens with vinaigrette to coat.

3. Divide among chilled serving plates and top with crumbled goat cheese.

THE DISH **Salad Spinner.** One of our favorite kitchen gadgets is a salad spinner, an ingenious tool that can wash and dry your lettuce to perfection. Make sure you tear the lettuce into bite-size pieces and wash the lettuce in cool water. Keep leftover lettuce in a resealable bag layered with paper towels. It will keep beautifully for 2 or 3 days.

Fashion Plate

This salad would be a wonderful starter or side dish for almost any meal. We especially like to serve it along with one of our homemade pizzas, starting on page 166.

Frisée Salad with Warm Bacon and Balsamic Vinaigrette

Warm vinaigrettes, especially when made with smoky bacon, create an entirely different ambiance for a salad than a traditional dressing, making it somehow more of a meal.

Serves 6

Hands-on time
20 minutes

Start to finish
20 minutes

- **Preheat broiler**

12	slices French baguette, cut into ½-inch (1 cm) thick slices	12
	Olive oil	
4 oz	soft fresh goat cheese	125 g
	Freshly ground black pepper	
8 cups	frisée lettuce, torn into bite-size pieces	2 L
3	slices bacon, chopped	3
1	recipe Balsamic Vinaigrette (page 62)	1

1. Brush both sides of bread slices lightly with olive oil. Toast both sides of bread until golden brown. Spread one side of each slice with goat cheese. Season with pepper to taste. Broil until cheese is lightly browned.

2. Place frisée in a bowl.

3. In a large skillet over medium heat, cook bacon until crisp and brown. Transfer to paper towels to drain. Discard all but 1 tbsp (15 mL) of fat from pan. Whisk balsamic vinaigrette into warm bacon fat. Immediately toss warm vinaigrette with frisée.

4. Divide salad equally among 6 serving plates. Place 2 croutons on top of each salad and sprinkle with crispy bacon. Serve immediately.

THE DISH **Frisée Lettuce.** Frisée is a sturdy, slightly bitter lettuce that can hold its own when paired with a warm vinaigrette that would render a more delicate green soggy and lifeless. Frisée also has a curly leaf that adds interest and unique texture to any salad.

Caesar Salad

For some reason, a Caesar salad seems like something bad for you and something good for you all at the same time. Perhaps the answer to that conundrum lies in the fact that it's a salad (the good part), coated in a rich garlicky dressing (some, not us, might call this the bad part), feathered with a generous amount of grated Parmesan (oh so bad, yet so good) and tossed with an obscene amount of buttery croutons (you get the picture). Some things in life should just be enjoyed and not over-analyzed.

Serves 6

Hands-on time
30 minutes

Start to finish
30 minutes

Tip

This recipe contains raw egg yolks. If you are concerned about the safety of using raw eggs, use pasteurized eggs in the shell or pasteurized liquid whole eggs instead.

Make Ahead

The dressing can be made 1 day ahead and kept covered and refrigerated.

- **Preheat oven to 400°F (200°C)**
- **Blender**

1/4 cup	unsalted butter	60 mL
4	cloves garlic, minced, divided	4
2 cups	rustic white bread cubes, 1/2-inch (1 cm) cubes	500 mL
1/2 tsp	salt	2 mL
3	anchovy fillets, finely chopped	3
1 tbsp	Dijon mustard	15 mL
1	egg yolk (see Tip, left)	1
2 tbsp	freshly squeezed lemon juice	15 mL
1 tsp	Worcestershire sauce	5 mL
1/3 cup	extra virgin olive oil	75 mL
	Salt and freshly ground black pepper	
8 cups	bite-size pieces romaine lettuce	2 L
1/2 cup	freshly grated Parmesan cheese	125 mL

1. In a medium saucepan, melt butter over medium heat. Add half of the garlic and cook for about 2 minutes, until it sizzles. Remove pan from heat.

2. On a large baking sheet, toss bread with garlic butter and salt. Spread in 1 layer and bake in preheated oven for about 10 minutes or until crisp. Let croutons cool on baking sheet on a wire rack.

3. In a blender, combine anchovies, mustard, egg yolk, remaining garlic, lemon juice and Worcestershire sauce. With blender running, slowly drizzle in olive oil. Season with salt and pepper to taste. Transfer to a bowl.

4. Add lettuce, Parmesan and garlic croutons and gently toss to coat with dressing.

Whole-Leaf Caesar Salad with Parmesan Fricos

Although the flavors are the same as in our traditional Caesar, this whole-leaf version, with Parmesan fricos, or crisps, has an entirely different attitude. Serving the lettuce leaves whole requires the diners to use their knives and forks to construct their own little bites out of all the elements. Doing this tends to focus everyone's attention more on the dish and slows the meal down, giving your guests a moment to relax and enjoy the food and the company.

Serves 6

Hands-on time
30 minutes

Start to finish
30 minutes

Make Ahead

The dressing can be made 1 day ahead and kept covered and refrigerated.

- **Preheat oven to 375°F (190°C)**
- **Baking sheet, lined with parchment paper**
- **Blender**

3 oz	Parmesan cheese, preferably Parmigiano-Reggiano, grated	90 g
1 tbsp	all-purpose flour	15 mL
1/4 tsp	freshly ground black pepper	1 mL
3	anchovy fillets, finely chopped	3
1 tbsp	Dijon mustard	15 mL
1	egg yolk (see Tip, page 64)	1
2	cloves garlic, minced	2
2 tbsp	freshly squeezed lemon juice	30 mL
1 tsp	Worcestershire sauce	5 mL
1/3 cup	extra virgin olive oil	75 mL
	Salt and freshly ground black pepper	
3	hearts of romaine lettuce, leaves separated	3
18	cherry tomatoes, halved	18

1. In a bowl, stir together cheese, flour and pepper. Spoon cheese mixture by generous tablespoonfuls (30 mL) into 6 mounds on prepared baking sheet, spacing 3 inches (7.5 cm) apart. Using your fingers, spread each mound evenly to 2 1/2-inch (6 cm) round.

2. Bake cheese in middle of preheated oven for about 10 minutes or until golden. Let cool for 2 minutes on baking sheet on a wire rack, then carefully transfer each frico with a metal spatula to rack and let cool completely.

3. In a blender, combine anchovies, mustard, egg yolk, garlic, lemon juice and Worcestershire sauce. With blender running, slowly drizzle in olive oil. Season with salt and pepper to taste.

4. Arrange 4 large romaine lettuce leaves on each of 6 plates. Top each with 4 smaller leaves. Top lettuce with tomatoes. Drizzle salads with dressing. Insert one Parmesan frico upright in the middle of the romaine leaves. Season generously with pepper and serve.

THE DISH **Crisp Romaine Lettuce.** Limp lettuce will absolutely ruin this salad. Look through the produce section for the best-looking lettuce with no tears or blemishes. Wash under cold water and store in a plastic bag layered between sheets of paper towels. Romaine will keep, refrigerated, for up to 5 days.

Fashion Plate

Pair this salad with Braised Short Ribs (page 192) and White Wine Poached Pears with Rosemary Syrup and Triple Crème Cheese (page 324).

Mediterranean Couscous Salad

Couscous can be a culinary lifesaver. It's so quick to make — just 5 minutes and it's ready to serve as a side dish, stuffing or in this case the foundation of a vegetarian salad. The mix of bell pepper, zucchini, chickpeas and pine nuts give this salad a Mediterranean feel, but it could just as easily swing into the Italian, French or California mood by substituting the vegetables, beans and herbs with whatever you have on hand.

Serves 6

Hands-on time
30 minutes

Start to finish
30 minutes

Make Ahead

The salad can be made 1 day ahead and kept covered and refrigerated.

⅓ cup	currants or raisins	75 mL
¼ cup	extra virgin olive oil, divided	60 mL
1½ tsp	salt, divided	7 mL
1½ cups	couscous	375 mL
1	red onion, cut into small dice	1
2	cloves garlic, minced	2
1	red bell pepper, seeded and cut into small dice	1
1	medium zucchini, trimmed and cut into small dice	1
3 tbsp	red wine vinegar	45 mL
1	can (14 to 19 oz/398 to 540 mL) chickpeas, drained and rinsed	1
½ cup	finely chopped flat-leaf parsley leaves	125 mL
⅓ cup	pine nuts, lightly toasted	75 mL
	Salt and freshly ground black pepper	

1. In a small saucepan over medium-high heat, bring 2 cups (500 mL) water to a boil with currants, 1 tbsp (15 mL) of the oil and 1 tsp (5 mL) of the salt. Stir in couscous. Remove from heat and let stand, covered, for 5 minutes. Fluff couscous with a fork and transfer to a bowl.

2. In a small skillet, heat 2 tbsp (30 mL) of oil over medium heat. Add red onion and sauté for about 6 minutes or until softened. Add garlic, bell pepper, zucchini and ½ tsp (2 mL) of salt and sauté for 2 minutes. The vegetables should still be crispy but tender. Stir vegetable mixture into couscous with vinegar, chickpeas, parsley, pine nuts, remaining oil and salt and pepper to taste. Serve cold or at room temperature.

THE DISH **Couscous.** Essentially the world's tiniest pasta, it's made from semolina and comes in regular and whole wheat varieties. We like both kinds and make sure we always have some sitting in our pantry.

Spiced Israeli Couscous and Chicken Salad

Warm spices of the Middle East like cinnamon, ginger, cumin and allspice come together to perfume this hearty main dish salad. Instead of the standard couscous, here we use the larger Israeli (sometimes called "pearl") type of couscous, which gives a chewier texture to the dish. Shredded chicken, an array of colorful vegetables and fresh herbs make it a meal. Try serving it in hollowed-out tomatoes for the perfect luncheon entrée.

Serves 6

Hands-on time
40 minutes

Start to finish
40 minutes

Make Ahead

The salad can be made 1 day ahead and kept covered and refrigerated.

⅓ cup	golden raisins	75 mL
¼ cup	extra virgin olive oil, divided	60 mL
1 tsp	salt	5 mL
1	box (8.8 oz/250 g) Israeli couscous	1
1	red onion, cut into small dice	1
2	cloves garlic, minced	2
2	medium zucchini, cut into small dice	2
1	red bell pepper, seeded and cut into small dice	1
½ tsp	ground cumin	2 mL
¼ tsp	ground ginger	1 mL
¼ tsp	ground cinnamon	1 mL
¼ tsp	ground allspice	1 mL
3 cups	shredded cooked or deli-roasted chicken	750 mL
¼ cup	pine nuts, toasted lightly	60 mL
¼ cup	finely chopped fresh cilantro	60 mL
¼ cup	finely chopped fresh mint	60 mL
2 tbsp	red wine vinegar	30 mL
	Salt and freshly ground black pepper	

1. In a small saucepan over medium-high heat, bring 2 cups (500 mL) water to a boil with raisins, 1 tbsp (15 mL) of the oil and salt. Stir in couscous and simmer for 8 minutes. Remove from heat and let stand for 5 minutes. Fluff couscous with a fork and transfer to bowl.

2. In a small skillet, heat 2 tbsp (30 mL) of oil over medium heat. Sauté red onion for about 6 minutes or until softened. Add garlic, zucchini, bell pepper, cumin, ginger, cinnamon and allspice and sauté for 2 minutes. The vegetables should still be crispy but tender. Stir vegetable mixture into couscous. Add chicken, pine nuts, cilantro, mint, remaining 1 tbsp (15 mL) of oil and vinegar. Season with salt and pepper to taste. Serve cold or at room temperature.

Mango, Jicama and Red Onion Salad

So simple and yet so good, this sweet and savory salad is our favorite foil to a spicy entrée. Although the ingredients are few, the salad seems complex, probably because of all the contrasting textures and flavors. Soft, sweet mango, crunchy jicama and thin slices of red onion are all bathed in a sweet-tart honey lime dressing.

Serves 8

Hands-on time
20 minutes

Start to finish
20 minutes

Make Ahead

The salad can be made up to 2 hours ahead and kept covered and refrigerated.

1	medium red onion, thinly sliced	1
	Zest of 1 lime	
3 tbsp	freshly squeezed lime juice	45 mL
2 tbsp	liquid honey	30 mL
⅓ cup	vegetable oil	75 mL
	Salt	
2	ripe mangos, cut into matchsticks	2
1	medium jicama (about 1½ lbs/750 g), peeled and cut into matchsticks	1
¼ cup	chopped fresh cilantro	60 mL

1. Place red onion in a medium bowl and cover with cold water. Let stand for 15 minutes.

2. Meanwhile, in a bowl, whisk together lime zest, lime juice and honey. Slowly whisk in oil. Season with salt to taste.

3. Drain onion in a colander and transfer to a large bowl. Add mango, jicama and cilantro. Drizzle honey lime vinaigrette over salad and toss to coat.

THE DISH **Jicama.** As the tuberous root of a large vine native to Mexico, jicama is a popular ingredient in Mexican cooking and tastes like a cross between a raw potato and apple. Its crunch is a welcome addition to any salad, and once you've tried it, you'll find a million other uses for it as well.

Mango, Jicama and Pecan Slaw with Honey Lime Dressing

Although mango and jicama might seem like intruders in this Southern-style coleslaw, when you taste it, it's easy to see that their sweetness and crunch are right at home. It's fun to serve something so unexpected. It adds a liveliness to gatherings and even gives guests something to talk about.

Serves 8

Hands-on time
35 minutes

Start to finish
35 minutes

Make Ahead

The dressing can be made up to 1 day ahead and kept covered and refrigerated. The slaw can be made up to 1 hour ahead and kept covered and refrigerated.

1	medium red onion, finely chopped	1
Honey Lime Dressing		
2 tbsp	heavy or whipping (35%) cream	30 mL
2 tbsp	mayonnaise	30 mL
	Zest of 1 lime	
3 tbsp	freshly squeezed lime juice	45 mL
2 tbsp	liquid honey	30 mL
½ cup	vegetable oil	125 mL
	Salt	
2	ripe mangos, cut into matchsticks	2
½	medium jicama (about 1½ lbs/750 g), peeled and cut into matchsticks	½
3 cups	shredded cabbage	750 mL
½ cup	chopped toasted pecans	125 mL
¼ cup	chopped fresh cilantro	125 mL

1. Place red onion in a medium bowl and cover with cold water. Let stand for 15 minutes.

2. *Honey Lime Dressing:* Meanwhile, in a bowl, whisk together cream, mayonnaise, lime zest, lime juice and honey. Slowly whisk in oil. Season with salt to taste.

3. Drain onion in a colander and transfer to a large bowl. Add mango, jicama, cabbage, pecans and cilantro. Drizzle honey lime dressing over salad and toss to coat.

THE DISH **Toasted Nuts.** We almost never use raw or untoasted nuts in a recipe and there's a good reason. Toasted nuts offer exponentially more flavor than their raw counterparts. Next time you're making cookies or a quick bread, try toasting the nuts first and you'll see what we mean.

Grilled Thai Chicken Salad with Spicy Mint Dressing

Grilled chicken salad has long been a favorite dish for ladies who "lunch." It's substantial enough to fill you up but light enough to make you comfortable eating it in front of the girls. The trouble is, most of those salads tend to be boring. Our Thai-inspired version is anything but. This zippy, citrusy version is a party in your mouth. The chicken is grilled and served on a bed of cold, crispy lettuce. The mint- and lime-based dressing is spicy enough to make you sit up, but not so incendiary that your hair goes up in flames.

Serves 4

Hands-on time
30 minutes

Start to finish
30 minutes

Make Ahead

The dressing can be made up to 2 days ahead and kept covered and refrigerated.

- **Preheat greased barbecue grill to medium-high or preheat broiler**

½ cup	freshly squeezed lime juice	125 mL
2 tbsp	Thai fish sauce or soy sauce	60 mL
3 tbsp	light brown sugar	45 mL
1 to 2	serrano chile peppers, seeded and minced	1 to 2
⅓ cup	thinly sliced fresh mint leaves	75 mL
¼ tsp	salt	1 mL
1½ lbs	chicken tenders	750 g
6 cups	romaine lettuce, torn into bite-size pieces	1.5 L
16	cherry tomatoes, quartered	16
½	medium red onion, sliced thinly	125 mL

1. In a medium bowl, whisk together lime juice, fish sauce, brown sugar, chile to taste, mint and salt. Toss chicken tenders in 2 tbsp (30 mL) of the dressing.

2. Grill or broil chicken tenders for 5 to 8 minutes per side or until nicely browned and no longer pink inside.

3. Divide lettuce among 4 serving plates. Sprinkle top with cherry tomatoes and red onion slices. Drizzle with some of the remaining dressing and top with grilled chicken.

THE DISH **Hot Chile Peppers.** Today's jalapeños just aren't what they used to be. Their degree of heat is so variable that you never know what you're getting. You could buy a dozen and only get two or three that have any heat at all. That's why we tend to stay away from jalapeños and veer toward predictable serranos.

Thai Chicken Lettuce Wraps with Two Dipping Sauces

Whoever thought of making a taco using lettuce leaves for the shell should be congratulated. Now we can enjoy the sensation of eating something decadent, when really we're just having salad. We love to serve this dish at dinner parties because it's so much fun to eat. Diners can construct their own lettuce wraps using delicious coconut curry-marinated grilled chicken, carrots, red peppers, bean sprouts and cilantro and dip them into a spicy lime-mint sauce or, our personal favorite, a Thai peanut sauce. Oh baby!

Serves 4

Hands-on time
1 hour

Start to finish
1 hour 30 minutes

Make Ahead

The marinade and both the dipping sauces can be made up to 2 days ahead and kept covered and refrigerated. The peanut sauce can be reheated in a saucepan over low heat.

Marinade

1 cup	unsweetened coconut milk	250 mL
2 tbsp	Thai fish sauce or soy sauce	30 mL
2 tbsp	freshly squeezed lime juice	30 mL
2 tbsp	light brown sugar	30 mL
1 tbsp	Thai red curry paste	15 mL
1½ lbs	chicken tenders	750 g

Peanut Dipping Sauce

1 cup	unsweetened coconut milk	250 mL
1 tbsp	light brown sugar	15 mL
1 tbsp	Thai red curry paste	15 mL
1 tbsp	Thai fish sauce or soy sauce	15 mL
½ cup	crunchy peanut butter	125 mL

Spicy Mint Dipping Sauce

½ cup	freshly squeezed lime juice	125 mL
2 tbsp	Thai fish sauce or soy sauce	30 mL
3 tbsp	light brown sugar	45 mL
1 to 2	serrano chile peppers, seeded and minced	1 to 2
⅓ cup	thinly sliced fresh mint leaves	75 mL
¼ tsp	salt	1 mL
2 cups	bean sprouts	500 mL
1	red bell pepper, cut into matchsticks	1
⅓ cup	whole cilantro leaves	75 mL
¼ cup	chopped roasted peanuts	60 mL
1	head butter lettuce, separated into individual leaves	1

1. *Marinade:* In a medium bowl, whisk together coconut milk, fish sauce, lime juice, brown sugar and curry paste. Add chicken tenders and toss to coat. Marinate in refrigerator for 1 hour.

2. *Peanut Dipping Sauce:* In saucepan over medium heat, combine coconut milk, brown sugar, curry paste and fish sauce. Bring to a gentle boil, stirring occasionally, for 3 minutes. Add peanut butter and continue to cook until peanut butter is well blended. Set aside.

3. *Spicy Mint Dipping Sauce:* In a small bowl, whisk together lime juice, fish sauce, brown sugar, chiles to taste, mint and salt. Set aside.

4. Preheat greased barbecue grill to medium-high or preheat broiler. Grill or broil chicken tenders for 5 to 8 minutes per side or until nicely browned and no longer pink inside. Set aside.

5. On a large platter, arrange bean sprouts, bell pepper, cilantro leaves, peanuts, lettuce leaves and chicken. Allow your guests to make their own lettuce wraps and serve with dipping sauces on the side.

THE DISH **Leftovers.** We can't get enough of these flavors, so when we make this dish, we always double the recipe, especially for the chicken and peanut sauce. They are perfect the next day tossed with spaghetti noodles and a handful of fresh cilantro.

Fashion Plate

For a fun soup and salad combo, combine this salad with Spicy Thai Sweet Potato Soup with Lemongrass and Coconut Milk (page 126).

Pasta Salad with Tomatoes and Corn

Pasta salad is one of our favorite dishes to bring to a potluck or casual cookout with friends and family. The most complicated step in this recipe is cooking the pasta. If you have a garlic press, you don't even need to pull a knife out of the drawer. So when easy and quick is the name of the game, this should be your go-to recipe for on the go entertaining.

Serves 8

Hands-on time
30 minutes

Start to finish
30 minutes

Make Ahead

The salad can be made up to 4 hours ahead and kept at room temperature.

1 tbsp	salt, divided	15 mL
1 lb	penne pasta	500 g
2 cups	frozen corn	500 mL
¼ cup	white wine vinegar (approx.)	60 mL
1	clove garlic, pressed in a garlic press or minced	1
	Freshly ground black pepper	
⅓ cup	extra virgin olive oil	75 mL
⅓ cup	pine nuts	75 mL
½ cup	julienned sun-dried tomatoes in oil, drained	125 mL
⅓ cup	freshly grated Parmesan cheese	75 mL
¼ cup	torn fresh basil	60 mL
½ tsp	hot pepper flakes, optional	2 mL

1. Bring a large pot of water to a boil over medium-high heat. Add 2 tsp (10 mL) of the salt and pasta and cook until al dente, following directions on box. Drain pasta and toss with frozen corn so that it stops the cooking. Set aside.

2. In a large bowl, combine vinegar, garlic, ½ tsp (2 mL) salt, and pepper to taste. Let stand for about 5 minutes for flavors to combine. Whisk in oil. Set aside.

3. In a small dry skillet, heat pine nuts over medium heat, shaking pan every now and then until they begin to brown. Transfer pine nuts to a large plate and set aside.

4. Add pasta and corn mixture to vinaigrette and toss to mix. Add pine nuts, sun-dried tomatoes, Parmesan, basil, hot pepper flakes, remaining salt and ¼ tsp (1 mL) pepper and toss to combine. Taste for seasoning and add more salt, pepper or vinegar to taste, if necessary. Serve at room temperature.

DOUBLE DISH

Pine Nuts. When toasted, pine nuts add that certain *je ne sais quoi* to everything from appetizers and salads to main dishes and desserts. Toasting them is as easy as heating them up for a few minutes in a dry skillet over medium heat. It's a great way to practice your chef skillet wrist-toss to make sure they brown evenly with no burned spots.

Julienned Sun-Dried Tomatoes. Sun-dried tomatoes can be messy, sticky and difficult to cut, so save yourself the trouble and buy them already cut down to size. If you'd like to cut some calories, buy your sun-dried tomatoes in dried form and reconstitute them in hot water until pliable.

Fashion Plate

Serve this hearty salad with Mustard and Garlic–Roasted Pork Loin (page 208) and Dark Chocolate–Hazelnut Biscotti (page 337).

Warm Pasta Salad with Roasted Corn and Poblanos

We've turned the previous recipe into a decidedly Mexican-inspired pasta salad. Here, we roast the corn and poblano chiles to give them a smoky flavor that blends nicely with the cumin, garlic and cilantro. We really prefer this salad warm, but at room temperature it is still a standout and sure to be something new for your guests to experience.

Serves 8

Hands-on time
40 minutes

Start to finish
1 hour

Make Ahead

This salad is best made and eaten right away. If you have to make it ahead, finish it 4 hours ahead of time and keep it at room temperature.

• **Preheat greased barbecue grill or broiler**

3	ears corn, husk and silk removed	3
3	poblano chiles	3
2 tbsp	vegetable oil	30 mL
1 cup	chopped onion	250 mL
1	clove garlic, minced	1
½ tsp	ground cumin	2 mL
¼ cup	white wine vinegar	60 mL
2½ tsp	salt, divided	12 mL
¼ tsp	freshly ground black pepper	1 mL
⅓ cup	extra virgin olive oil	75 mL
2 cups	grape tomatoes, halved	500 mL
1	can (14 to 19 oz/398 to 540 mL) black beans, drained and rinsed	1
1 cup	queso fresco (fresh Mexican cheese), crumbled	250 mL
¼ cup	roasted sunflower seeds	60 mL
¼ cup	minced fresh cilantro	60 mL
1 lb	penne pasta	500 g

1. Grill corn on prepared grill or place on a baking sheet under a broiler over high heat for about 20 minutes or until it blackens slightly, turning occasionally to cook evenly. Let cool until it can be handled. Remove kernels and set aside in a bowl. Discard cobs.

2. Over a gas stove-top burner or under a broiler over high heat, blacken chiles on all sides, using tongs to turn them, about 10 minutes. Transfer to a bowl. Cover with plastic wrap and let cool until they can be handled. Peel blackened skin from chiles and discard. Cut peppers into strips, discarding seeds.

3. In a skillet, heat vegetable oil over medium heat. Sauté onion for 6 minutes or until softened. Add garlic, cumin and corn and sauté for 1 minute or until garlic is fragrant.

4. Bring a large pot of water to a boil.

5. In a large bowl, combine vinegar, ½ tsp (2 mL) of the salt and pepper until salt dissolves. Whisk in olive oil. Add corn mixture, chiles, tomatoes, black beans, cheese, sunflower seeds and cilantro. Toss to coat.

6. Add remaining salt to boiling water along with pasta and cook until al dente, following directions on box. Drain pasta and add to vegetables. Toss to blend salad. Taste for seasoning and add more salt or pepper to taste, if necessary. Serve warm or at room temperature.

THE DISH **Queso Fresco.** Similar to farmer's cheese, salty queso fresco is also called queso blanco, or white cheese. If you can't find it, try using Italy's version, ricotta salata.

Fashion Plate

Start off with Tequila Bloody Mary Shrimp Cocktails (page 42) and serve Warm Pasta Salad with Roasted Corn and Poblanos alongside Chicken Chorizo Enchiladas with Creamy Tomatillo Sauce (page 246).

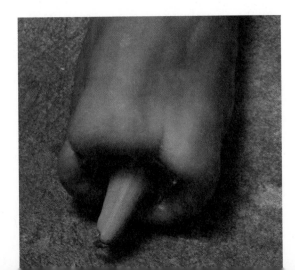

Panzanella

Whenever we eat this delightful tomato, cucumber and bread salad, we think of sitting on the patio of a scenic Italian coastal restaurant, sipping a refreshingly light red wine and nibbling our afternoon away. The view from the restaurant may be difficult to duplicate, but this salad is no problem to throw together on a sunny day — or any day, for that matter.

Serves 6

Hands-on time
30 minutes

Start to finish
1 hour 15 minutes

Make Ahead

The vinaigrette can be made up to 2 days ahead and kept covered and refrigerated.

● **Preheat oven to 375°F (190°C)**

Croutons

12 oz	rustic Italian bread, cut into 1-inch (2.5 cm) cubes (6 cups/1.5 L)	375 g
2 tbsp	extra virgin olive oil	30 mL
	Salt and freshly ground black pepper	

Vinaigrette

2	cloves garlic, minced	2
3 tbsp	red wine vinegar	45 mL
½ cup	extra virgin olive oil	125 mL
2	large ripe tomatoes, cut into 1-inch (2.5 cm) cubes	2
1	English cucumber, unpeeled, seeded and sliced ½ inch (1 cm) thick	1
½ cup	thinly sliced red onion	125 mL
¼ cup	coarsely chopped fresh basil	60 mL

1. *Croutons:* On a large baking sheet, toss bread with oil to coat. Season with ½ tsp (2 mL) salt and ¼ tsp (1 mL) pepper. Bake in preheated oven, stirring once or twice, for 8 to 9 minutes or until croutons are lightly golden. Let cool.

2. *Vinaigrette:* In a medium bowl, combine garlic, vinegar and ½ tsp (2 mL) each salt and pepper. Slowly whisk in oil.

3. In a large bowl, mix together tomatoes, cucumber, red onion and basil. Add bread cubes and vinaigrette and toss to coat. Taste and season with salt and pepper, if necessary. Let stand for 30 minutes at room temperature for the flavors to blend.

THE DISH **Leftover Bread.** Just pop it into a freezer bag and store it frozen until you are ready to make croutons or bread crumbs or this summery salad.

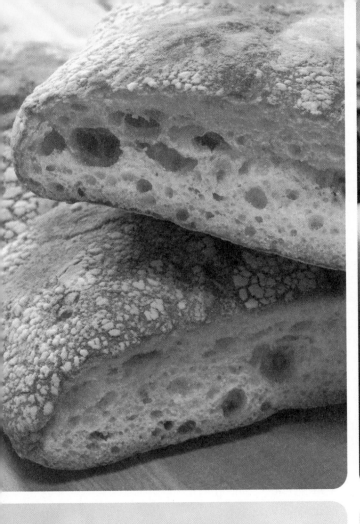

Grilled Summer Vegetable Salad on Sourdough Croutons

One of our favorite ways to entertain is to grill and eat outside, and no dish lends itself better to that kind of get-together than this pretty as a picture salad. In a twist on our traditional panzanella, we grill our bread and vegetables, adding sweet peppers and zucchini to the mix. We keep them separate and reunite them all just before serving, ladling the vegetable salad on top of our sourdough slices and allowing them to soak up all the mouth-watering flavors.

Serves 6

Hands-on time
30 minutes

Start to finish
30 minutes

Make Ahead

The bread can be grilled up to 2 hours ahead and kept at room temperature. The vegetables can be grilled up to 2 hours ahead and kept at room temperature. The dressing can be made up to 2 days ahead and kept covered and refrigerated.

• **Preheat greased barbecue grill to medium-high**

6	1-inch (2.5 cm) slices sourdough bread	6
	Olive oil	
	Salt and freshly ground black pepper	
1	red bell pepper	1
1	yellow bell pepper	1
1	zucchini, cut lengthwise in half	1
1	onion, cut into thick slices	1
2	cloves garlic, minced	2
3 tbsp	balsamic vinegar	45 mL
1/2 tsp	salt	2 mL
1/4 tsp	freshly ground black pepper	1 mL
1/2 cup	extra virgin olive oil	125 mL
2	large ripe tomatoes, cut into 1-inch (2.5 cm) cubes	2
1/2 cup	Pesto (page 25) or store-bought	125 mL

1. Lightly brush both sides of bread equally with 3 tbsp (45 mL) olive oil and lightly season with salt and pepper. Grill for about 1 minute per side, until toasted. Set aside.

2. Brush red and yellow peppers, zucchini and onion lightly with olive oil. Grill, turning occasionally, for about 10 minutes or until peppers are blackened and zucchini and onion are softened and have grill marks. Remove vegetables from grill and place peppers in a bowl, covered tightly with plastic wrap. Let steam for 5 minutes. Peel, seed and core.

3. Cut peppers, zucchini and onion into 1-inch (2.5 cm) pieces and place in a large bowl.

4. In a medium bowl, add garlic, vinegar, salt and pepper. Slowly whisk in oil.

5. Add dressing and tomatoes to vegetables in large bowl and gently toss to combine.

6. Slather one side of grilled bread slices with pesto and place on serving plates, pesto side up. Spoon vegetables on top of bread slices, making sure to spoon any leftover juices on as well.

THE DISH **Linen and Candlelight.** Just because you're eating outside doesn't mean you have to break out the paper plates and plastic forks. Throwing a lovely tablecloth on your patio table and setting out candles can turn a casual evening into a magical night. Arrange the table with white pillar candles of varying heights and don't forget the sparkly tea lights to fill up the spaces in between.

Fashion Plate

Sometimes, when serving a hearty salad, it makes sense to serve it alongside a light entrée. We'd serve this "big" salad with Nothin'-But-Crab Cakes (page 254) and a Rustic Plum Tart (page 362).

Lentil Salad with Feta Cheese

There are countless versions of this healthful salad served along the Mediterranean from North Africa and Spain all the way to Turkey and beyond. Not only is it delicious and good for you, but the flavors are bright with lemon and mint, while the tomatoes and feta cheese add color and punch.

Serves 6

Hands-on time
20 minutes

Start to finish
30 minutes

Tip

Add a combination of green French lentils du Puy, orange or red Indian lentils and the easy-to-find brown lentils. The colors are very pretty.

Make Ahead

The salad can be made up to 1 day ahead, covered and refrigerated. Add feta cheese just before serving.

1 cup	lentils, washed and picked over	250 mL
1 tsp	salt, divided	5 mL
1	shallot, minced	1
1	clove garlic, minced	1
¼ cup	white wine vinegar	60 mL
1 tsp	liquid honey	5 mL
¼ tsp	freshly ground black pepper	1 mL
⅓ cup	extra virgin olive oil	75 mL
2 cups	grape tomatoes, halved	500 mL
¼ cup	chopped fresh mint	60 mL
2 tsp	freshly squeezed lemon juice, optional	10 mL
½ cup	crumbled feta cheese	125 mL

1. In a medium saucepan over medium heat, cover lentils and ¼ tsp (1 mL) of the salt with water by 2 inches (5 cm) and bring to a boil. Reduce heat to low, cover and simmer lentils for 15 minutes or until tender. Drain and set aside

2. In a large bowl, combine shallot, garlic, vinegar, honey, ¼ tsp (1 mL) of salt and pepper. Let stand for a few minutes for flavors to blend. Whisk in olive oil. Taste and adjust with more salt or pepper, if necessary.

3. Add warm lentils and remaining ½ tsp (2 mL) of salt to bowl with dressing and toss to mix. Add tomatoes and mint. Taste and add lemon, if desired. Refrigerate if not eating right away. Bring to room temperature before serving and top with feta cheese.

THE DISH **Lentils.** Lentils come in quite a few shapes and sizes. There are the usual brown lentils at most grocery stores, the green lentils from France (lentils du Puy), lentils from India (dal) and the black beluga lentils at specialty markets. Like a mother with many children, we love them all equally, but sometimes prefer one type over another depending on the occasion. They all cook basically in the same way, so use whichever lentil strikes your fancy.

Lentil Salad with Dried Cranberries and Pistachios

You will be surprised at how the addition of cranberries, celery, carrot and pistachios adds sweetness and crunch to this salad. The colors in this mélange remind us of bright and breezy Lily Pulitzer dresses from the '60s. The flavors, however, are very today.

Serves 6

Hands-on time
30 minutes

Start to finish
30 minutes

Variation

Substitute raisins or dried cherries for the cranberries.

Make Ahead

The salad can be made up to 1 day ahead, covered and refrigerated. Stir in pistachios and sprinkle with feta just before serving.

½ cup	dried cranberries	125 mL
1	recipe Lentil Salad with Feta Cheese (page 84)	1
½ cup	finely diced carrot	125 mL
½ cup	finely diced celery	125 mL
½ cup	pistachios	125 mL
	Zest of 1 lemon	
1 tbsp	freshly squeezed lemon juice	15 mL
1	8-oz (250 g) empty can with both ends removed, optional	1
½ cup	crumbled feta cheese	125 mL

1. In a bowl, soak dried cranberries in hot water for 10 minutes. Drain.

2. Make Lentil Salad with Feta Cheese recipe, adding cranberries, carrot, celery, pistachios, lemon zest and lemon juice, through Step 3.

3. For a more structured look on your plate, place an empty 8-oz (250 g) can with both ends removed on the plate. Spoon salad into can and compress lightly with back of a fork. Lift can directly up and it will leave a lovely disk of molded salad on the plate. Garnish with feta.

THE DISH **Pistachios.** It is easier than ever to find shelled pistachios. You should look for unsalted natural (green) pistachios. If you can't find them, slivered almonds will work in a pinch.

Fashion Plate

Begin with this lentil salad and follow with Prosciutto-Wrapped Salmon with Rosemary Butter (page 272) and Vanilla Gelato with Summer Berries and Limoncello (page 350).

Arugula Salad with Grape Tomatoes and Shallot Vinaigrette

Sharp, peppery arugula makes one of our favorite winter salads. Try the baby arugula if you see it. The tiny, tender leaves pack a powerhouse of flavor that is a sure bet to wake up sleepy appetites.

Serves 6

Hands-on time
15 minutes

Start to finish
15 minutes

Make Ahead

The vinaigrette can be made up to 4 hours ahead and kept covered and refrigerated. Toss the arugula and tomatoes with the dressing moments before serving.

- **6 chilled plates**

Shallot Vinaigrette

1	shallot, minced	1
2 tbsp	white wine or sherry vinegar	30 mL
1 tsp	Dijon mustard	5 mL
½ tsp	lightly chopped fresh thyme	2 mL
¼ tsp	salt	1 mL
Pinch	freshly ground black pepper	Pinch
¼ cup	extra virgin olive oil	60 mL
2 cups	halved grape tomatoes	500 mL
1½ cups	arugula	375 mL
	Coarsely ground black pepper, optional	

1. *Shallot Vinaigrette:* In a large bowl, whisk together shallot, vinegar, mustard, thyme, salt and pepper. Let stand for at least 5 minutes for salt to dissolve and flavors to blend.

2. Slowly whisk in olive oil until dressing forms an emulsion or blends together.

3. Toss tomatoes and arugula into bowl with dressing. Season with salt and pepper to taste. Divide arugula and tomato mixture among 6 chilled plates. Top with a generous grinding of black pepper, if desired.

THE DISH **Vinaigrette.** If diamonds are a girl's best friend, then a great vinaigrette recipe can't be far behind. Making this vinaigrette is as easy as 1, 2, 3 and will reward your taste buds with a more delicate flavor than most packaged dressings provide. We think the shallot makes this dressing come alive, but don't underestimate the value of quality white wine or sherry vinegar along with a fine extra virgin olive oil.

Arugula Salad with Shaved Fennel and Prosciutto

One of the best reasons to wear perfume is that its scent precedes you. It relays a silent message of great expectations. Similarly, we love how the peppery arugula brings out the best in savory, roasted fennel, with salty prosciutto chiming in. A simple browning of the shallots will give you a vinaigrette with out of this world taste.

Serves 6

Hands-on time
30 minutes

Start to finish
45 minutes

Make Ahead

The vegetables, dressing and Parmesan curls can be made up to 4 hours ahead of time and kept, covered, at room temperature. Toss arugula and dressing together moments before serving.

- **Preheat greased barbecue grill to medium-high or preheat oven to 400°F (200°C)**
- **6 chilled plates**

Caramelized Shallot Vinaigrette

2	shallots, peeled and quartered	2
1 tbsp plus 1/4 cup	extra virgin olive oil, divided	75 mL
	Salt and freshly ground black pepper	
2 tbsp	white wine or sherry vinegar	30 mL
1/2 tsp	minced fresh thyme	2 mL
1/4 tsp	salt	1 mL
Pinch	freshly ground black pepper	Pinch
2	heads fennel, trimmed and sliced crosswise into 1/8-inch (3 mm) slices	2
1 tbsp	olive oil	15 mL
	Salt and freshly ground black pepper	
1 1/2 cups	arugula	375 mL
8	slices prosciutto, coarsely chopped	8
1/2 cup	chopped toasted walnuts	125 mL
18	curls Parmesan cheese, preferably Parmigiano-Reggiano, shaved with a vegetable peeler	18

1. *Caramelized Shallot Vinaigrette:* Spread shallots on a grill basket if grilling or a baking sheet if roasting in oven. Drizzle shallots with 1 tbsp (15 mL) of the olive oil and season with salt and pepper to taste. Grill or roast for about 15 minutes or until shallots have caramelized and softened. Let cool. Mince and transfer to a large bowl.

Continued on next page

2. Add vinegar, thyme, salt and pepper to shallots. Let stand for at least 5 minutes or for up to 1 hour. Whisk in $\frac{1}{4}$ cup (60 mL) olive oil. Set aside.

3. Spread fennel on a grill basket if grilling or a baking sheet if roasting in oven. Drizzle fennel with 1 tbsp (15 mL) of olive oil and salt and pepper to taste. Grill or roast for 7 to 8 minutes or until fennel softens slightly. Transfer to a medium bowl. Toss fennel with 2 tbsp (30 mL) of the vinaigrette. Set aside.

4. Add arugula to a large bowl and toss with 2 tbsp (30 mL) of the vinaigrette until well coated. Be careful not to overdress the salad. There shouldn't be any dressing pooling in the bottom of the bowl.

5. Divide arugula among 6 chilled plates and arrange roasted fennel decoratively on top. Sprinkle prosciutto and walnuts over top and garnish with Parmesan curls.

THE DISH **Caramelized Shallot.** Grilling or roasting the shallot brings out its sweeter nature. Once the sugars have browned, the shallot morphs from sharp to sweet, providing a rich, full-bodied background flavor. Once you've become familiar with shallots, your kitchen will never be without them.

Fashion Plate

Begin with this salad and follow with simple Steak with Simple Deglazing Sauce (page 182), Crispy Potato Cakes (page 304) and Almond Cake with Apricot Filling and Whipped Cream (page 334).

Roasted Beet Salad on Endive Spears

Who knew that beets could be so charming? As children, we wanted nothing to do with tired old beets from a can, but now we know that when you cook them up fresh, delicious happens. Beets are the master of clever understatement. There they sit, unassuming, just waiting to be made fabulous with a little garlic vinaigrette.

Serves 4

Hands-on time
10 minutes

Start to finish
1 hour

Make Ahead

The beets can be made 1 day ahead, mixed with the dressing and kept covered and refrigerated. Assemble the salad just before serving.

- **Preheat oven to 375°F (190°C)**

1 lb	medium-size beets, red, orange chiogga or golden	500 g
¼ cup	olive oil, divided	60 mL
	Salt and freshly ground black pepper	
2 tbsp	sherry vinegar	30 mL
1	small clove garlic, minced	1
Pinch	salt	Pinch
Pinch	freshly ground black pepper	Pinch
1	head Belgian endive, leaves separated	1
2 tsp	minced flat-leaf parsley	10 mL

1. Scrub beets and cut into 4 wedges or 6 to 8 wedges, if very large. Divide beets between two separate sheets of foil and drizzle with 1 tbsp (15 mL) of the olive oil. Sprinkle with salt and pepper. Bring up corners of foil to tightly enclose the packages. Roast packages in middle of preheated oven for 45 minutes to 1 hour or until beets are tender. To test for doneness, open a package and insert the tip of a knife into middle of one of the sections. If it enters easily, the beets are done. If there is some resistance, cook beets for 10 minutes more and check again. Remove from oven, open packages and let beets stand until cool enough to handle.

2. Meanwhile, in a medium bowl, combine vinegar, garlic, salt and pepper. Let stand for 5 minutes for flavors to blend. Whisk in remaining olive oil. Taste dressing for seasoning, adding more salt or pepper to taste, if necessary.

3. Using a paring knife, slip skins from the still warm beets and cut into ½-inch (1 cm) dice. Add beets to vinaigrette and toss to mix.

4. Just before serving, add 1 tsp (5 mL) or so of beet salad to fat end of 12 endive spears. Arrange spears in a spoke fashion onto individual serving plates. Sprinkle parsley over plates. Serve at room temperature.

Beet Salad with Ricotta Salata, Walnuts and Micro Greens

Roasted beets and tasty micro greens unite for a beautiful plate of vegetables that really sings. This is our go-to recipe in the fall, whether we take it to a friend's house for a potluck or serve it to our very lucky families. Either way, the combination of roasted beets, ricotta salata cheese, walnuts and spunky greens makes for a ravishing plate of color, texture and taste.

Serves 4

Hands-on time
20 minutes

Start to finish
1 hour

Tip

Ricotta salata is a firm, mild, slightly salty cheese made from sheep's milk. If you can't find it, go ahead and use feta instead.

Make Ahead

The beets can be made 1 day ahead, mixed with the dressing and kept covered and refrigerated. The micro greens can be dressed moments before serving.

1	recipe Roasted Beets (page 90)	1
2 cups	micro greens	500 mL
½ cup	ricotta salata cheese, cut into small dice	125 mL
½ cup	chopped toasted walnuts	125 mL
	Freshly ground black pepper	

1. Make Roasted Beets as directed in previous recipe. Toss with a little more than half of the vinaigrette and set aside. Thinly slice endive.

2. In a large bowl, combine micro greens and endive with remaining vinaigrette.

3. Divide salad among 4 plates. Top with beets and finish with a sprinkling of ricotta salata, walnuts and a generous grind of black pepper.

THE DISH **Micro Greens.** Combined with blends of itty bitty, delicate salad greens, edible flowers and herbs, micro greens can often be found prepackaged in grocery stores these days. Cutting-edge chefs brought them to our attention a few years ago, and now it's our turn to create innovative salads with these trendy greens. If you can't find them, just use the mesclun mix or a combination of tender baby greens and sprouts.

Fashion Plate

Partner this salad with various small bites, such as Wild Mushroom and Thyme Spread (page 56) and Smoked Salmon on toast points (page 18).

Seared Scallop Salad with Chicory and Sherry Vinaigrette

Scallops make such a nice beginning to a meal. They are light but flavorful, especially when quickly seared and paired with chewy frisée lettuce. The enticing red and green lettuces on the plate will stir your appetite, as will the tart, shallot-infused vinaigrette. This combo is a party on a plate, and we think it's time you joined the party!

Serves 6

Hands-on time
20 minutes

Start to finish
20 minutes

Make Ahead

The Sherry Vinaigrette can be made up to 4 hours ahead and kept at room temperature.

Sherry Vinaigrette

2 tbsp	sherry wine vinegar	30 mL
1	small shallot, minced	1
Pinch	each salt and freshly ground black pepper	Pinch
¼ cup	extra virgin olive oil	60 mL
1	small head radicchio or chicory, thinly sliced	1
1	small head frisée lettuce (curly escarole), torn into small pieces	1
1 tbsp	unsalted butter	15 mL
12	scallops, U-10, day boat or dry pack	12
	Fleur de sel or sea salt	

1. *Sherry Vinaigrette:* In a small bowl, combine vinegar, shallots, salt and pepper. Let stand for 5 minutes for flavors to blend. Whisk in olive oil. Taste for seasoning, adding more salt or pepper to taste.

2. Ten minutes before serving, in a large bowl, combine radicchio and frisée lettuce and toss with half the dressing. Set aside.

3. Heat a large skillet over medium-high heat and add butter. When butter sizzles, add scallops and cook for about 2 minutes. Turn and cook for 1 minute more. Transfer to a plate and lightly season with salt and pepper.

4. Divide lettuce among 6 plates and arrange scallops on top. Drizzle remaining dressing over scallops.

THE DISH **Fleur de Sel.** If you have fleur de sel in your pantry, this dish is a good use for it. French fleur de sel is the "flower of salts" because it has concentrated salty flavor and a clean taste that other salts wish they could mimic. Another of our salty favorites is Maldon salt, which comes from the English coastal flats.

Seared Scallop Salad with Grapefruit, Avocado and Fennel

A perfectly seared scallop is an impressive dish, but pairing it with this combination of tart grapefruit, buttery avocado and crunchy fennel gives it superstar status. This dish will soon be your favorite starter for a more formal dinner or as a casual main course dinner for two.

Serves 6

Hands-on time
30 minutes

Start to finish
30 minutes

Tip

To section a grapefruit, peel away the skin and pith with a sharp paring knife. Over a large bowl, make cuts between the membranes and release each section of the fruit into the bowl. The bowl will also catch any stray juices that release from the grapefruit. When all the fruit has been released from the membrane, squeeze the membrane to release the last of the juice. To keep the avocado from browning, add it to the bowl and toss to mix. The acid in the juice will keep the green color bright.

Make Ahead

The Sherry Vinaigrette can be made up to 4 hours ahead and kept at room temperature. The fruit can be cut and kept, covered and refrigerated, in the same bowl for up to 4 hours.

1	recipe Sherry Vinaigrette (page 92)	1
1	small head radicchio or chicory, thinly sliced	1
1	small head frisée lettuce (curly escarole), torn into small pieces	1
½	head fennel, trimmed and thinly sliced	½
1 tsp	black sesame seeds (nigella)	5 mL
12	scallops, U-10, day boat or dry pack	12
1 tbsp	unsalted butter	15 mL
	Salt and freshly ground black pepper	
1	pink grapefruit, sectioned (see Tip, left)	1
1	avocado, cut into thin slices	1

1. Ten minutes before serving, make Sherry Vinaigrette in previous recipe. In a large bowl, combine radicchio, frisée and fennel and toss with half the dressing. Set aside.

2. Sprinkle sesame seeds over scallops. Heat a large skillet over medium-high heat and add butter. When butter sizzles, add scallops, seed side down, and cook for about 2 minutes. Turn and cook for 1 minute more. Transfer to a plate and season lightly with salt and pepper.

3. Divide greens among plates and arrange grapefruit and avocado decoratively on top. Sprinkle with a little salt and pepper, if desired. Top with scallops and drizzle with remaining dressing.

THE DISH **Black Sesame Seeds (Nigella).** Sesame seeds can come in brown, red or black and have a nutty taste. Nigella is in fact a black onion seed that has an oniony, peppery flavor. Both seeds can be found in Middle Eastern or Indian grocery stores or online. If you can't find them, just use garden-variety sesame seeds. When browned, they taste fabulous.

Pear Salad with Hazelnuts and Gorgonzola

You'll love the color, crunch and creamy richness of this fall classic. Nothing tastes better on a crisp autumn day than the match of Gorgonzola, hazelnuts and pears. We could serve this salad for dinner with bread and a glass or two of a fine Pinot Gris. So go ahead and bundle up for that last dinner outside before winter weather chases us indoors.

Serves 6

Hands-on time
30 minutes

Start to finish
30 minutes

Make Ahead

The dressing can be made up to 24 hours ahead and kept covered and refrigerated. Cut the pears and toss the salad just before serving.

2 tbsp	freshly squeezed lemon juice	30 mL
1 tbsp	white wine vinegar	15 mL
2 tbsp	minced shallot	30 mL
1 tsp	liquid honey	5 mL
1 tsp	Dijon mustard	5 mL
½ cup	olive oil	125 mL
2	heads Boston lettuce, torn into bite-size pieces	2
1	head radicchio, cut into thin slivers	1
3	ripe pears, such as Bartlett or Anjou, cored and each cut into 8 slices	3
1 cup	crumbled Gorgonzola cheese	250 mL
1 cup	hazelnuts, skinned and chopped	250 mL
	Salt and freshly ground black pepper	

1. In a medium bowl, combine lemon juice, vinegar and shallot. Let stand for about 5 minutes for flavors to blend. Add honey and mustard and vigorously whisk in olive oil until blended and emulsified. Set aside.

2. In a large bowl, combine lettuce and radicchio and toss with half the dressing. Arrange salad on serving plates.

3. Add 2 tbsp (30 mL) of the dressing to a medium bowl. Add pears and toss gently. Arrange pears decoratively on salads and sprinkle with Gorgonzola and hazelnuts. Season with salt and pepper to taste. Drizzle over a little more dressing, if desired.

Fashion Plate

Serve this salad with Potato and Leek Soup (page 108) and Chocolate Mousse (page 338).

Roasted Pear Salad with Gorgonzola Rounds

Once you try roasted pears, you will always want to eat them this way. The heat tenderizes them, but also concentrates their sweetness. In this dressed-up version, we've also roasted the nuts, which imparts a toasty edge. One of our favorite things about this recipe is the technique of pressing the disks of cheese into the warm nuts. The hot nuts melt the cheese slightly, which gives it a different character in the vinaigrette-tossed salad.

Serves 6

Hands-on time
30 minutes

Start to finish
40 minutes

Make Ahead

The dressing can be made up to 24 hours in advance and kept covered and refrigerated. The pears can be roasted up to 8 hours in advance and kept at room temperature. The nut-crusted Gorgonzola can be assembled and just reheated in a 350°F (180°C) oven along with the pears for about 3 minutes. Toss the salad with the dressing just before serving.

- **Preheat greased barbecue grill to medium-high**
- **Preheat oven to 350°F (180°C)**
- **Baking sheet, lined with parchment paper**

2 tbsp	freshly squeezed lemon juice	30 mL
1 tbsp	white wine vinegar	15 mL
2 tbsp	minced shallot	30 mL
1 tsp	liquid honey	5 mL
1 tsp	Dijon mustard	5 mL
½ cup	olive oil	125 mL
3	ripe pears, such as Bartlett or Anjou, cored and each cut into 8 slices	3
1 cup	hazelnuts, skinned and chopped	250 mL
1 cup	Gorgonzola cheese	250 mL
2	heads Boston lettuce, torn into bite-size pieces	2
1	head radicchio, cut into thin slivers	1
	Salt and freshly ground black pepper	

1. In a medium bowl, combine lemon juice, vinegar and shallot. Let stand for about 5 minutes for flavors to blend. Add honey and mustard and vigorously whisk in olive oil until blended and emulsified. Set aside.

2. Toss the pears with 2 tbsp (30 mL) of the dressing. Arrange on prepared grill or on prepared baking sheet. Grill or roast for about 4 minutes on grill or 10 minutes in oven or until lightly browned on both sides. Let cool.

3. Spread hazelnuts on a baking sheet and toast in preheated oven for about 7 minutes or until lightly golden and fragrant.

Continued on next page

4. Meanwhile, shape cheese into 6 disk-shaped rounds. Press both sides of rounds into the warm toasted nuts. Set aside on a plate.

5. Toss lettuce and radicchio with half the remaining dressing. Divide salad among 6 serving plates. Place grilled pears decoratively on top. Top with warm-nut-covered cheese. Season with salt and pepper to taste. Top each salad with a drizzle of remaining dressing.

DOUBLE DISH

Radicchio. We'd like to crown magenta-colored radicchio as the Miss Congeniality of salad competitions.

Of course it is beautiful, but what we really love about radicchio is that it gets along so well with every kind of salad greens, adding color, crunch and a slightly bitter flavor that we find irresistible. Cut the head of radicchio in half and then into thin slices so that the color is incorporated throughout the salad and each bite contains a bit of radicchio.

Pears. Pears are harvested in the fall but are available year-round as a result of sophisticated storage methods. For the best flavor and texture, try to buy locally grown pears at farmers' markets from September through November, and by all means try some of the local varieties. Choose firm fruit with no bruises or flaws. Store pears at room temperature for 4 to 6 days or until they turn yellow and lose some of their firmness. Refrigerate to slow further ripening.

Fashion Plate

Serve this salad with French Onion Soup (page 128), followed by Individual Chocolate and Almond Bread Puddings (page 329).

Winter Salad with Orange Vinaigrette

Quick and easy to pull together, this salad features the bright note of citrus, making it one of our weeknight standbys. The charm of this salad is its simplicity, so buy the freshest, most perfect greens you can find. This salad is a perfect accompaniment to stews, braises or soups.

Serves 6

Hands-on time
15 minutes

Start to finish
15 minutes

Tip

Keep washed lettuce refrigerated and layered between paper towels in a resealable bag. The leaves will remain crispy and fresh for days.

Variations

Swap out the orange juice for lemon, pineapple, pomegranate or grapefruit juices. Add zest. Or skip the fruit and just use sherry vinegar, balsamic, cider, red wine, champagne or a herbal vinegar. Taste and add more extra virgin oil as needed.

Make Ahead

The vinaigrette can be made up to 4 hours ahead and kept covered and refrigerated.

Orange Vinaigrette

	Grated zest of 1 orange	
2 tbsp	freshly squeezed orange juice	30 mL
2 tsp	white wine vinegar	10 mL
¼ tsp	salt	1 mL
	Freshly ground black pepper	
3 tbsp	extra virgin olive oil	45 mL

Winter Salad

1	head escarole or frisée lettuce, torn into bite-size pieces (about 6 cups/1.5 L)	1
1	head radicchio, thinly sliced (about 2 cups/500 mL)	1

1. *Orange Vinaigrette:* In a large bowl, combine orange zest, orange juice, vinegar, salt and pepper until salt dissolves, about 3 minutes. Whisk in olive oil.

2. *Winter Salad:* Just before serving, add escarole and radicchio to vinaigrette in bowl and toss to coat.

THE DISH

Winter Greens. Winter greens have thicker, hardier leaves than their counterparts such as Bibb, Boston or leaf. They are also a little bit on the bitter side, which makes them more assertive and able to hold up to vinaigrettes containing a little more acid. Look for escarole, frisée, mizuna, radicchio and endive to perk up winter plates and alleviate the winter doldrums.

Citrus-Seared Tuna Salad with Winter Greens and Orange

In the winter, citrus fruits and hardy lettuces like escarole and frisée are at their peak of flavor. This fresh salad, bright with color, really perks up a gray winter's day and is guaranteed to wake up your taste buds as well. The tuna benefits from a short bath in an Asian vinaigrette, which marries the greens with the fish. We like our tuna a bit on the rare side. Be careful. It cooks up really fast.

Serves 4 as a lunch or 6 as a starter

Hands-on time
30 minutes

Start to finish
30 minutes

Tip

If you want to eat your tuna rare, sushi-grade tuna is what you are looking for. It is the highest grade, quality-wise, and will reward you with the freshest taste as well. If rare tuna isn't your bag, don't hesitate to top this salad with a good can of drained oil-packed tuna.

Make Ahead

The vinaigrette can be made up to 4 hours ahead and kept covered and refrigerated.

Tuna

1 tbsp	soy sauce	15 mL
1 tbsp	rice vinegar	15 mL
1 tbsp	dark sesame oil	15 mL
1½ lbs	sushi-grade tuna steaks (see Tip, left)	750 g
	Salt and freshly ground black pepper	
2 tbsp	black sesame seeds	30 mL
2 tbsp	white sesame seeds	30 mL

Salad

1	recipe Orange Vinaigrette (page 98)	1
½	head fennel, trimmed and very thinly sliced	½
1	head escarole or frisée lettuce, torn into bite-size pieces (about 6 cups/1.5 L)	1
1	head radicchio, thinly sliced (about 2 cups/500 mL)	1
2	navel oranges, peeled and sectioned	2
1	green onion, thinly sliced	1

1. *Tuna:* In a resealable plastic bag, combine soy sauce, vinegar and oil. Pat tuna dry and add to bag. Let stand for 30 minutes at room temperature, turning bag occasionally to coat tuna.

2. Remove tuna from marinade and pat dry. Season with salt and pepper to taste. Combine black and white sesame seeds on a plate. Coat one side of tuna with seeds.

3. Heat a skillet over medium-high heat. When hot, add tuna and sear about 1 minute per side for very rare, or 2 minutes per side for medium. Transfer to a cutting board and let stand for 2 or 3 minutes. Cut tuna into 1-inch (2.5 cm) wide strips.

4. *Salad:* Add fennel to orange vinaigrette in bowl and let stand for 1 minute or so. Add escarole and radicchio and toss to coat. Arrange salad on serving plates and top with strips of tuna. Garnish with oranges and green onion. Sprinkle a little salt and pepper over plates to finish.

Yukon Gold Salad

When the French go on a "peek-neek," a version of this potato salad is often included in their picturesque woven straw hamper. When accompanied by a thinly sliced sausage or salami, good bread, wine and seasonal fruit, this portable feast is just the ticket to a romantic Sunday dinner under a very large old tree.

Serves 6

Hands-on time
20 minutes

Start to finish
1 hour

Make Ahead

The salad can be made a day ahead and kept covered and refrigerated. Let come to room temperature before serving. It can also be made up to 4 hours ahead and kept, covered, at room temperature.

¼ cup	white wine vinegar	60 mL
2	cloves garlic, minced	2
½ cup	minced red onion	125 mL
1 tsp	freshly ground black pepper	5 mL
2 tsp	salt, divided	10 mL
2 lbs	Yukon gold potatoes, cut into 2-inch (5 cm) cubes	1 kg
1 lb	green beans, trimmed and halved	500 g
¼ cup	torn fresh basil (approx.)	60 mL
¼ cup	minced flat-leaf parsley (approx.)	60 mL
2 tbsp	extra virgin olive oil	30 mL
2 cups	grape tomatoes	500 mL

1. In a large bowl, combine vinegar, garlic, red onion, pepper and 1 tsp (5 mL) of the salt. Let stand for about 5 minutes to allow flavors to blend.

2. In a large pot of water over medium-high heat, add potatoes and bring to a boil. Add remaining 1 tsp (5 mL) of salt. Reduce heat and simmer potatoes, about 5 minutes. Add green beans and cook for 5 minutes or until potatoes and beans are tender. Drain vegetables. Add hot potatoes and green beans to bowl with dressing and toss to mix. Toss in basil, parsley, olive oil and grape tomatoes. Taste for seasoning and add more salt and pepper to taste, if necessary.

3. Transfer to an attractive serving bowl and garnish with extra basil and parsley.

THE DISH **Good White Wine Vinegar.** There is a world of difference among vinegars, and the only way to discover the good ones is to actively seek them out. Small-production vinegars aged in toasted oak barrels seem to have a rounder and smoother taste, so check the label. If it has been aged in oak, it should say so. Sorry to say that these better vinegars cost a little more than the larger-production labels, but we find them to be worth every penny.

Potato Salad à la Niçoise

The beauty of this dish is that it appears as individually seasoned components. Nothing is lovelier when this salad is composed on a large white serving platter. Diners can assemble their own salads, taking a combination of whatever vegetables most strike their fancy.

Serves 6

Hands-on time
30 minutes

Start to finish
1 hour

Make Ahead

The salad can be made 1 day ahead and kept covered and refrigerated. Let come to room temperature before serving. It can also be made up to 4 hours ahead and kept, covered, at room temperature before adding the eggs at the last moment.

2 lbs	Yukon gold potatoes, cut into 2-inch (5 cm) cubes	1 kg
2 tsp	salt, divided	10 mL
1 lb	green beans, trimmed and halved	500 g
2 cups	grape tomatoes	500 mL
2	cans (each 6 oz/170 g) tuna, packed in oil, drained	2
1/3 cup	white wine vinegar	75 mL
2	cloves garlic, minced	2
1/2 cup	minced red onion	125 mL
1 tsp	freshly ground black pepper	5 mL
1/4 cup	extra virgin olive oil	60 mL
1/4 cup	torn fresh basil	60 mL
1/4 cup	minced flat-leaf parsley	60 mL
1/2 cup	niçoise olives	125 mL
8	anchovies	8
2	hard-boiled eggs, grated	2

1. In a large pot of water over medium-high heat, add potatoes and bring to a boil. Add 1 tsp (5 mL) of salt. Reduce heat and simmer potatoes, about 5 minutes. Remove potatoes with a slotted spoon and transfer to a bowl. Add green beans to boiling water and blanch for 5 minutes. Drain green beans and transfer to another bowl. Add grape tomatoes to another bowl. Add tuna to another bowl.

2. In a medium bowl, combine vinegar, garlic, red onion, and remaining salt and pepper. Let stand for about 5 minutes to allow flavors to blend. Whisk in olive oil, basil and parsley.

3. Toss hot potatoes with half the dressing and divide remaining dressing among hot green beans, tomatoes and tuna. Taste for seasoning and add more salt and pepper to taste, if necessary.

4. On a large serving platter, arrange potatoes in one area, green beans next to them, tomatoes in a group next to them and then tuna. Scatter olives, anchovies and grated egg over top. Serve at room temperature.

Soulful Bowlfuls
Soups

Gazpacho

Summer is hot in the south of Spain, where this cool blend of vegetables, olive oil and vinegar quenches and revives overheated bodies and spirits alike. Gazpacho usually combines uncooked tomatoes, cucumber, sweet peppers, garlic and onion for what amounts to a liquid salad on a spoon. Our only break with tradition here is the addition of just a teeny tiny bit of vodka, which improves the flavor and kicks up the revivifying quality of this potent potation.

Serves 6

Hands-on time
30 minutes

Chilling time
3 hours

Start to finish
3 hours 30 minutes

Tip

Because the quality of tomatoes can vary widely, be sure to taste your soup with a discerning palate and remedy any flavor deficiency with more salt, pepper, vinegar or even a touch of honey, if necessary.

Make Ahead

Go ahead and make this soup a day ahead. Keep covered and refrigerated.

- **Food processor or blender**

2 lbs	medium tomatoes (about 7)	1 kg
1 cup	crustless baguette or country-style bread cubes	250 mL
1 cup	peeled seeded chopped cucumber	250 mL
¾ cup	seeded diced green bell pepper	175 mL
¾ cup	chopped red onion	175 mL
1	clove garlic, minced	1
¼ cup	vodka	60 mL
3 tbsp	sherry wine vinegar	45 mL
	Salt and freshly ground black pepper	
¼ cup	extra virgin olive oil	60 mL
2 cups	bread cubes, toasted	500 mL

1. In a large pot, bring 1 quart (1 L) water to a simmer over medium-high heat. Cut an X into bottom of each tomato and drop 3 at a time into simmering water. Blanch tomatoes for 1 minute. Using a slotted spoon, transfer to a bowl of cold water to stop cooking. Repeat with remaining tomatoes. It should be easy to peel the skin from their flesh. Discard skin and cut each tomato in half.

2. In a large bowl with a strainer over it, squeeze tomatoes so that seeds and juices run into the strainer. Discard seeds and drop tomato halves into the bowl with the juice. Add bread, cucumber, bell pepper, red onion, garlic, vodka, sherry vinegar, ¾ cup (175 mL) water, 2 tsp (10 mL) salt and ¼ tsp (1 mL) pepper.

3. Transfer mixture to a food processor or a blender and blend, in batches if necessary, until smooth. While food processor is running, add olive oil through the feed tube. Taste and adjust seasoning with salt, pepper and more vinegar, if necessary. Transfer to a large pitcher, cover and refrigerate for at least 3 hours or until cold. Taste and add more seasoning, if necessary.

4. To serve, pour soup into bowls and garnish with bread cubes.

Yellow Tomato Gazpacho with Spicy Crab Relish

Simply substituting yellow tomatoes for the red tomatoes in our basic Gazpacho (page 104) creates a completely different dish. Yellow tomatoes have less acidity than the usual red suspects, and the addition of the rich and spicy crab relish harmonizes beautifully with this smooth but still tart golden soup.

Serves 6

Hands-on time
30 minutes

Chilling time
3 hours

Start to finish
3 hours 30 minutes

Tip

The unexpected yellow of this gazpacho contrasts beautifully with a green or cobalt blue soup bowl.

- **Food processor or blender**

4 oz	backfin or lump crabmeat	125 g
2 tbsp	mayonnaise	30 mL
	Zest and juice of 1 lemon, divided	
1 tbsp	minced chives, divided	15 mL
1/4 tsp	salt	2 mL
Pinch	freshly ground black pepper	Pinch
Pinch	cayenne pepper	Pinch
2 lbs	yellow tomatoes (about 7)	1 kg
1 cup	crustless baguette or country-style bread cubes	250 mL
1 cup	peeled seeded chopped cucumber	250 mL
3/4 cup	seeded diced green bell pepper	175 mL
3/4 cup	chopped red onion	175 mL
1	clove garlic, minced	1
2 tbsp	sherry wine vinegar	30 mL
2 tbsp	vodka	30 mL
2 tsp	salt	10 mL
1/4 tsp	freshly ground black pepper	1 mL
1/4 cup	extra virgin olive oil	60 mL

1. In a large bowl, combine crab, mayonnaise, half the lemon zest, 1 tbsp (15 mL) of the lemon juice, 2 tsp (10 mL) of the minced chives, salt, pepper and cayenne. Taste the crab salad and adjust the seasoning to taste with more lemon juice, salt, pepper and cayenne. Refrigerate crab salad if not using immediately.

2. In a large pot, bring 1 quart (1 L) water to a simmer over medium-high heat. Cut an X into bottom of each tomato and drop 3 at a time into simmering water. Blanch tomatoes for 1 minute. Using a slotted spoon, transfer to a bowl of cold water to stop cooking. Repeat with remaining tomatoes. It should be easy to peel the skin from their flesh. Discard skin and cut each tomato in half.

3. In a large bowl with a strainer over it, squeeze tomatoes so that seeds and juices run into the strainer. Discard seeds and drop tomato halves into the bowl with the juice. Add bread, cucumber, bell pepper, red onion, garlic, sherry vinegar, $\frac{1}{2}$ cup (125 mL) water, vodka, salt and pepper.

4. Transfer mixture to a food processor or a blender and blend, in batches if necessary, until smooth. While food processor is running, add olive oil through the feed tube. Taste and adjust seasoning with salt, pepper and more vinegar, if necessary. Transfer to a large pitcher, cover and refrigerate for at least 3 hours or until cold. Taste and add more seasoning, if necessary.

5. To serve, ladle cold soup into chilled bowls. Garnish with crab salad and a sprinkling of remaining lemon zest and chives.

THE DISH   **Vodka.** There are many obvious reasons why we enjoy vodka, but the reason we enjoy it in this soup is not obvious. The alcohol in vodka actually helps enhance the flavors of this vibrant soup. Just taste it before you add the vodka and after. You'll notice the difference.

Potato and Leek Soup

One thing is for certain: some version of this classic soup has been slurped up through the ages, whether in modest homes or palatial estates. Silky potatoes and oniony leeks combine to make the simplest and maybe the best soup in our repertoires. Lest we forget, there is one other thing we know for sure: delicious is always in style.

Serves 6

Hands-on time
10 minutes

Start to finish
30 minutes

Make Ahead

This soup can be made up to 2 days ahead and kept covered and refrigerated.

- **Immersion blender, food processor or blender**
- **6 heated soup bowls**

2 lbs	potatoes, peeled and diced	1 kg
2	leeks, white and tender green parts only, sliced	2
6 cups	Brown or Quick Chicken Stock (pages 110 and 119) or ready-to-use broth	1.5 L
2 tsp	freshly squeezed lemon juice	10 mL
1½ tsp	salt	7 mL
½ tsp	freshly ground black pepper	2 mL
Pinch	ground nutmeg	Pinch
Pinch	cayenne pepper	Pinch
1 cup	heavy or whipping (35%) cream	250 mL
2 tbsp	minced chives	30 mL

1. In a large pot over medium-high heat, combine potatoes, leeks and chicken stock and bring to a simmer. Reduce heat to low and simmer for 20 minutes or until potatoes and leeks are tender.

2. Using an immersion blender, food processor or blender, process soup until smooth. Return soup to pot and add lemon juice, salt, pepper, nutmeg and cayenne. Taste for seasoning and adjust with more salt, pepper or lemon juice, if necessary.

3. Add cream and reheat over medium heat. Taste for seasoning again and adjust, if necessary. Ladle soup into heated bowls and garnish with chives.

THE DISH **Whipping Cream.** Heavy, or whipping, cream gives this soup a backdrop that allows the other, more subtle flavors to march forward. Just taste the soup before adding the cream and then after. You won't believe the difference in depth and flavor.

Vichyssoise with Tarragon Pesto

Just saying the word "vichyssoise" makes you seem smart and sophisticated. The good news is, eating it also makes you feel good. This creamy, velvety blend of potato and leek is topped with a dollop of tarragon pesto, which adds a flavorful herbal note to this subtly seasoned potage.

Serves 6

Hands-on time
30 minutes

Chilling time
3 hours

Start to finish
3 hours 30 minutes

Make Ahead

This soup can be made up to 2 days ahead and kept covered and refrigerated. The pesto can be made up to 1 week ahead and kept covered and refrigerated.

- **Food processor**
- **6 chilled soup bowls**

1	recipe Potato and Leek Soup (page 108)	1
Tarragon Pesto		
2 tbsp	pine nuts (walnuts in a pinch)	30 mL
1	clove garlic	1
¼ cup	coarsely chopped fresh tarragon	60 mL
¼ cup	coarsely chopped flat-leaf parsley	60 mL
1 tbsp	freshly squeezed lemon juice	15 mL
¼ tsp	salt	1 mL
Pinch	freshly ground black pepper	Pinch
⅓ cup	extra virgin olive oil	75 mL
2 tbsp	minced chives	30 mL

1. Make Potato and Leek Soup and refrigerate until chilled, for at least 3 hours or overnight. Once cold, taste soup for seasoning again and adjust with salt and pepper, if necessary.

2. *Tarragon Pesto:* In a food processor, pulse pine nuts and garlic until finely chopped. Add tarragon, parsley, lemon juice, salt and pepper and pulse until puréed. While food processor is running, pour olive oil through the feed tube and process until well mixed.

3. Ladle soup into chilled bowls and garnish with a dollop of pesto. Draw a skewer through the middle of the dollop to make a swirl design on the surface of the soup. Garnish with chives.

THE DISH **Big Soup Spoons.** It is so much more fun to eat soup with a large spoon. If you've ever tried to eat soup with a teaspoon, you know how frustrating it can be. We can't have enough of these big spoons and scout them out in antique or thrift shops, scoring occasional silver-plated and engraved spoons that make us wonder about all the many soups that they've dipped into over the past 100 years. That's probably a lot of soup!

Brown Chicken Stock

Brown chicken stock is our all-purpose most used stock. It is brown because we roast the bones in a hot oven before adding them to the vegetables in the stockpot.

Makes 10 quarts (10 L) or 3 quarts (3 L) reduced

Tip

Stock can be made ahead and refrigerated for up to 4 days or frozen for up to 4 months. When you want to use the stock, just add water in increments until it tastes right to you. Begin by adding 2 parts water to 1 part stock. If it tastes too strong, add a little more water until you get the flavor just right.

- **Preheat oven to 425°F (220°C)**
- **Rimmed baking sheets**
- **Chinois or fine-mesh strainer**

12 lbs	chicken bones, such as necks, backs, breast bones, wings, etc.	6 kg
2 lbs	onions, quartered	1 kg
1 lb	carrots, peeled and quartered	500 g
4	stalks celery, quartered	4
3	leeks, green tops only	3
1	head garlic, cut in half crosswise	1
1	tomato, cut in half	1
1	bunch parsley stems	1
2	bay leaves	2
1 tbsp	whole black peppercorns	15 mL
1 tbsp	dried thyme	15 mL

1. Arrange chicken bones on baking sheets, leaving space between bones so they brown nicely. Roast bones in preheated oven for 45 minutes to 1 hour or until golden brown.

2. In an extra-large stockpot, combine roasted bones, onions, carrots, celery, leeks, garlic, tomato, parsley stems, bay leaves, peppercorns and thyme. Add enough cold water to cover by at least 2 inches (5 cm). Bring to a simmer over medium-low heat, about 1 hour. Skim scum off surface as it forms and discard it. Watch pot so that it doesn't boil and turn heat down accordingly. Simmer very gently (you will see a bubble every 10 seconds or so) for at least 4 hours, until stock is flavorful, or for up to 8 hours.

3. *To strain stock:* The best tool for this job is a chinois, or China cap strainer with a very fine mesh, or a very fine-mesh strainer. Place strainer over a large pot and ladle stock through strainer. Using the back of a ladle, push as much liquid out as possible, discarding solids.

4. *To degrease stock:* Once the stock is strained, it must be degreased. Using a large shallow serving spoon, run lip of spoon just under the grease-slicked top of stock, discarding grease into a throwaway container. Remove as much of the grease as possible for the best-looking, clear stock.

5. *To reduce stock:* Once stock is degreased, it can be reduced. Reduce stock for two reasons: so that it can store efficiently and for a richer and fuller flavor. At this point, boil stock until it has reduced by about 75%. It sounds like a lot of reduction, but the more the stock is reduced, the more space you have in your freezer. Highly reduced stock also keeps longer than less reduced stock. Boil stock until reduced to your specifications.

Chicken Soup with Corn and Leeks

When you're in that limbo between seasons in late summer and fall, a satisfying soup like this one, rich with chicken, delicate leek and corn, will help you welcome in the cooler weather. So go ahead and put away all those cute sandals and pull out those warm fuzzy boots — it's soup season again.

Serves 6 to 8

Hands-on time
30 minutes

Start to finish
1 hour

Make Ahead

The soup can be made 2 days ahead and kept covered and refrigerated.

2 tbsp	unsalted butter or vegetable oil	30 mL
2	leeks, white and light green parts, chopped	2
2	carrots, peeled and chopped	2
1	stalk celery, chopped	1
1 tsp	each dried thyme and salt	5 mL
1/4 tsp	freshly ground black pepper	1 mL
1	bay leaf	1
8 cups	Brown or Quick Chicken Stock (pages 110 and 119)	2 L
2 lbs	bone-in chicken thighs	1 kg
8 oz	egg noodles	250 g
2 cups	frozen corn, thawed	500 mL
	Salt and freshly ground black pepper	
1/4 cup	minced flat-leaf parsley	60 mL

1. In a large soup pot, heat butter over medium heat. Sauté leeks for about 3 minutes or until softened. Add carrots, celery, thyme, salt, pepper and bay leaf and sauté for 5 minutes or until vegetables begin to soften.

2. Add chicken stock and chicken to pot and simmer, about 5 minutes. Reduce heat to low, cover and simmer chicken and vegetables for 30 minutes or until chicken juices run clear when thighs are pierced.

3. Meanwhile, in a large pot of boiling salted water over medium-high heat, cook egg noodles according to package directions. Drain noodles and run under cold water to stop the cooking. Set aside.

4. Transfer chicken to a platter and let cool. When cool enough to handle, cut meat from bones. Return meat and add corn to soup and bring to a simmer and cook for about 5 minutes or until corn is tender. Taste for seasoning and adjust with salt and pepper, if necessary.

5. Place a large helping of noodles into each heated bowl and ladle soup over all. Garnish with parsley.

EVERYDAY

Chipotle Chicken Soup with Black Beans and Grilled Corn

For this soup, we combine the smokiness of grilled corn and chipotle chile. To pull even more corn flavor into the pot, we've simmered the corn cobs in this south-of-the-border soup. The chipotle chile adds a touch of Mexican flair when paired with the black beans and cilantro. Just reading the recipe makes us long for an icy cold Corona.

Serves 6 to 8

Hands-on time
30 minutes

Start to finish
1 hour

Make Ahead

The soup can be made up to 2 days ahead and kept covered and refrigerated.

- **Preheat greased barbecue grill to high or preheat broiler**
- **6 to 8 heated soup bowls**

3	ears corn, husk and silk removed	3
2 tbsp	unsalted butter or vegetable oil, divided	30 mL
2	leeks, white and light green parts, chopped	2
2	carrots, peeled and chopped	2
1	stalk celery, chopped	1
1 tsp	dried thyme	5 mL
1 tsp	salt	5 mL
1/4 tsp	freshly ground black pepper	1 mL
1	bay leaf	1
8 cups	Brown or Quick Chicken Stock (pages 110 and 119) or ready-to-use broth	2 L
2 lbs	bone-in chicken thighs	1 kg
1 tbsp	finely chopped chipotle chile in adobo sauce	15 mL
1	can (14 to 19 oz/398 to 540 mL) black beans, drained and rinsed	1
	Salt and freshly ground black pepper	
1/4 cup	minced fresh cilantro	60 mL
1	lime, cut into 4 sections	1

1. Grill corn or place under broiler for about 20 minutes or until corn has colored, turning as it browns. Let cool. When cool enough to handle, cut corn from cobs and set aside. Reserve cobs.

2. In a large soup pot, heat butter over medium heat. Sauté leeks for about 4 minutes or until softened. Add carrots, celery, thyme, salt, pepper and bay leaf and sauté for 5 minutes, until vegetables begin to soften.

3. Add cobs (save corn to add later), chicken stock, chicken and chipotle to pot and bring to a simmer, about 5 minutes. Reduce heat to low, cover and simmer chicken and vegetables for 30 minutes or until chicken juices run clear when thighs are pierced.

4. Remove chicken pieces and corn cobs from soup. Transfer chicken to a platter to cool off and discard cobs. When chicken is cool enough to handle, cut meat from bones. Return meat, reserved corn and black beans to soup and bring to a simmer for about 5 minutes or until corn is heated through. Taste for seasoning and adjust with more salt, pepper or chipotle chile, if necessary.

5. Ladle into heated bowls and serve garnished with cilantro and lime wedges.

THE DISH **Chipotle Chile.** Chipotle chiles are smoked jalapeños often canned in a spicy, vinegary tomato sauce called adobo. Look for them in the Mexican foods section at your grocery store. After they are opened, drop the remaining chiles in an ice cube tray, freeze and then store in a resealable freezer bag for the next time you want to add zip to soups, stews or casseroles.

Fashion Plate

For a great make-ahead meal worthy of company, prepare this soup a day ahead along with the Tres Leches Cake (page 342). Serve this soup with warm flour tortillas and the moist rich cake for dessert.

Herbed Tomato Soup with Grilled Cheese Croutons

Most of us have fond childhood memories of eating tomato soup, even if it was from a can. Since grilled cheese sandwiches are the classic partner to this tomatoey blend, we've cut to the chase and just added the sandwich right into the bowl. This soup will take you back, but in a good way, to those carefree days playing out in the snow and coming in wet and cold to a bowl of love served up by Mom.

Serves 6

Hands-on time
10 minutes

Start to finish
1 hour

Make Ahead

The soup can be made up to 24 hours in advance and kept covered and refrigerated. The croutons can be made up to 4 hours in advance and kept, covered, at room temperature. Reheat croutons in a dry skillet over medium heat for about 4 minutes or until cheese melts.

- **Immersion blender, food processor or blender**
- **6 heated soup bowls**

3 tbsp	olive oil	45 mL
1 cup	chopped onion	250 mL
6	cloves garlic, minced	6
1/4 tsp	hot pepper flakes	1 mL
1	can (28 oz/796 mL) diced tomatoes with juice	1
4 cups	Brown or Quick Chicken Stock (pages 110 and 119) or ready-to-use broth	1 L
1 tsp	salt	5 mL
1/2 tsp	freshly ground black pepper	2 mL

Grilled Cheese Croutons

2 tbsp	unsalted butter, softened	30 mL
6	slices country-style bread	6
4 oz	Colby Jack cheese, thinly sliced	125 g
1/4 cup	torn fresh basil	60 mL

1. In a large pot, heat olive oil over medium heat. Sauté onion, garlic and hot pepper flakes for 10 minutes or until onions start to brown. Add tomatoes with juice, chicken stock, salt and pepper. Bring to a boil. Reduce heat and simmer for 40 minutes. Blend with an immersion blender, food processor or blender until smooth. Return to the pot. Taste and adjust seasoning with salt and pepper, if necessary.

2. *Grilled Cheese Croutons:* Meanwhile, spread butter over one side of each slice of bread. Place cheese on 3 slices of bread, butter side down, and top with remaining bread, butter side up. Heat a skillet over medium heat and cook croutons for about 4 minutes on one side, until browned and cheese begins to melt. Turn and brown other side, about 3 minutes. Cut each into quarters.

3. Ladle soup into heated serving bowls. Garnish soup with torn basil and place 2 croutons in each soup bowl, pointed end down, so that they can be picked up and dunked into the soup.

THE DISH **Freshly Ground Black Pepper.** There's hardly a recipe in this book that doesn't call for freshly ground black pepper. We love it because it is so aromatic and full of taste when ground fresh. And it is so easy to make it happen in your house. Just buy a mill and some whole peppercorns, fill up the mill and grind away. It is one of the best ways we know to add spice to your life.

Fashion Plate

Serve this childhood favorite with Caesar Salad (page 64) and Chocolate Chip and Ice Cream Cookie-wiches (page 368).

Roasted Cherry Tomato Soup with Basil Cream

The partnership of basil and tomato is a classic in the culinary world. And we all know that classics never go out of style. We've taken this popular duo and combined them in a new way by mixing pesto into a whipped cream topper that carries this slightly sweet and deeply tomato-flavored soup to new heights.

Serves 6

Hands-on time
20 minutes

Start to finish
1 hour

Make Ahead

The soup can be made up to 24 hours in advance and kept covered and refrigerated. The Basil Cream can be made up to 4 hours in advance and kept covered and refrigerated.

- **Preheat oven to 400°F (200°C)**
- **Immersion blender, food processor or blender**
- **6 heated soup bowls**

2 cups	cherry tomatoes	500 mL
3 tbsp	olive oil, divided	45 mL
1 tsp	salt	5 mL
1/2 tsp	freshly ground black pepper	2 mL
1	onion, chopped	1
4	cloves garlic, minced	4
1/4 tsp	hot pepper flakes	1 mL
1	can (28 oz/796 mL) diced tomatoes with juice	1
4 cups	Brown or Quick Chicken Stock (pages 110 and 119) or ready-to-use broth	1 L

Basil Cream

1/2 cup	heavy or whipping (35%) cream	125 mL
2 tbsp	Pesto (page 25) or store-bought	30 mL

1. In a bowl, toss together tomatoes, 2 tbsp (30 mL) of the olive oil, salt and pepper. Spread tomatoes in 1 layer on a baking sheet and roast in preheated oven for 20 minutes.

2. In a large pot, heat remaining olive oil over medium heat. Sauté onion, garlic and hot pepper flakes for 10 minutes or until onions start to brown. Add canned tomatoes with juice and chicken stock. Add oven-roasted tomatoes, including liquid on baking sheet. Bring to a boil. Reduce heat and simmer for 40 minutes. Blend with an immersion blender, food processor or blender until smooth and return to pot. Taste and adjust seasoning with salt and pepper, if necessary.

3. *Basil Cream:* In a bowl, using an electric mixer, whip together cream and pesto until soft peaks form. Ladle soup into heated serving bowls and top with a dollop of Basil Cream.

Quick Chicken Stock

Sometimes we want the flavor of homemade stock but don't have time to make it. That's when we compromise and make this quick version. Cooking a good store-bought chicken stock with extra chicken bones and vegetables results in a better-than-canned-flavored chicken stock in less than an hour.

Makes about 4 quarts (4 L)

Hands-on time
20 minutes

Start to finish
1 hour 30 minutes

Tip

Stock can be made ahead and refrigerated for up to 4 days or frozen for up to 4 months.

4 quarts	ready-to-use chicken broth	4 L
2 lbs	chicken necks and backs	1 kg
2	onions, sliced	2
1	carrot, sliced	1
1	stalk celery, sliced	1
2	cloves garlic, smashed	2
3	parsley stems	3
6	whole black peppercorns	6
½ tsp	dried thyme	2 mL
1	bay leaf	1

1. In a large stock pot, combine chicken broth, chicken parts, onions, carrot, celery, garlic, parsley, peppercorns, thyme and bay leaf. Bring to a simmer over medium-low heat. Reduce heat and simmer gently for about 45 minutes, until very flavorful. Strain solids from stock, degrease if necessary (see Steps 3 and 4, page 111).

Fresh Corn Chowder with Ham

A simple chowder is a thing of beauty, and at no time is it more beautiful than in the summer, when fresh ingredients are just a farmers' market away. This treatment highlights the idea that when something is already great, don't mess with it too much. So when corn is in season, all that's needed is a little cream, a little ham and little else to make a memorable bowl of chowder.

Serves 6

Hands-on time
20 minutes

Start to finish
50 minutes

Tip

You can make this chowder in the winter with frozen corn with good results, and let's face it, we have done it ourselves when we need a spoonful of summer to shake off the winter blues. It is an entirely different creature, though, when made with fresh sweet corn picked at the height of corn season, which is mid to late summer.

Make Ahead

The soup can be made up to 24 hours before serving and kept covered and refrigerated.

- **Immersion blender, food processor or blender**
- **6 heated soup bowls**

¼ cup	unsalted butter	60 mL
1	medium onion, chopped	1
2	cloves garlic, minced	2
3	ears corn, husked and corn cut from cobs, reserving cobs (see Tip, left)	3
2	potatoes, diced	2
1 tbsp	chopped flat-leaf parsley	15 mL
2 tsp	chopped fresh thyme	10 mL
¼ tsp	cayenne pepper	1 mL
6 cups	Brown or Quick Chicken Stock (pages 110 and 119) or ready-to-use broth	1.5 L
2 cups	diced ham	500 mL
1 cup	half-and-half (10%) cream	250 mL
	Salt and freshly ground black pepper	

1. In a large soup pot, melt butter over medium heat. Sauté onion for 6 minutes or until it begins to soften. Add garlic and sauté for 1 minute or until garlic is fragrant.

2. Add corn kernels, potatoes, parsley, thyme and cayenne and sauté for 3 minutes or until vegetables begin to soften. Add stock and corn cobs and bring to a simmer. Reduce heat to low and simmer for about 15 minutes or until vegetables are tender. Remove corn cobs and discard.

3. Process half the soup in a blender or food processor and return to pot or pulse with an immersion blender a few times. Add ham.

4. Add cream and reheat over medium heat, if necessary. Avoid boiling as cream will curdle. Season with salt and pepper to taste. Ladle into heated bowls.

EVERYDAY

Silky Corn Soup with Caramelized Bacon

Contrasting flavors and textures turns our Fresh Corn Chowder on its high heels. While all the key elements are the same, this dish looks nothing like its soupy sibling. Here, we've taken our corn chowder and puréed it to create a smooth soup that glides right off the spoon. As a garnish, we're using caramelized bacon, which may sound strange at first, but come on. Who doesn't love to dredge their bacon through their maple syrup on Sunday morning? The salty/sweet combo gets us every time, and it's a wonderful foil for our sublime corn soup.

Serves 6

Hands-on time
20 minutes

Start to finish
1 hour

Make Ahead

The soup can be made up to 24 hours before serving and kept covered and refrigerated.

- **Preheat oven to 350°F (180°C)**
- **Rimmed baking sheet**
- **Immersion blender, food processor or blender**
- **6 heated soup bowls**

⅔ cup	packed brown sugar	150 mL
8	slices bacon	8
¼ cup	unsalted butter	60 mL
1	medium onion, chopped	1
2	cloves garlic, minced	2
4	ears corn, husked and corn cut from cobs, reserving cobs	4
1 tbsp	chopped flat-leaf parsley	15 mL
2 tsp	chopped fresh thyme	10 mL
¼ tsp	cayenne pepper	1 mL
4 cups	Brown or Quick Chicken Stock (pages 110 and 119) or ready-to-use broth	1.5 L
	Salt and freshly ground black pepper	
1 cup	half-and-half (10%) cream	250 mL

1. Place brown sugar in a shallow pan. Add bacon and turn to coat completely with sugar. Transfer bacon to a large broiler pan or rack set over a rimmed baking sheet. Bake bacon in preheated oven, turning once, for about 8 minutes per side or until dark golden brown. Using tongs, transfer to a wire rack and let cool. When cool enough to handle, cut bacon crosswise in half. Set aside.

2. In a large soup pot, melt butter over medium hat. Sauté onion for 6 minutes or until it begins to soften. Add garlic and sauté for 1 minute or until garlic is fragrant.

3. Add corn kernels, parsley, thyme and cayenne and sauté for 3 minutes or until vegetables begin to soften. Add stock and corn cobs and bring to a simmer. Reduce heat to low and simmer for about 15 minutes or until vegetables are tender. Remove corn cobs and discard.

4. Process half the soup in a blender or food processor and return to pot or pulse with an immersion blender a few times.

5. Add cream and reheat over medium heat, if necessary. Avoid boiling as cream will curdle. Season with salt and pepper to taste. Ladle into heated bowls and garnish with caramelized bacon.

THE DISH **Shallow Glass Soups Bowls.** We love a sound investment, and a set of simple glass soup bowls certainly fall in that category. They're versatile and make anything you put into them look even better. Need we say more?

Fashion Plate

Pair up this luscious soup with Seared Scallop Salad with Chicory and Sherry Vinaigrette (page 92) and end with Individual Plum Tartlets with Frangipane and Plum Brandy (page 364).

Sweet Potato Chowder

Sweet potatoes make some of the most delicious soups. They go beautifully with holiday meals or even just a regular dinner with pork chops. This soup is a little chunky with potatoes and flavored with fried sage leaves. If you've never tried fried sage leaves, you're in for a treat. The crispy leaves' sagey flavor softens and mellows, making them less likely to overwhelm the delicate sweetness of this seductive soup.

Serves 6

Hands-on time
30 minutes

Start to finish
1 hour 10 minutes

Make Ahead

The soup can be made 1 day ahead and kept covered and refrigerated.

- **Preheat oven to 400°F (200°C)**
- **Baking sheet, lined with parchment paper**
- **6 heated soup bowls**

3 lbs	sweet potatoes, halved	1.5 kg
¼ cup	olive oil, divided	60 mL
10	thinly sliced sage leaves	10
1	large onion, diced	1
1	clove garlic, minced	1
1 cup	dry white wine	250 mL
6 cups	Brown or Quick Chicken Stock (pages 110 and 119) or ready-to-use vegetable or chicken broth or a blend of the two	1.5 L
2	Yukon gold or baking potatoes, peeled and diced	2
1 tsp	salt	5 mL
1 tsp	freshly squeezed lemon juice	5 mL
Pinch	cayenne pepper	Pinch
Pinch	freshly grated nutmeg	Pinch
	Freshly ground black pepper	
1 cup	half-and-half (10%) cream	250 mL
½ cup	heavy or whipping (35%) cream	125 mL

1. Rub cut side of sweet potatoes with 1 tbsp (15 mL) of the olive oil and place cut side down on prepared baking sheet. Roast in preheated oven for about 40 minutes or until tender when a knife pierces easily into thickest part. Let cool on baking sheet.

2. Meanwhile, heat remaining oil in a large pot over medium-high heat. Add sage leaves and sauté for 1 minute or until fragrant. Add onion and sauté for 6 minutes or until softened. Add garlic and sauté for 1 minute or until fragrant.

3. Add wine and cook for about 5 minutes or until reduced somewhat. Add chicken stock, diced potato and salt and bring to a simmer. Reduce heat and simmer for 20 minutes or until potato is tender.

4. Scoop roasted sweet potato from shell, mash and add to soup. Season soup with lemon juice, cayenne, nutmeg, and pepper to taste. Add half-and-half (10%) cream and whipping (35%) cream. Taste again and adjust seasoning with more salt, pepper, nutmeg or cayenne pepper, if necessary. Ladle soup into heated bowls.

THE DISH **Freshly Grated Nutmeg.** Maybe you've noticed that we like nutmeg in many soups. That's because its sweet aroma and flavor go as well with savory dishes as it does with desserts. Invest in a nutmeg grater and buy a container of whole nutmeg. Freshly grated nutmeg is a world apart from the stale spice sold already ground on the grocery shelf.

Fashion Plate

Roasted Pear Salad with Gorgonzola Rounds (page 95) is a nice start to this hearty meal in a bowl. Finish up with rustic but delicious Fudgy Brownie Cake (page 358).

Spicy Thai Sweet Potato Soup with Lemongrass and Coconut Milk

Sweet potatoes and coconut milk have a natural affinity. They both share a sweet richness that is amplified when paired with the spicy fresh ginger and fragrant lemongrass. Add a bit of curry paste and you've got a whole lot of flavor going on. The soup is best eaten the day it is made. The flavors from the lemongrass tend to become woody and overwhelm the soup after a day of refrigeration.

Serves 6

Hands-on time
30 minutes

Start to finish
1 hour 10 minutes

- **Preheat oven to 400°F (200°C)**
- **Baking sheet, lined with parchment paper**
- **6 heated soup bowls**

3 lbs	sweet potatoes, halved	1.5 kg
¼ cup	olive oil, divided	60 mL
1	large onion, diced	1
1	clove garlic, minced	1
1 tbsp	minced fresh gingerroot	15 mL
1	stalk lemongrass, bulbous end very thinly sliced (see The Dish, right)	1
2 tsp	Thai red curry paste or ½ tsp (2 mL) cayenne pepper	10 mL
6 cups	Brown or Quick Chicken Stock (pages 110 and 119) or ready-to-use vegetable or chicken broth or a blend of the two	1.5 L
2	Yukon gold or baking potatoes, peeled and diced	2
1 tsp	salt	5 mL
1	can (14 oz/400 mL) unsweetened coconut milk	1
1 tsp	freshly squeezed lime juice	5 mL
	Salt and freshly ground black pepper	
2 tbsp	minced fresh cilantro	30 mL

1. Rub cut side of sweet potatoes with 1 tbsp (15 mL) of the olive oil and place cut side down on prepared baking sheet. Roast in preheated oven for about 40 minutes or until tender when a knife pierces easily into thickest part. Let cool on baking sheet.

2. Meanwhile, in a large pot, heat remaining oil over medium-high heat. Add onion and sauté for 5 minutes or until softened. Add garlic, ginger, lemongrass and curry paste and sauté for 1 minute or until fragrant.

3. Add chicken stock, diced potato and salt and bring to a simmer. Reduce heat and simmer for 20 minutes or until potato is tender.

4. Scoop roasted sweet potato from shell, mash and add to soup along with coconut milk. Season soup with lime juice, and salt and pepper to taste.

5. Ladle soup into heated bowls and top each with a sprinkle of cilantro.

THE DISH **Lemongrass.** Lemongrass is a tropical grass with long, greenish stalks. We find it in Asian grocery stores and some grocery stores. The exterior leaves are very tough and should be peeled off to display the tender, more palatable inner leaves. For this recipe, trim the root end off the stalk and use the 5 inches (12.5 cm) closest to the root end for slicing. If you can't find it, just go ahead and use the grated zest of 2 lemons.

Fashion Plate

Thai Chicken Lettuce Wraps with Two Dipping Sauces (page 74) pairs with this Asian-inspired soup. Oranges and Pink Grapefruit with Cardamom and Ginger (page 373) is a tasty way to end the meal.

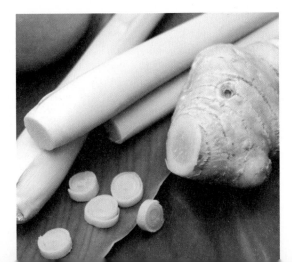

French Onion Soup

Nothing makes you feel more like a kid again than tugging on the stretchy strings of melted Gruyère cheese as you pull your spoon away from a bowl of this deeply flavorful soup. The foundation of French onion soup is the caramelized onions. Their sweet, slightly smoky character is a lovely contrast to the earthy beef broth and Madeira wine.

Serves 6

Hands-on time
40 minutes

Start to finish
1 hour 30 minutes

Make Ahead

The soup can be made up to 24 hours before serving and kept covered and refrigerated. Top with bread and cheese just before serving and proceed with recipe as directed.

- **6 heatproof soup bowls**

2 tbsp	unsalted butter	30 mL
2 tbsp	olive oil	30 mL
6	large yellow onions, thinly sliced	6
Pinch	salt	Pinch
3	cloves garlic, minced	3
⅓ cup	Madeira wine	75 mL
6 cups	Beef Stock (page 132) or ready-to-use broth	1.5 L
1	bay leaf	1
6	slices French bread	6
1 tsp	white wine vinegar	5 mL
	Salt and freshly ground black pepper	
8 oz	Gruyère cheese, shredded	250 g

1. In a large soup pot, heat butter and vegetable oil over medium heat. Sauté onions and a pinch of salt for about 10 minutes or until onions begin to brown. Reduce heat to low and continue to sauté, scraping bottom of pot to release the browned bits, for 30 to 40 minutes or until onions are soft and a deep mahogany brown. Add garlic and sauté for 2 minutes or until garlic is fragrant.

2. Increase heat to medium-high and add wine. Scrape up all the brown bits and cook for about 5 minutes or until wine has reduced to 2 to 3 tbsp (30 to 45 mL). Add stock and bay leaf and partially cover pot. Cook at a gentle simmer for 30 minutes or until flavors have blended and onions are very tender.

3. Meanwhile, preheat broiler and toast bread on both sides.

4. Add vinegar and taste soup for seasoning, adding salt and pepper to taste, if necessary.

5. Arrange heatproof bowls on a baking sheet and ladle in soup. Sprinkle half the cheese over soup, top with toasted bread and then remaining cheese. Place under broiler and toast until cheese has melted and is lightly browned. Serve immediately.

Creamy Three-Onion Soup with Crispy Shallots

Why is it that simply adding more than one variety of a particular ingredient to a dish makes it sound classier? Quattro fromaggio pizza (four cheeses), Tres Leches Cake (three milks), and the list goes on. We don't know why, but who are we to fight a trend? With that in mind, we decided to take our basic version of French Onion Soup and add leeks and white onions to the mix, which, as we discovered, adds a different element of sweetness and complexity. And yes, a little cream and our favorite version of onion rings as a garnish didn't hurt either.

Serves 6

Hands-on time
40 minutes

Start to finish
1 hour 30 minutes

Make Ahead

The soup can be made up to 24 hours before serving and kept covered and refrigerated.

- **Immersion blender, food processor or blender**
- **6 heated soup bowls**

2 tbsp	unsalted butter	30 mL
2 tbsp	olive oil	30 mL
3	medium leeks, white and pale green part only, sliced thinly	3
2	large yellow onions, thinly sliced	2
1	large white onion, thinly sliced	1
Pinch	salt	Pinch
2	cloves garlic, minced	2
4 cups	Beef Stock (page 132) or ready-to-use broth	1 L
4	thyme sprigs	4
	Vegetable oil	
6	shallots, thinly sliced	6
1 cup	heavy or whipping (35%) cream	250 mL
2 tbsp	red wine vinegar	30 mL
	Salt and freshly ground black pepper	

1. In a large soup pot, heat butter and olive oil over medium-high heat. Sauté leeks, yellow onions, white onions and a pinch of salt for 15 to 20 minutes or until onions begin to brown. Reduce heat to medium and continue to sauté, scraping bottom of the pot to release the browned bits, for about 35 minutes or until onions are soft and a deep mahogany brown. Add garlic and sauté for 2 minutes or until garlic is fragrant.

2. Add stock, 1 cup (250 mL) water and thyme and bring to a boil. Cover, reduce heat and simmer for 30 to 40 minutes.

3. Meanwhile, in a medium saucepan, pour vegetable oil to a depth of 1 inch (2.5 cm) and heat over medium heat until hot but not smoking. Fry shallots in 2 batches, stirring frequently and being careful not to burn, 3 to 4 minutes or until golden brown. Remove shallots with a slotted spoon and drain on paper towels. Immediately sprinkle lightly with salt and set aside.

4. Remove thyme sprigs from soup and using an immersion blender, food processor or blender, blend soup until smooth. Return to pot and stir in cream, vinegar, and salt and pepper to taste. Heat thoroughly. Ladle into heated serving bowls and top with crispy shallots.

THE DISH **Clean Leeks.** Leeks are grown in troughs of dirt and sand, which finds its way into every nook and cranny of the plant. That's why it is so important to clean your leeks well before using. Here's how we do it: Trim off the root end and about $1/4$ inch (0.5 cm) of the white base. Trim each of the darkest portions of the leaves down to the light green, tender part. Slice the leeks down the center and rinse under cold running water to remove all dirt and sand, being careful to get in between the layers. Drain on paper towels and you're ready to go.

Fashion Plate

This elegant onion soup makes a lovely start to a classic steakhouse meal of Steak with Red Wine Sauce and Mushrooms (page 183), Potato Haystacks with Gruyère (page 283) and for the finale, Chocolate Mousse–Filled Profiterole (page 340).

Beef Stock

There's no equal to hardy homemade beef stock. The difference it can make to a beef or even vegetable soup can be the difference between an OK bowl and something truly special. Canned beef stock tends to taste more like salt than beef and will never come close to giving you the depth of flavor you get by browning bones and simmering them with hardy vegetables for hours.

Makes about 6 quarts (6 L) stock or 2 quarts (2 L) reduced

Hands-on time
20 minutes

Start to finish
9 hours

Tip

Stock can be made ahead and refrigerated for up to 4 days or frozen for up to 4 months. When you want to use the stock, just add water in increments until it tastes right to you. Begin by adding 2 parts water to 1 part stock. If it tastes too strong, add a little more water until you get the flavor just right.

- **Preheat oven to 450°F (230°C)**
- **Large rimmed baking sheets**

8 lbs	beef bones, such as necks, shanks, knuckles, oxtails or a mixture, cut into 2-inch (5 cm) pieces by your butcher	4 kg
3	onions, quartered	3
3	carrots, peeled and quartered	3
3	stalks celery, quartered	3
2	tomatoes, halved	2
4	cloves garlic, smashed	4
3	leeks, green tops only, chopped	3
1	bunch parsley stems	1
2	bay leaves	2
2 tsp	whole black peppercorns	10 mL
1 tsp	whole allspice	5 mL

1. Arrange beef bones on baking sheets, leaving space between bones so they brown nicely. Roast bones in preheated oven for 25 minutes. Scatter onions, carrots, celery, tomatoes and garlic around bones. Continue to roast for about 20 minutes or until bones and vegetables are well browned.

2. Transfer browned bones and vegetables to an extra-large stockpot, pouring off and discarding any accumulated fat.

3. While baking sheets are still hot from oven, deglaze by pouring 1 cup (250 mL) water onto sheets and scraping up any browned bits. Pour into stockpot.

4. Add enough cold water to cover bones and vegetables by at least 2 inches (5 cm). Add leeks, parsley, bay leaves, peppercorns and allspice. Bring to a simmer over medium-low heat, about 1 hour. Skim scum as it forms on surface and discard it. Watch pot so that it doesn't boil and turn the heat down accordingly. Simmer very gently (you will see a bubble every 10 seconds or so) for at least 4 hours, until stock is flavorful, or up to 8 hours.

5. *To strain stock:* Place a strainer over a large pot and ladle stock through strainer. Using the back of a ladle, push as much liquid out as possible, discarding solids.

6. *To degrease stock:* Once the stock is strained, it must be degreased. Using a large shallow serving spoon, run lip of spoon just under the grease-slicked top of stock, discarding grease into a throwaway container. Remove as much of the grease as possible for the best-looking, clear stock.

7. *To reduce stock:* Reduce stock for two reasons: so that it can store efficiently and for a richer and fuller flavor. At this point, boil stock until it has reduced by about 75%. It sounds like a lot of reduction, but the more the stock is reduced, the more space you have in your freezer. Highly reduced stock also keeps longer than less reduced stock. Boil stock until reduced to your specifications.

Italian White Bean Soup with Pesto

Italians love beans, and we love Italians, so if you follow the logic, this soup has to be good. Here, we've simply sautéed vegetables, added tons of fresh herbs and simmered it all with cannellini beans until the beans are tender and the broth is infused with flavor. Top it all off with a dash of pesto and that's amore!

Serves 6 to 8

Hands-on time
20 minutes

Start to finish
40 minutes

Make Ahead

The soup can be made up to 24 hours before serving and kept covered and refrigerated.

2 tbsp	olive oil	30 mL
1	yellow onion, diced	1
1	carrot, diced	1
1	stalk celery, diced	1
½	fennel bulb, diced	½
5 cups	Brown or Quick Chicken Stock (pages 110 and 119) or ready-to-use broth	1.25 L
3	cans (each 14 to 19 oz/398 to 540 mL) cannellini beans, drained and rinsed	3
4	cloves garlic, chopped	4
5	rosemary sprigs	5
2	thyme sprigs	2
1	bunch fresh sage	1
½ tsp	salt	2 mL
¼ tsp	freshly ground black pepper	1 mL
1	recipe Pesto (page 25) or store-bought	1
	Freshly grated Parmesan cheese	

1. In a large pot, heat oil over medium heat. Sauté onion, carrot, celery and fennel for about 6 minutes or until softened. Add stock, beans, garlic, rosemary, thyme, sage and salt and bring to a boil. Reduce heat and simmer for 20 minutes to allow flavors to develop.

2. Remove herb stems and season soup with salt and pepper.

3. To serve, ladle into soup bowls and garnish with a dollop of pesto and sprinkling of Parmesan.

THE DISH **Herb Garden.** This is a great dish to make in the fall when your herb garden is at the end of its season and you're trying to figure out what to do with all the bounty before you hit the first frost.

Tuscan Bean and Barley Soup with Crispy Pancetta

Once you understand how to make a good bean soup, like the Italian White Bean Soup with Pesto, it's easy to transform it into elegant fare by simply puréeing it, as we've done with this recipe. OK, we've added a few other things too, like barley, which gives a wonderful contrasting chew to the otherwise smooth soup, and crispy pancetta, which, like American bacon, makes everything taste better and never has to justify its existence.

Serves 6 to 8

Hands-on time
40 minutes

Standing time
1 hour

Start to finish
3 hours 10 minutes

Make Ahead

The soup can be made up to 24 hours before serving and kept covered and refrigerated.

- **Immersion blender, food processor or blender**

2 cups	dried cranberry beans	500 mL
3 oz	pancetta, finely diced	90 g
1	yellow onion, diced	1
1	carrot, diced	1
1	stalk celery, diced	1
½	fennel bulb, diced	½
4	cloves garlic	4
5	rosemary sprigs	5
2	thyme sprigs	2
1	bunch fresh sage	1
½ cup	pearl barley	125 mL
	Salt and freshly ground black pepper	
	Extra virgin olive oil	

1. Place beans in a large pot and cover with 3 inches (7.5 cm) water. Bring to a boil over high heat. Remove from heat and let stand for 1 hour.

2. In a large pot over medium heat, sauté pancetta for 5 minutes or until golden brown and crispy. Remove pancetta with a slotted spoon and drain on paper towels. Set aside.

3. In remaining fat, sauté onion, carrot, celery and fennel for about 4 minutes. Add drained beans, garlic, rosemary, thyme and sage and cover with water by about 2 inches (5 cm). Bring to a boil and then reduce heat and simmer for 1½ hours or until beans are just tender.

4. Meanwhile, cook barley according to package directions and set aside.

Continued on next page

5. When beans are cooked, remove herb stems and, using an immersion blender, food processor or blender, purée soup until smooth. Return soup to pot and add barley. Bring back to a simmer. Season with salt and pepper to taste.

6. To serve, ladle into soup bowls and garnish with crispy pancetta and a drizzle of extra virgin olive oil.

THE DISH **Pancetta.** Often referred to as Italian bacon, pancetta is salt-cured pork belly that hasn't been smoked. You can certainly substitute regular bacon in a pinch.

Fashion Plate

Nothing pairs better with this hearty bean-filled soup than a Pizza Bianca with Chard and Chorizo Sausage (page 170). Keep dessert a light affair with White Wine Poached Pears with Rosemary Syrup and Triple Crème Cheese (page 324).

ENTERTAINING

Black Bean and Chorizo Soup

Black beans are the new black, as far as soups go at least. Black beans have a distinctively deep, earthy flavor and a gorgeous color, which makes them a good pick for the base of this spicy soup. Chorizo is a sausage that is sold in fresh and cured forms. For this recipe, we're using the fresh variety, which in this case is mildly spicy with just a hint of cinnamon in the background.

Serves 6 to 8

Hands-on time
20 minutes

Start to finish
50 minutes

Make Ahead

The soup can be made up to 24 hours before serving and kept covered and refrigerated.

1 tbsp	vegetable oil	15 mL
6 oz	fresh chorizo sausage, removed from casings	175 g
1	onion, diced	1
2	cloves garlic, minced	2
2	jalapeños, seeded and minced	2
5 cups	Brown or Quick Chicken Stock (pages 110 and 119) or ready-to-use broth (approx.)	1.25 L
3	cans (each 14 to 19 oz/398 to 540 mL) black beans, drained and rinsed	3
½ tsp	salt	2 mL
¾ cup	crumbled queso fresco, salted farmer's or feta cheese	175 mL

1. In a large pot, heat oil over medium heat. Sauté chorizo, breaking up with a spoon, for about 4 minutes or until lightly browned. Add onion and sauté for about 6 minutes or until softened. Add garlic and jalapeños and sauté for 2 minutes. Reduce heat to low.

2. Add stock, beans and salt and bring to a simmer for 20 minutes to allow flavors to develop. Taste and season with more salt, if necessary.

3. Ladle soup into bowls. Garnish with a little cheese.

Caribbean Black Bean Soup with Mango Habanero Salsa

There's nothing like a jolt of Caribbean flavor to put a little cha-cha-cha into a meal. Of course, a habanero chile doesn't hurt either. The habanero is extremely close in heat (very hot), color (varies from orange to red) and shape (short and stout) to the Scotch bonnet, which is commonly used in the Caribbean but not easy to get in North America. The habanero has a fruity flavor, which is a nice match to the mango in our salsa topper.

Serves 6

Hands-on time
40 minutes

Start to finish
50 minutes

Make Ahead

The soup can be made up to 24 hours before serving and kept covered and refrigerated. The salsa can be made up to 4 hours ahead and kept covered and refrigerated.

1 tbsp	vegetable oil	15 mL
6	slices bacon, chopped	6
1	onion, diced	1
2	cloves garlic, minced	2
2	jalapeños, seeded and minced	2
1 tsp	ground cumin	5 mL
5 cups	Brown or Quick Chicken Stock (pages 110 and 119) or ready-to-use broth (approx.)	1.25 L
3	cans (each 14 to 19 oz/398 to 540 mL) black beans, drained and rinsed	3
½ tsp	salt	2 mL
¼ cup	chopped fresh cilantro	60 mL
3	mangos, cut into small dice	3
1	habanero, seeded and finely chopped	1
½ cup	diced red onion	125 mL
2 tbsp	freshly squeezed lime juice	30 mL
1	lime, cut into 8 sections	1

1. In a large pot, heat oil over medium heat. Add bacon and cook for about 2 minutes or until fat renders but bacon is still soft. Add onion and sauté for about 6 minutes or until softened. Add garlic, jalapeños and cumin and sauté for 2 minutes. Reduce heat to low.

2. Add stock, beans and salt and bring to a simmer for 20 minutes to allow flavors to develop. Taste and season with more salt, if necessary.

3. In a small bowl, combine cilantro, mangos, habanero, red onion and lime juice.

4. Ladle soup into bowls. Garnish with a dollop of salsa and serve lime wedges on the side.

Fast and Fresh Vegetable Soup

A fresh and speedy vegetable soup is a dish in every food fashionista's culinary repertoire. The vegetables used in this dish are always available, so this soup is just a moment away from serving your friends and family their daily vegetable requirements.

Serves 6 to 8

Hands-on time
20 minutes

Start to finish
40 minutes

Variation

Don't let the absence of one or two vegetables stop you from making this tasty potage. Substitute with vegetables in your refrigerator, such as carrots, parsnips, yellow squash, asparagus, cauliflower, etc.

Make Ahead

The soup can be made up to 24 hours before serving and kept covered and refrigerated.

- **Immersion blender, food processor or blender**
- **6 to 8 heated soup bowls**

3 tbsp	olive oil, divided	45 mL
1	red onion, chopped	1
4	zucchini, chopped	4
2	eggplants, chopped	2
1	red bell pepper, chopped	1
3	cloves garlic, minced	3
6 cups	Brown or Quick Chicken Stock (pages 110 and 119) or ready-to-use broth	1.5 L
¼ cup	chopped flat-leaf parsley	60 mL
	Zest and juice of 1 lemon	
	Salt and freshly ground black pepper, optional	
½ cup	crumbled feta cheese	125 mL

1. In a large soup pot, heat olive oil over medium-high heat. Sauté red onion for 6 minutes or until it begins to soften. Add zucchini, eggplant, bell pepper and garlic and sauté for 5 minutes or until vegetables begin to soften.

2. Add stock and bring soup to a simmer. Reduce heat and simmer for 20 minutes or until vegetables are completely tender.

3. In a food processor or blender, process half the soup or give it a few pulses in the pot with an immersion blender. Return to the pot with the unprocessed soup. Add parsley, lemon zest and lemon juice. Taste and season with salt and pepper, if necessary, but remember that the feta cheese you will be adding later is on the salty side.

4. Ladle soup into heated bowls and garnish with feta cheese.

Roasted Vegetable Soup with Harissa

Harissa is a spicy North African condiment made from oil, chiles, garlic, cumin, coriander and sometimes cinnamon and dried mint. We've combined it with roasted vegetables, which always taste so much better than boiled.

Serves 6 to 8

Hands-on time
20 minutes

Start to finish
1 hour

Tip

Harissa can be found in a can or a jar at Middle Eastern grocers and at some large grocery stores, or make your own (page 143). It gives depth and flavor to soups, stews and vegetables and can also be used as a rub on roasted or grilled meats.

Make Ahead

The soup can be made up to 24 hours before serving and kept covered and refrigerated.

- **Preheat oven to 425°F (220°C)**
- **Immersion blender, food processor or blender**
- **6 to 8 heated soup bowls**

4	zucchini, chopped	4
2	eggplant, chopped	2
1	red bell pepper, chopped	1
1	red onion, chopped	1
¼ cup	olive oil, divided	60 mL
	Salt and freshly ground black pepper	
3	cloves garlic, minced	3
1 tbsp	Harissa (page 143) or to taste (see Tip, left)	15 mL
6 cups	Brown or Quick Chicken Stock (pages 110 and 119) or ready-to-use vegetable or chicken broth	1.5 L
¼ cup	chopped flat-leaf parsley	60 mL
	Zest and juice of 1 lemon	
½ cup	crumbled feta cheese	125 mL

1. On a baking sheet, combine zucchini, eggplant, bell pepper and red onion. Toss with 2 tbsp (30 mL) of the olive oil and salt and pepper to taste. Roast in preheated oven for about 20 minutes or until vegetables are tender and browned around edges.

2. In a large soup pot, heat remaining olive oil over medium-high heat. Add garlic and sauté for 1 minute or until fragrant. Add harissa and roasted vegetables and sauté for 2 minutes or until harissa is fragrant. Add chicken stock and bring to a simmer. Taste soup for level of heat and add more harissa as taste dictates. Reduce heat and simmer soup for 20 minutes or until vegetables are completely tender.

Continued on next page

3. Process half the soup in a food processor or blender or give it a few pulses in the pot with an immersion blender. Return to the pot with the unprocessed soup. Add parsley, lemon zest and lemon juice. Taste and season with salt and pepper, if necessary, but remember that the feta cheese you will be adding later is on the salty side.

4. Ladle soup into heated bowls and garnish with feta cheese.

THE DISH **Immersion Blender.** Once you have one, you will wonder how you ever got along without it. An immersion blender is essentially a stick with a little blade on the working end that acts as a blender. It won't blend as completely as a food processor or blender, but it does a superb job of blending soups when you want the texture in them to be a bit creamy or thick. Best of all, the job can be completed in the pan on the stove so that you won't be obliged to transfer the blazing hot soup to another appliance.

Fashion Plate

A Mediterranean-inspired soup like this pairs nicely with Pizza with Kalamata Olives, Red Peppers and Mozzarella (page 162). Dessert could include Vanilla Gelato with Summer Berries and Limoncello (page 350).

Harissa

This spicy North African condiment is easily made using a blender or food processor and is perfect on anything from omelets to grilled meats or seafood.

Makes ½ cup (125 mL)

Hands-on time
10 minutes

Start to finish
10 minutes

Make Ahead

The paste keeps frozen for up to 1 year.

- **Blender or mini food processor**

1	roasted red bell pepper	1
2	cloves garlic, crushed	2
2 tbsp	hot pepper flakes	30 mL
1 tsp	salt	5 mL
½ tsp	ground coriander	2 mL
½ tsp	ground cumin	2 mL
	Extra virgin olive oil	

1. In a blender or mini food processor, process roasted pepper, garlic, hot pepper flakes, salt, coriander and cumin until a thick paste. Pack mixture in a small dry jar. Cover harissa with a thin layer of oil. Close lid and keep refrigerated for up to 1 month.

When In Rome
Pasta and Pizza

Creamy Macaroni and Cheese

Once you've had this cheesy, buttery version of the old-time classic, you'll never look at one of those boxes of elbow macaroni and mysterious orange powder the same way again.

Serves 6 to 8

Hands-on time
25 minutes

Start to finish
1 hour

- **Preheat oven to 400°F (200°C) with rack in middle**
- **12-cup (3 L) shallow baking dish, buttered**

½ cup	unsalted butter, divided	125 mL
2 cups	panko bread crumbs	500 mL
6 tbsp	all-purpose flour	90 mL
3 cups	whole milk	750 mL
1 cup	heavy or whipping (35%) cream	250 mL
	Salt	
¼ tsp	freshly ground black pepper	1 mL
¼ tsp	freshly grated nutmeg	1 mL
1 lb	coarsely shredded extra-sharp (aged) Cheddar cheese	500 g
1 lb	elbow macaroni	500 g

1. In a skillet, melt 2 tbsp (30 mL) of the butter over medium-high heat. Add panko and stir together until coated. Set aside.

2. In a large pot, bring 6 quarts (6 L) of water to a boil over high heat.

3. Meanwhile, in a large saucepan, melt remaining butter over medium heat. Stir in flour and sauté for 2 minutes. Gradually whisk in milk, cream, 1 tsp (5 mL) salt, pepper and nutmeg and bring to a boil, whisking constantly. Reduce heat and simmer, stirring occasionally, for 3 minutes or until slightly thickened. Add cheese, a handful at a time, whisking until smooth after each addition (do not let boil). Remove from heat.

4. Meanwhile, add 2 tbsp (30 mL) salt to the pot of boiling water. Stir in macaroni and boil for about 5 minutes or until almost al dente. Drain well.

5. In a large bowl, combine cooked macaroni and cheese sauce. Transfer to prepared baking dish. Sprinkle buttered bread crumbs evenly over macaroni. Bake in preheated oven for 20 to 25 minutes or until golden and bubbling. Let stand for 10 minutes before serving.

THE DISH **Extra-Sharp Cheddar.** Mild Cheddar cheese just doesn't have enough oomph to make this dish memorable. Choose extra-sharp (sometimes called extra-old) Cheddar for a powerful punch of flavor.

Fashion Plate

For a tasty meatless Monday meal, add Roasted Asparagus (page 290) to this creamy, cheesy favorite. For a decadent dessert, add Chocolate Chip Bread Pudding (page 328).

Quattro Fromaggio Baked Penne with Wild Mushrooms and Pancetta

Italians know how to live, and certainly how to make a version of mac and cheese that will drive you to the fridge, fork in hand, in the middle of the night. Pancetta, the Italian version of bacon, and wild mushrooms are sautéed and added to a creamy fontina, mozzarella, Asiago and Parmesan sauce, which is tossed with hot pasta and baked until golden and bubbling. All this extravagance in one dish should be illegal, but you only live once — unless you're Shirley MacLaine.

Serves 6 to 8

Hands-on time
35 minutes

Start to finish
1 hour 10 minutes

- **Preheat oven to 400°F (200°C) with rack in middle**
- **12-cup (3 L) shallow baking dish, buttered**

4 oz	pancetta, chopped	125 g
½ cup	unsalted butter, divided	125 mL
I lb	assorted wild mushrooms, such as cremini, oyster and stemmed shiitake, thinly sliced	500 g
6 tbsp	all-purpose flour	90 mL
3 cups	whole milk	750 mL
1 cup	heavy or whipping (35%) cream	250 mL
	Salt	
¼ tsp	freshly ground black pepper	1 mL
¼ tsp	freshly grated nutmeg	1 mL
2½ cups	coarsely shredded fontina cheese (about 10 oz/300 g)	625 mL
1½ cups	coarsely shredded mozzarella cheese (about 6 oz/175 g)	375 mL
½ cup	coarsely shredded Asiago cheese	125 mL
1 cup	freshly grated Parmesan cheese, preferably Parmigiano-Reggiano, divided	250 mL
1 lb	penne pasta	500 g

1. In a large skillet over medium heat, sauté pancetta with 2 tbsp (30 mL) of the butter for about 3 minutes or until lightly browned. Add mushrooms and sauté for about 5 minutes or until brown. Set aside.

2. In a large pot, bring 6 quarts (6 L) water to a boil over high heat.

3. Meanwhile, in a medium heavy saucepan, melt remaining 6 tbsp (90 mL) of butter over medium heat. Stir in flour and sauté for 2 minutes. Gradually whisk in milk, cream, $\frac{1}{2}$ tsp (2 mL) salt, pepper and nutmeg and bring to a boil, whisking constantly. Reduce heat and simmer, stirring occasionally, for 3 minutes or until thickened. Add fontina, mozzarella, Asiago and half of the Parmesan, a handful at a time, whisking until smooth after each addition (do not let boil). Remove from heat.

4. Add 2 tbsp (30 mL) salt to the pot of the boiling water. Stir in penne and boil for about 6 minutes or until almost al dente. Drain well.

5. In a large bowl, combine pasta with cheese sauce and pancetta mixture. Transfer to prepared baking dish. Sprinkle remaining Parmesan evenly over pasta and bake in preheated oven for 20 to 25 minutes or until golden and bubbling. Let stand for 10 minutes before serving.

THE DISH **Imported Dried Pasta.** We've found many domestic brands of dried pasta become too mushy in the boiling and baking process. For that reason, we like to use imported Italian pasta, which is relatively inexpensive and is made from durum flour. This results in pastas that are sturdier, with a nice al dente bite when cooked.

Fashion Plate

This uptown version of mac and cheese deserves a salad starter like Arugula Salad with Shaved Fennel and Prosciutto (page 87). A finale such as Dark Chocolate Hazelnut Biscotti with Mexican Coffee (page 337) would finish off the meal to a T.

Simple Summer Pasta with Fresh Tomatoes and Basil

You won't believe how fast and easy this pasta dish comes together. It is one of our favorites and should be reserved for that time of year when local tomatoes are at their peak of flavor. The crispy, buttery croutons add a welcome crunch, so don't even think about making this dish without them. Serve this dish al fresco with a tossed salad and lots of chilled light red wine, such as a Beaujolais.

Serves 4 to 6

Hands-on time
20 minutes

Start to finish
40 minutes

Make Ahead

The recipe can be completed through Step 4 up to 4 hours ahead and kept at room temperature.

- **Preheat oven to 375°F (190°C)**
- **Rimmed baking sheet**

¼ cup	unsalted butter, melted	60 mL
4	cloves garlic, minced, divided	4
2 cups	cubes (1 inch/2.5 cm) French- or Italian-style bread	500 mL
3	large tomatoes, diced	3
⅓ cup	thinly sliced fresh basil	75 mL
¼ cup	extra virgin olive oil	60 mL
1 tbsp	balsamic vinegar (approx.)	15 mL
¼ tsp	hot pepper flakes (approx.)	1 mL
¼ tsp	freshly ground black pepper	1 mL
	Salt	
1 lb	penne pasta	500 g

1. In a small saucepan, melt butter over medium-high heat. Add 1 clove garlic and sauté for about 1 minute or until fragrant. Set aside.

2. Place bread on baking sheet and pour butter mixture over top, tossing with your hands to distribute butter evenly. Bake in preheated oven for 15 minutes or until croutons are crispy and lightly browned. Let cool.

3. Meanwhile, in a large pot, bring 4 quarts (4 L) water to a boil over high heat.

4. In a large bowl, toss together remaining garlic, tomatoes, basil, olive oil, vinegar, hot pepper flakes, black pepper and 1 tsp (5 mL) salt. Taste for seasoning and adjust to your taste with more salt, hot pepper flakes or vinegar, if necessary.

5. When water comes to a boil, stir in 2 tsp (10 mL) salt. Stir in penne and boil for 10 minutes or until pasta is al dente. (Begin checking for doneness after 8 minutes of cooking. Bite down on the pasta and look for a tiny white dot in the center of the noodle. It should be firm, but not hard.) Drain well.

6. Add hot pasta to bowl of tomatoes. Toss for 1 minute to make sure pasta absorbs liquid at bottom of bowl. Add croutons. Toss again and serve immediately.

THE DISH **Extra Virgin Olive Oil.** The flavor of olive oils can vary from bottle to bottle. Some are peppery. Others are grassy. Because quality extra virgin olive oil can be pricey, it pays to taste first and decide which flavors you enjoy. You can often find a specialty grocery store that allows you to taste their offerings before you buy. No matter which one you choose, olive oil is best stored in a cool, dark place and should be used within a year of purchasing it.

Fashion Plate

Because this pasta dish is really like a salad in the pasta, complete the meal with Limoncello Shortcakes with Berries and Vanilla Gelato (page 352).

Fettuccini with Pesto, Mozzarella and Fresh Tomatoes

Whether you make your own or buy a good-quality pesto from the grocery store, this condiment is an easy addition that makes a big impact on any dish. In this hearty pasta dish, we combine it with chunky tomatoes and fresh mozzarella cheese for a taste of summer that you'll yearn for all through the cold winter months.

Serves 4 to 6

Hands-on time
20 minutes

Start to finish
40 minutes

¼ cup	Pesto (page 25) or store-bought	60 mL
¼ cup	extra virgin olive oil	60 mL
1 tbsp	balsamic vinegar (approx.)	15 mL
¼ tsp	hot pepper flakes	1 mL
	Freshly ground black pepper	
2	cloves garlic, minced, divided	2
	Grated zest of 1 lemon	
2½ tsp	salt, divided	12 mL
1 lb	fresh fettuccine pasta	500 g
3	large tomatoes, diced	3
¼ cup	freshly grated Parmesan cheese	60 mL
1 cup	bocconcini (fresh mozzarella), cut into 1-inch (2.5 cm) pieces	250 mL
2 tbsp	sliced fresh basil	30 mL

1. In a large pot, bring 4 quarts (4 L) water to a boil over high heat.

2. In a large bowl, whisk together pesto, olive oil, vinegar, hot pepper flakes, ¼ tsp (1 mL) black pepper, garlic, lemon zest and ½ tsp (2 mL) of the salt.

3. Stir remaining 2 tsp (10 mL) salt into the pot of boiling water. Stir in fettuccine and boil for 4 to 5 minutes or until pasta is tender and cooked through to the center. Drain well.

4. Add pasta to pesto mixture and toss gently to coat. Add tomatoes, Parmesan and bocconcini and toss to combine. Taste for seasoning and add more salt, pepper or vinegar to taste, if necessary. Serve immediately garnished with basil.

THE DISH **Fresh Pasta.** Most grocery stores sell fresh pasta these days. Whether you make your own or purchase it from the grocery store, fresh pasta gives this dish a chewy texture that makes us want to keep eating long after our appetites have been satisfied.

Penne with Roasted Tomatoes and Basil

Roasted tomatoes are another one of our "gold in the refrigerator" items. We use them all the time. From soup to bruschetta to all manner of pastas, these little nuggets are worth keeping on hand on a regular basis. This effortless dish combines the roasted tomatoes with fresh basil, balsamic vinegar and a generous scattering of Parmigiano-Reggiano.

Serves 4

Hands-on time
15 minutes

Start to finish
35 minutes

Make Ahead

The tomatoes can be roasted and cooled up to 3 days ahead and kept covered and refrigerated. Reheat in a saucepan over low heat.

- **Preheat oven to 450°F (230°C)**
- **2 rimmed baking sheets**

¼ cup	extra virgin olive oil, divided	60 mL
3 cups	cherry or grape tomatoes, cut in half	750 mL
	Salt and freshly ground black pepper	
12 oz	penne pasta	375 g
2 tbsp	balsamic vinegar	30 mL
1	clove garlic, finely minced	1
¾ cup	freshly grated Parmesan cheese, preferably Parmigiano-Reggiano (approx.)	175 mL
½ cup	chopped fresh basil	125 mL

1. In a large pot, bring 6 quarts (6 L) water to a boil over high heat.

2. Drizzle 2 tbsp (30 mL) of olive oil evenly over each baking sheet. Add tomatoes to prepared baking sheets and sprinkle with salt and pepper to taste. Toss to coat with oil. Roast in preheated oven for 15 to 20 minutes or until very tender and browned.

3. Meanwhile, stir 2 tbsp (30 mL) salt into pot of boiling water. Stir in penne and boil for about 10 minutes or until al dente. (Begin checking for doneness after 8 minutes of cooking. Bite down on the pasta and look for a tiny white dot in the center of the noodle. It should be firm, but not hard.) Drain well.

4. In serving bowl, combine pasta, roasted tomatoes, vinegar, garlic, Parmesan and basil. Taste to correct seasonings and serve with extra Parmesan on the side.

THE DISH **Balsamic Vinegar.** Always look at the ingredient list on a bottle of balsamic vinegar. If red wine vinegar is listed, it's not real balsamic vinegar. Balsamic vinegar is made from concentrated grape juice that has been aged in wooden casks for years. It is possible to spend hundreds of dollars for a small vial of the best-quality vinegar that has been aged more than 25 years. However, most grocery stores carry a range of balsamic vinegars for you to choose from. We can usually find a reasonably priced 6-year-old bottle that works beautifully in almost any recipe.

Fashion Plate

Serve this simple pasta dish with Prosciutto-Wrapped Salmon with Rosemary Butter (page 272) and end with Almond Cornmeal Cake with Balsamic Strawberries (page 332).

Crispy Penne with Roasted Mediterranean Vegetables

If you've ever tried the crispy noodle cakes at your local Asian restaurant, you know how wonderful crispy pasta can be. With that in mind, we set about finding a way to use this technique in some of our other favorite pasta dishes. For this recipe, we sauté penne pasta until it's browned and combine it with roasted eggplant, zucchini and cherry tomatoes for a delicious dish you'll want to sneak back down for in the middle of the night. Just repeat after us: "Any food I eat in my nightgown by the light of my refrigerator doesn't count."

Serves 4

Hands-on time
40 minutes

Start to finish
1 hour

Make Ahead

The vegetables can be roasted and cooled up to 3 days ahead and kept covered and refrigerated. Reheat in a saucepan over low heat.

- **Preheat oven to 450°F (230°C)**
- **2 rimmed baking sheets**
- **Large warm serving bowl**

½ cup	extra virgin olive oil, divided	125 mL
1	medium eggplant, cut into ½-inch (1 cm) cubes	1
2	medium zucchini, cut into ½-inch (1 cm) cubes	2
2 cups	cherry tomatoes, cut in half	500 mL
	Salt and freshly ground black pepper	
12 oz	penne pasta	375 g
4 oz	feta cheese, crumbled	125 g
½ cup	pine nuts, toasted	125 mL

1. In a large pot, bring 6 quarts (6 L) water to a boil over high heat.

2. Drizzle 2 tbsp (30 mL) of the oil evenly over each baking sheet. Divide eggplant, zucchini and cherry tomatoes between prepared baking sheets. Sprinkle with salt and pepper to taste and toss to coat with oil. Roast in preheated oven for 15 to 20 minutes or until very tender and browned.

3. Meanwhile, stir 2 tbsp (30 mL) of salt into pot of boiling water. Stir in penne and boil for about 10 minutes or until al dente. (Begin checking for doneness after 8 minutes of cooking. Bite down on the pasta and look for a tiny white dot in the center of the noodle. It should be firm, but not hard.) Drain well.

4. In a large nonstick skillet, heat 2 tbsp (30 mL) of remaining olive oil over medium-high heat. Add half of the pasta and sauté to ensure even browning, for about 10 minutes or until penne becomes a crispy, golden brown. Transfer to a large warm serving bowl and set aside. Repeat with remaining oil and pasta.

5. Add roasted vegetables, feta cheese and pine nuts to pasta in bowl and toss gently to combine. Taste to correct the seasonings and serve.

THE DISH **A Large Sauté Pan.** A large sauté pan is a thing of beauty. It not only will allow you to cook more quickly and efficiently, but it might even make your food taste better because less crowding in the pan means better browning and caramelization of whatever you're cooking.

Fashion Plate

Butterflied Herb-Roasted Chicken (page 236) pairs beautifully with this Mediterranean-themed pasta dish. For dessert just add White Chocolate Soup with Chilled Berries (page 346).

Lemony Fettuccine Alfredo

If heaven has a restaurant, Lemony Fettuccine Alfredo is definitely on the menu. This indulgent, ultra-creamy pasta comes together in no time and the tart lemon juice cuts through just enough of the richness to make it even more interesting. You could resist the urge to eat the whole thing all by yourself — in the dark, wearing sweatpants in the closet — but why would you?

Serves 4

Hands-on time
15 minutes

Start to finish
25 minutes

2 tbsp	salt	30 mL
12 oz	fettuccine pasta	375 g
1 cup	heavy or whipping (35%) cream	250 mL
¼ cup	butter	60 mL
	Grated zest of 1 lemon	
2 tbsp	freshly squeezed lemon juice	30 mL
¼ cup	freshly grated Parmesan cheese	60 mL
	Salt and freshly ground black pepper	
2 tbsp	finely chopped parsley	30 mL

1. In a large pot, bring 6 quarts (6 L) water to a boil over high heat. Stir in 2 tbsp (30 mL) salt.

2. Stir in fettuccini and boil for 10 minutes or until al dente or just cooked through, but not flabby. (Begin checking for doneness after 8 minutes of cooking. Bite down on the pasta and look for a tiny white dot in the center of the noodle. It should be firm, but not hard.).

3. Meanwhile, in a large skillet, bring cream, butter and lemon juice to a boil over medium-high heat. Stir in lemon zest. Season with salt and pepper to taste. Cover and set aside.

4. Drain pasta and add to pan with sauce and cook, tossing gently to coat, for 1 minute. Taste again to adjust seasonings, if necessary. Transfer pasta to a serving platter and garnish with parsley.

THE DISH **A Black Platter.** Something as pristinely white as this dish needs a black platter for contrast. Serving this pasta on a white plate would be like looking for a cotton ball in a snowstorm. Basic black is always in style, but any other brightly colored platter would work in a pinch.

Fettuccini with Roasted Asparagus and Tarragon Lemon Cream Sauce

Some dried herbs make more of an impact than others, and tarragon is one of them. Not only does it have a lovely licorice flavor, it has the power to transport us to another place. We always think of France when we use tarragon, and since French food is usually delicious, the smell of tarragon has a Pavlovian effect on us. Not pretty, but true. Here, we use it, along with roasted asparagus, to bring our already celestial Alfredo to an even higher level. Is there a higher level? You be the judge.

Serves 4

Hands-on time
35 minutes

Start to finish
45 minutes

- **Preheat the oven to 425°F (220°C)**
- **Rimmed baking sheet**

2 tbsp	salt	30 mL
12 oz	fettuccine pasta	375 g
1½ lbs	asparagus	750 g
1½ tbsp	olive oil	22 mL
	Salt and freshly ground black pepper	
1 cup	heavy or whipping (35%) cream	250 mL
½ tsp	dried tarragon	2 mL
¼ cup	unsalted butter	60 mL
	Grated zest of 1 lemon	
2 tbsp	freshly squeezed lemon juice	30 mL
¼ cup	freshly grated Parmesan cheese	60 mL

1. In a large pot, bring 6 quarts (6 L) water to a boil over high heat. Stir in 2 tbsp (30 mL) salt.

2. Stir in fettuccini and boil for 10 minutes or until al dente or just cooked through, but not flabby. (Begin checking for doneness after 8 minutes of cooking. Bite down on the pasta and look for a tiny white dot in the center of the noodle. It should be firm, but not hard.).

3. Snap tough ends off asparagus and cut spears on the diagonal into 1½-inch (4 cm) pieces. Drizzle olive oil on baking sheet. Add asparagus, ¼ tsp (1 mL) each salt and pepper and toss together until asparagus is well coated. Arrange in a single layer and roast in preheated oven for about 12 minutes or until tender.

Continued on next page

4. Meanwhile, in a large skillet over medium-high heat, bring cream, tarragon, butter and lemon juice to a boil. Cook for about 3 minutes so the liquid can reduce to a sauce consistency. Stir in lemon zest. Season with salt and pepper to taste. Set aside.

5. Drain pasta and add it and asparagus to skillet with sauce. Return heat to medium and cook pasta with sauce, tossing gently to coat, for 1 minute or until heated through. Taste to correct the seasonings. Garnish with Parmesan and serve.

THE DISH **Fresh Dried Herbs.** When purchasing dried herbs, the best advice we can give you is to buy from a quality source. Dried herbs that have been sitting on the grocery shelf for a long time have already lost a lot of their flavor. We like to buy our herbs from stores that specialize in herbs and spices, because they are constantly refreshing their stock. If you still have that jar of beau monde seasoning from back in the '70s still lurking in your cabinet (remember the dill dip?), it's time to pitch it. Herbs and spices are typically only good for up to a year after purchase.

Fashion Plate

To accompany this rich dish, add Arugula Salad with Grape Tomatoes and Shallot Vinaigrette (page 86) and for dessert a decadent Pear Jalousie with Marsala Mascarpone Cream (page 356).

Pizza with Kalamata Olives, Red Peppers and Mozzarella

Not only does homemade pizza taste better, but it helps out in the battle of the bulge. The contrast of sweet red peppers, salty olives and gooey mozzarella is not one you're likely to find on the menu at your local pizza joint. Kids (or grownups) will love making their very own pizza pies. Don't fret if you're not an experienced roller-outer of dough. So what if your pizza is in the shape of, say, Spain or Australia or even Italy? Flip on the soundtrack to Big Night *and segue into a geography lesson. Mangia!*

Makes two 12-inch (30 cm) pizzas

Hands-on time
30 minutes

Start to finish
1 hour 30 minutes

Make Ahead

The pizza dough can be divided, placed in resealable freezer bags and kept frozen for up to 4 weeks. Just thaw at room temperature for about 2 hours, or if you're in a hurry, we've had good luck microwaving the dough for about 30 seconds and then letting it finish thawing on the counter, about 30 minutes. The toppings can be assembled 1 day ahead and kept covered and refrigerated.

- **Pizza stone with peel (see The Dish, page 163), sprinkled with cornmeal (see Tip, page 174), or rimless baking sheet**
- **Preheat oven to 450°F (230°C) with pizza stone on lower rack**

1	recipe Basic Pizza Dough (page 174)	1
4	red bell peppers, thinly sliced	4
½ cup	chopped kalamata olives	125 mL
3 cups	shredded mozzarella cheese	750 mL
	Salt and freshly ground black pepper	

1. Roll out dough into two 12-inch (30 cm) circles. Place one circle of dough on top of cornmeal. Arrange half each of the red peppers, olives and cheese evenly over pizza. Season with salt and pepper to taste.

2. Open oven door and place front edge of peel to back edge of stone. Tilt peel slightly and pull back toward you (kind of like the magician who pulls the tablecloth from under a table laid with dishes), effectively transferring the pizza to the stone. Bake for 12 to 15 minutes or until bottom is crispy and cheese has browned slightly.

3. Meanwhile, assemble second pizza with remaining dough and toppings.

4. To retrieve baked pizza, just reverse the movement by sliding peel under cooked pizza, scooping it up. Transfer the pizza to a cutting board and let stand for 5 minutes before cutting into slices. The pizza will cut more neatly if you do.

DOUBLE DISH

Pizza Stone. Baking pizza directly on a hot stone in your oven results in pizza that cooks fast with a nice crispy bottom and thin crust. We are also fond of unglazed 6-inch (15 cm) tiles that you can configure on the oven rack in myriad ways. The tiles or stone need to go in the oven before it preheats. Otherwise, the clay can fracture. We just leave them in our ovens on the lowest rack. It's a great place to bake rustic breads and roasts, and even roasted vegetables brown up faster when sitting on the pizza stone.

A Peel or Thin Sheet. The peel or thin sheet is used to transfer the pizza to the hot stone. The best pizzas all have one thing in common: a crispy crunchy bottom thanks to a direct bake on a hot, hot, hot pizza stone. The peel can be made of metal or thin wood with a handle. They can be bought at cookware stores, or maybe you have something lying around that would work splendidly, such as a thin cookie sheet with no sides or a 16-inch (40 cm) square of thin wood paneling.

Fashion Plate

Get the party started with Tequila Bloody Mary Shrimp Cocktails (page 42) and Arugula Salad with Shaved Fennel and Prosciutto (page 87). End the night with Coffee Cookie Tower with Espresso Hot Fudge Sauce (page 370).

Pizza with Red Pepper Sauce, Kalamata Olives, Caramelized Onions and Feta Cheese

Once you've roasted the peppers, sweet red pepper sauce is just a food processor pulse away, and with the addition of garlic and a touch of balsamic vinegar, a vibrant-hued pizza sauce is born. Just a little more complicated than its sister recipe, the extra effort really pays off. It looks almost too good to eat, but go ahead. You won't be sorry.

Makes two 12-inch (30 cm) pizzas

Hands-on time
45 minutes

Start to finish
2 hours

Tip

Red pepper sauce is so scrumptious that you will want to use up every last bit. Try making it with fresh-from-the-farm-stand produce when local peppers are at their peak, then freeze the sauce in the portions in which you will use it. That way, you will have it on hand to make not only pizza but pasta or to use as a sauce for simple grilled meat, fish or poultry.

- **Preheat broiler**
- **Food processor or blender**
- **Pizza stone with peel, sprinkled with cornmeal (see Tip, page 174), or rimless baking sheet**

1/4 cup	olive oil, divided	60 mL
2	large sweet onions, thinly sliced	2
4	red bell peppers	4
2	cloves garlic, minced	2
1 tsp	balsamic vinegar	5 mL
	Salt and freshly ground black pepper	
1	recipe Basic Pizza Dough (page 174)	1
1/2 cup	chopped kalamata olives	125 mL
3 cups	shredded mozzarella cheese	750 mL
1 cup	crumbled feta cheese	250 mL

1. In a large skillet, heat 2 tbsp (30 mL) of the olive oil over medium-high heat. Add onions and cook, stirring occasionally, until they begin to color. Reduce heat to medium-low and cook, stirring occasionally, for about 30 minutes or until evenly golden.

2. Core bell peppers, flatten them and place on a baking sheet skin side up. Broil on top rack until skins blacken. Using tongs, transfer peppers to a heatproof bowl and cover with plastic wrap. When cool enough to handle, peel blackened skin away with the edge of a knife. It's okay if some of the black skin remains.

3. Preheat oven to 450°F (230°C) with pizza stone on lower rack.

4. Transfer peppers to a food processor or blender. Add remaining oil, garlic, vinegar, salt to taste and a few grindings of pepper. Process until smooth. Taste for seasoning and adjust with more salt and pepper, if desired. Set aside.

5. Roll out dough into two 12-inch (30 cm) rounds. Transfer one pizza dough to prepared peel. Spread a layer of red pepper sauce over all. Scatter half of the caramelized onions over and dot with half of the olives. Sprinkle with half each of the mozzarella and feta cheese.

6. Open oven door and place front edge of peel to back edge of stone. Tilt peel slightly and pull back toward you (kind of like the magician who pulls the tablecloth from under a table laid with dishes), effectively transferring the pizza to the stone. Bake in preheated oven for 12 to 15 minutes or until bottom is crispy and cheese has browned slightly.

7. Meanwhile, assemble second pizza with remaining dough and toppings.

8. To retrieve baked pizza, just reverse the movement by sliding peel under cooked pizza, scooping it up. Transfer pizza to a cutting board. Let pizza stand for about 5 minutes before cutting into slices. The pizza will cut more neatly if you do.

Make Ahead

The red pepper sauce can be made weeks ahead and kept frozen for up to 3 months or made 5 days ahead and kept covered and refrigerated.

THE DISH **Roasted Red Bell Peppers.** When sweet red peppers are roasted, their skins blacken while the flesh underneath gently steams and softens. Once the blackened skins are removed, these tender red beauties are ready to give themselves up so that you can tuck into red bell pepper sauce, one of the most versatile and delicious sauces on the planet. If you are time-pressed, go ahead and use a jar of roasted red peppers from the grocery shelf. It won't be quite as sweet but will still taste delicious.

Fashion Plate

Start the night with Crab Dip with Artichokes and Jalapeño (page 44) or Crab and Goat Cheese Bouchées (page 47) and Tuscan Bean and Barley Soup with Crispy Pancetta (page 135). For dessert, keep it light with Navel Oranges with Caramel (page 371).

Pizza Margherita

Pizza Margherita is the best that pizza has to offer. Fresh ripe tomatoes, basil and mozzarella make up the major components with little else to get in the way. The result is a powerful punch of summer flavor.

Makes two 12-inch (30 cm) pizzas

Hands-on time
30 minutes

Start to finish
1 hour 30 minutes

Make Ahead

The tomato mixture can be completed up to 4 hours ahead and kept at room temperature.

- **Preheat oven to 450°F (230°C)**
- **Pizza peel or rimless baking sheet, sprinkled with cornmeal**

1 lb	ripe tomatoes, chopped	500 g
1	clove garlic, minced	1
2 tbsp	extra virgin olive oil (approx.)	30 mL
½ tsp	salt	2 mL
24	fresh basil leaves, divided	24
1	recipe Basic Pizza Dough (page 174)	1
12 oz	bocconcini (fresh mozzarella), cut into 16 slices	375 g
	Extra virgin olive oil	

1. In a large bowl, combine tomatoes, garlic, olive oil, salt and 6 basil leaves. Using a potato masher or back of a wooden spoon, mash mixture slightly. Let stand for 20 minutes.

2. Roll out dough into two 12-inch (30 cm) circles. Transfer pizza dough to prepared peel or baking sheet. Spread ½ cup (125 mL) of the tomato mixture on dough, leaving a ½-inch (1 cm) border around the surface. Top with 8 slices of the bocconcini. Tear 6 of the remaining basil leaves into small pieces and sprinkle on top of pizza. Brush edges of pizza with more olive oil.

3. Open oven door and place front edge of peel to back edge of stone. Tilt peel slightly and pull back toward you (kind of like the magician who pulls the tablecloth from under a table laid with dishes), effectively transferring pizza to the stone. Bake in preheated oven 10 to 12 minutes or until cheese is bubbling and crust is golden brown.

4. Meanwhile, assemble second pizza with remaining dough and toppings.

5. To retrieve baked pizza, just reverse the movement by sliding peel under cooked pizza, scooping it up. Transfer pizza to a cutting board. Let stand about 5 minutes before slicing. The pizza will cut more neatly if you do.

Four-Cheese Pizza with Pesto

An intense hit of basil pesto, mixed with an ooey gooey combo of Pecorino, fontina, mozzarella and Parmesan and juicy ripe red tomato slices, make for a fun twist on the more straightforward Pizza Margherita.

Makes two 12-inch (30 cm) pizzas

Hands-on time
30 minutes

Start to finish
1 hour 25 minutes

- **Preheat oven to 450°F (230°C)**
- **Pizza peel or rimless baking sheet, sprinkled with cornmeal**

1	recipe Basic Pizza Dough (page 174)	1
1 cup	Pesto (page 25) or store-bought	250 mL
1 cup	shredded fontina cheese	250 mL
1 cup	shredded partly skim mozzarella	250 mL
½ cup	freshly grated Pecorino-Romano cheese	125 mL
2	ripe tomatoes, thinly sliced	2
	Salt and freshly ground black pepper	
1 cup	freshly grated Parmesan cheese, preferably Parmigiano-Reggiano	250 mL
	Olive oil	

1. Roll out dough into two 12-inch (30 cm) circles. Transfer pizza dough to prepared peel or baking sheet. Spread ½ cup (125 mL) of the pesto on dough, leaving a ½-inch (1 cm) border around the surface. Sprinkle with half each of the fontina, mozzarella and Pecorino cheeses. Top with half of the tomato slices and season lightly with salt and pepper. Sprinkle half of the Parmesan on top. Brush edges of pizza with olive oil.

2. Open oven door and place front edge of peel to back edge of stone. Tilt peel slightly and pull back toward you (kind of like the magician who pulls the tablecloth from under a table laid with dishes), effectively transferring pizza to the stone. Bake in preheated oven 10 to 12 minutes or until bubbling and golden brown.

3. Meanwhile, assemble second pizza with remaining dough and toppings.

4. To retrieve baked pizza, just reverse the movement by sliding peel under cooked pizza, scooping it up. Transfer pizza to a cutting board. Let stand about 5 minutes before slicing. The pizza will cut more neatly if you do.

Pizza Bianca

Pizza doesn't get much simpler than pizza bianca, or white pizza. Garlicky olive oil, spicy hot pepper flakes and three cheeses layered on top of a crispy thin crust makes us wish it was pizza night seven nights a week. But best of all, making it yourself means that it will be just the way you like it.

Makes two 12-inch (30 cm) pizzas

Hands-on time
20 minutes

Start to finish
1 hour 15 minutes

Make Ahead

The pizza dough can be divided, placed in resealable freezer bags and kept frozen for up to 4 weeks. Just thaw at room temperature for about 2 hours, or if you're in a hurry, we've had good luck microwaving the dough for about 30 seconds and then letting it finish thawing on the counter, about 30 minutes. The toppings can be assembled 1 day ahead and kept covered and refrigerated.

- **Preheat oven to 450°F (230°C)**
- **Pizza peel or rimless baking sheet, sprinkled with cornmeal**

3 tbsp	extra virgin olive oil	45 mL
2	cloves garlic, minced	2
Pinch	hot pepper flakes	Pinch
1	recipe Basic Pizza Dough (page 174)	1
1 cup	shredded mozzarella cheese	250 mL
1 cup	shredded Asiago cheese	250 mL
½ cup	freshly grated Parmesan cheese	125 mL

1. In a small saucepan, heat olive oil over medium heat. Add garlic and hot pepper flakes and let sizzle for 30 seconds. Set aside and let cool.

2. Roll out dough into two 12-inch (30 cm) circles. Transfer dough to prepared peel or baking sheet. Brush pizza with half of the garlic oil and spread half each of the mozzarella, Asiago and Parmesan cheeses over top.

3. Open oven door and place front edge of peel to back edge of stone. Tilt peel slightly and pull back toward you (kind of like the magician who pulls the tablecloth from under a table laid with dishes), effectively transferring pizza to the stone. Bake in preheated oven for 10 minutes or until bottom is crispy and cheese has browned slightly.

4. Meanwhile, assemble second pizza with remaining dough and toppings.

5. To retrieve baked pizza, just reverse the movement by sliding peel under cooked pizza, scooping it up. Transfer pizza to a cutting board. Let pizza stand for about 5 minutes before cutting into 6 slices. The pizza will cut more neatly if you do.

EVERYDAY

Pizza Bianca with Chard and Chorizo Sausage

It all started with the crème fraîche and smoked salmon pizzas fed to Hollywood starlets back in the early '80s. That was when Wolfgang Puck burst on the scene with his first pizza innovations, and we've been topping our pizzas with unusual ingredients ever since. Although tender sautéed chard and spicy chorizo are not your typical pizza toppings, the combination is strangely at home on a hot-out-of-the-oven pizza.

Makes two 12-inch (30 cm) pizzas

Hands-on time
30 minutes

Start to finish
1 hour 25 minutes

Variation

Top pizzas with mushrooms instead of chard. Sauté 12 oz (375 g) sliced wild mushrooms in 1 tbsp (15 mL) olive oil. Sprinkle with salt and pepper. Cook until tender, about 5 minutes.

- **Preheat oven to 450°F (230°C)**
- **Pizza peel or rimless baking sheet, sprinkled with cornmeal**

¼ cup	olive oil, divided	60 mL
2	cloves garlic, minced, divided	2
Pinch	hot pepper flakes	Pinch
1 lb	chard, tough ribs discarded, leaves chopped (about 4 cups/1 L)	500 g
	Salt and freshly ground black pepper	
8 oz	fresh chorizo sausage, removed from casings	250 g
1	recipe Basic Pizza Dough (page 174)	1
1 cup	shredded mozzarella cheese	250 mL
1 cup	shredded Asiago cheese	250 mL
½ cup	freshly grated Parmesan cheese	125 mL

1. In a small saucepan, heat 2 tbsp (30 mL) of the olive oil over medium heat. Add half the garlic and hot pepper flakes and let sizzle for 30 seconds. Set aside and let cool.

2. In a large skillet, heat 1 tbsp (15 mL) of the remaining olive oil over medium-high heat. Add chard, a pinch of salt and pepper to taste and sauté for about 2 minutes or until wilted. Add remaining garlic and sauté for 1 to 2 minutes or until garlic is fragrant. Set aside.

3. In another skillet, heat remaining olive oil over medium-high heat. Add chorizo sausage, breaking up with a spoon into small chunks, and cook for 5 minutes or until no pink remains. Set aside and let cool.

4. Roll out dough into two 12-inch (30 cm) circles. Transfer dough to prepared peel or rimless baking sheet. Brush pizza with half of the garlic oil. Top with half each of the cooked chard and sausage. Spread half each of the mozzarella, Asiago and Parmesan cheeses over top. Open oven door and place front edge of peel to back edge of stone. Tilt peel slightly and pull back toward you (kind of like the magician who pulls the tablecloth from under a table laid with dishes), effectively transferring pizza to the stone. Bake in preheated oven 12 minutes or until bottom is crispy and cheese has browned slightly.

5. Meanwhile, assemble second pizza with remaining dough and toppings.

6. To retrieve baked pizza, just reverse the movement by sliding peel under cooked pizza, scooping it up. Transfer pizza to a cutting board. Let pizza stand for 5 minutes before cutting into slices. The pizza will cut more neatly if you do.

THE DISH **Pizza Wheel.** If you are committed to making your own pizza, a pizza wheel will make short work of slicing it up. The best thing about a pizza wheel is that the cutting disk rolls over the pizza, cutting through the crust instead of dragging a knife across the pizza, which pulls the soft, melted cheese and leaves a big mess.

Make Ahead

The pizza dough can be divided, placed in resealable freezer bags and kept frozen for up to 4 weeks. Just thaw at room temperature for about 2 hours, or if you're in a hurry, we've had good luck microwaving the dough for about 30 seconds and then letting it finish thawing on the counter, about 30 minutes. The toppings can be assembled 1 day ahead and kept covered and refrigerated.

Fashion Plate

Begin this meal with Gazpacho (page 104) and wrap it up with Vanilla Gelato with Summer Berries and Limoncello (page 350).

Parmesan Flatbread

For everyone that enjoys a good honest pizza, with or without the tomatoes, we've included a few recipes for white pizza. This Parmesan and roasted garlic version is as simple as it gets, combining the sweet flavor of roasted garlic and the nuttiness of Parmesan cheese.

Makes two 12-inch (30 cm) flatbreads

Hands-on time
30 minutes

Start to finish
40 minutes

- **Preheat oven to 450°F (230°C)**
- **Pizza peel or rimless baking sheet, sprinkled with cornmeal**

1	recipe Basic Pizza Dough (page 174)	1
¼ cup	olive oil, divided (approx.)	60 mL
	Salt and freshly ground black pepper	
1½ cups	freshly grated Parmesan cheese, preferably Parmigiano-Reggiano	375 mL

1. Roll out dough into two 12-inch (30 cm) circles. Place pizza dough on prepared peel or baking sheet. Brush half of the oil over entire surface of crust. Sprinkle with half of the Parmesan. Brush edges of the pizza with olive oil.

2. Open oven door and place front edge of peel to back edge of stone. Tilt peel slightly and pull back toward you (kind of like the magician who pulls the tablecloth from under a table laid with dishes), effectively transferring pizza to the stone. Bake in preheated oven 10 to 12 minutes or until bubbling and golden brown.

3. Meanwhile, assemble second pizza with remaining dough and toppings.

4. To retrieve baked pizza, just reverse the movement by sliding peel under cooked pizza, scooping it up. Transfer pizza to a cutting board. Let stand about 5 minutes before slicing. The pizza will cut more neatly if you do.

THE DISH **Real Parmesan Cheese.** Parmigiano-Reggiano is simply one of the best cheeses in the world. It can be found cut into wedges in the specialty cheese section of most grocery stores, and its nutty flavor is the real deal. It has a dot matrix pattern on the rind that spells out its name, and it's well worth hunting down. The shredded or pregrated cheeses labeled Parmesan are typically of much lower quality and can often have a strange texture. And if they have any flavor at all, it tends to be less than appealing.

Parmesan Flatbread with Roasted Pears, Arugula and Gorgonzola

Roasted pears and a fresh green salad, right on top of flatbread. Are we crazy? Au contraire, this combination has found its way onto pizzas in many stylish restaurants, and there's a good reason: the flavor works. It goes back to the sweet and savory combination that everyone loves.

Makes two 12-inch (30 cm) pizzas

Hands-on time
45 minutes

Start to finish
1 hour 40 minutes

- **Preheat oven to 425°F (220°C)**
- **Pizza peel or rimless baking sheet, sprinkled with cornmeal**

4	red-skinned pears, such as Red Bartlett	4
1 tbsp	freshly squeezed lemon juice	15 mL
2 tbsp	granulated sugar	30 mL
Balsamic Vinaigrette		
2 tbsp	balsamic vinegar	30 mL
2 tsp	Dijon mustard	10 mL
1	clove garlic, minced	1
1/4 cup	extra virgin olive oil	60 mL
	Salt and freshly ground black pepper	
8 cups	arugula	2 L
4 oz	Gorgonzola cheese, crumbled	125 g
1	recipe Parmesan Flatbread (page 172), baked	1
1/4 cup	chopped peeled toasted hazelnuts	60 mL

1. Peel, core and cut pears into 1/2-inch (1 cm) thick slices. In a large bowl, toss pear slices with lemon juice. Add sugar and toss once again. Transfer to a baking sheet large enough to hold slices in a single layer. Roast in preheated oven, stirring occasionally to prevent scorching, for 35 to 40 minutes or until pears are tender and golden brown.

2. *Balsamic Vinaigrette:* Meanwhile, in a small bowl, combine vinegar, mustard and garlic. Add oil in a slow, steady stream, whisking constantly. Season with salt and pepper to taste.

3. In a large bowl, gently toss arugula with vinaigrette to coat and top with Gorgonzola.

4. Arrange roasted pears evenly on top of baked flatbreads. Top each pizza with half of the arugula salad and sprinkle with half of the chopped hazelnuts.

Basic Pizza Dough

One of the best things about making your own pizza is that you get to make it just the way you like it. One of the other best things is that it's much easier to do than you think.

Makes two 12-inch (30 cm) pizza shells

Hands-on time
15 minutes

Start to finish
1 hour 25 minutes

Tip

If you don't have a stone, invert a large baking sheet on a lower rack in the oven and preheat as instructed. A rimless cookie sheet makes a good substitute for a peel.

- **Instant-read thermometer**
- **Pizza stone or unglazed tiles, sprinkled with cornmeal (see Tip, left)**
- **Food processor**

3⅓ cups	unbleached all-purpose flour	825 mL
1 tbsp	salt	15 mL
1 tbsp	granulated sugar	15 mL
1	package (¼ oz/8 g) active dry yeast	1
1⅓ cups	warm water (110°F/43°C)	325 mL
	Extra virgin olive oil	

1. Place pizza stone or unglazed tiles on rack in oven. Preheat oven to 450°F (230°C).

2. In a food processor, pulse flour and salt a few times to blend salt evenly into flour.

3. Add sugar and yeast to warm water and stir. Let yeast mixture stand for 3 or 4 minutes, until foamy. Add 1 tbsp (15 mL) olive oil and stir.

4. With the processor running, quickly pour yeast mixture through feed tube and process until dough forms a ball. Remove dough from processor and shape into a ball. Place in a large bowl that has been brushed with olive oil. Roll ball around in bowl to coat with oil. Cover with plastic wrap or a clean dish towel and let rise for about 45 minutes or until doubled in size. Deflate the dough with your hands and cut into two pieces.

5. On a floured surface, using a rolling pin, roll dough out to two 12-inch (30 cm) rounds.

Two Pizza Dough Methods

The traditional pizza method, where the toppings are placed on uncooked pizza dough and then baked, results in a chewier crust, more along the line of a New York–style pizza.

The prebaked version, where the shell is partially baked before topping, allows for much of the work to be done ahead and results in a crispier, more cracker-like crust.

Traditional Method: Sprinkle cornmeal over the surface of a rimless baking sheet or pizza peel. Place rolled-out dough on top of cornmeal. Jerk baking sheet or peel slightly to make sure dough will slide off easily. If it sticks, lift up dough and sprinkle a little more cornmeal underneath. Top pizza as desired and brush rim of dough with olive oil.

Prebaked Method: Sprinkle cornmeal over surface of a rimless baking sheet or pizza peel. Place rolled-out dough on top of cornmeal. Pierce dough a few times with a fork to keep it from puffing up in the oven and slide dough off the sheet or peel onto the hot stone or tiles in hot oven. Bake for 3 to 4 minutes or until the crust has firmed up and is easy to handle, then remove from oven by sliding the crust onto the baking sheet or peel. Top your pizza as desired.

Make Ahead

The dough can be made 1 day ahead and kept in a bowl, tightly covered with plastic wrap, in the refrigerator for 24 hours. The pizza dough can be divided, sealed in resealable freezer bags and kept frozen for up to 4 weeks. Just let thaw at room temperature for about 2 hours or overnight in the refrigerator. If you're in a hurry, we've had good luck microwaving the dough for about 30 seconds and then letting it finish thawing on the counter, about 30 minutes.

The Meat of the Matter
Beef, Pork and Lamb

Beef Kabobs with Ras al Hanout

What is it about meat on a stick? It's festive, fun, and with the addition of a few vegetables, it becomes — ta-da — a meal on a stick! Because they can be assembled ahead of time, kabobs are an easy solution for the well-dressed but time-pressed. Now there's time for more important things, like a relaxing mani and pedi before the guests begin to arrive.

Serves 4

Hands-on time
30 minutes

Marinating time
8 hours

Start to finish
9 hours

Tip

Once you've discovered it you'll find many uses for ras al hanout, a North African spice blend of cinnamon, ginger, anise, nutmeg, cardamom and cloves.

Make Ahead

The meat can be marinated up to 24 hours ahead and kept covered and refrigerated.

- **Four 6-inch (15 cm) bamboo skewers**

1 lb	boneless beef top sirloin, cut into 1-inch (2.5 cm) cubes	500 g
2 tbsp	olive oil	30 mL
1 tbsp	Ras al Hanout (see Tip, left, and page 179)	15 mL
2	cloves garlic, minced	2
	Juice of 1 lime	
	Salt and freshly ground black pepper	
2 cups	cherry tomatoes	500 mL
1	medium zucchini, quartered lengthwise and cut into 1-inch (2.5 cm) pieces	1

1. In a medium bowl, combine beef, olive oil, ras al hanout, garlic, lime juice, 1 tsp (5 mL) salt, and pepper to taste and toss to coat. Cover for at least 8 hours or overnight.

2. Thirty minutes before cooking, remove meat from refrigerator and toss in tomatoes and zucchini. Let stand at room temperature.

3. Meanwhile, soak wooden bamboo skewers in a shallow dish filled with water. Preheat barbecue grill to medium-high or preheat broiler.

4. Alternately skewer beef, tomatoes and zucchini, starting and ending with a piece of zucchini. Sprinkle with salt and pepper.

5. Grill skewers for 4 minutes. Turn and cook for 3 minutes more for medium or until desired doneness. If broiling, arrange in a broiler pan and broil on the top rack for 3 minutes per side for medium.

Fashion Plate

Serve this summer classic with Turkish-Spiced Rice Pilaf with Dried Fruits (page 281) and Navel Oranges with Caramel (page 372).

Ras al Hanout

Ras al hanout is a complex Moroccan spice blend that can include ginger, anise, cinnamon, nutmeg, peppercorns, cardamom and turmeric. This exotic mixture lends a unique flavor to grilled meats and vegetables. Although some recipes call for up to 50 ingredients, our simpler version still adds a touch of the Kasbah to anything you sprinkle it on.

**Makes about
⅓ cup (75 mL)**

Hands-on time
5 minutes

Start to finish
5 minutes

1 tbsp	cumin seeds	15 mL
1 tbsp	coriander seeds	15 mL
1 tbsp	black peppercorns	15 mL
2 tsp	whole cloves	10 mL
2 tsp	whole allspice	10 mL
1 tsp	ground ginger	5 mL
1 tsp	salt	5 mL
1 tsp	ground cinnamon	5 mL
½ tsp	cayenne pepper	2 mL

1. In a spice mill, combine cumin, coriander, peppercorns, cloves and allspice and grind to a fine powder. Transfer to a bowl and add ginger, salt, cinnamon and cayenne. Stir to blend. Keep spice blend in a jar with a tight-fitting lid (an old empty spice jar works well). Label it and keep in a dark, dry place for up to 6 months.

Middle Eastern Beef Kabobs with Garlic Hummus Sauce

We don't know which we like the best, the kabobs or the hummus sauce. When paired together, these spicy, perfumed kabobs moistened with the blend of chickpeas, garlic and lemon are one of our new favorite things to put in our mouths. Serve this dish with lots of flatbread to sop up what's left on the plate.

Serves 4

Hands-on time
40 minutes

Marinating time
8 hours

Start to finish
9 hours

Make Ahead

The meat can be marinated and chickpea sauce made up to 24 hours ahead and kept covered and refrigerated.

- **Food processor**

1	recipe Beef Kabobs with Ras al Hanout (page 178)	1

Garlic Hummus Sauce

2	cloves garlic	2
1	can (14 to 19 oz/398 to 540 mL) chickpeas, drained and rinsed	1
¼ cup	Brown or Quick Chicken Stock (pages 110 and 119) or ready-to-use chicken or vegetable broth	60 mL
2 tbsp	freshly squeezed lime juice (approx.)	30 mL
1	green onion, chopped	1
1 tsp	salt	5 mL
¼ tsp	hot pepper flakes	1 mL
	Freshly ground black pepper	
⅓ cup	extra virgin olive oil	75 mL
2 tbsp	chopped fresh cilantro (approx.)	30 mL
1	lime, cut into wedges, optional	1
	Flatbread, optional	

1. Complete Beef Kabobs with Ras al Hanout through Step 2.

2. *Garlic Hummus Sauce:* While meat marinates, make sauce. In a food processor, process garlic until finely chopped. Add chickpeas, stock, lime juice, green onion, salt, hot pepper flakes and black pepper to taste and process until a smooth purée forms. Taste for seasoning and adjust with more lime juice, salt or pepper, if necessary. Stir in cilantro. If too thick, add more stock or water to thin.

3. Preheat barbecue grill or broiler to high heat. Assemble and grill kabobs as directed in previous recipe.

4. To serve, add a dollop of sauce on a platter or individual serving plates and lay kabobs over top. Garnish with more cilantro and lime wedges, if desired. Serve with flatbread, if desired.

DOUBLE DISH

Chickpeas. Did you know that the base of the best sauces and dips could be sitting right there on your pantry shelf? Chickpeas, also known as ceci or garbanzo beans, are delicious when whirred up in a food processor with lemon juice and garlic. We make it a habit to always have a can or two on hand, whether for an instant appetizer or a nutritious addition to soups and salads.

Herbs. Though we prefer our herbs clean, and always wash thoroughly before using, we don't enjoy chopping soft herbs such as cilantro, basil and parsley while still wet. This will result in a dark green, largely unusable smear on the cutting board. To get the lightly, fluffy, nicely chopped effect that you're looking for, make sure to carefully dry your herbs before cutting them. It's so disappointing for your herbs to plop into a dish instead of lightly sprinkle.

Fashion Plate

Add Basmati Rice Pilaf (page 280) and Oranges and Pink Grapefruit with Cardamom and Ginger (page 373) and call it dinner.

Steak with Simple Deglazing Sauce

When we think of steak, most of us attach the word "grilled" to it. The grill does have its place, and though steaks cooked on it are delicious, all the delectable juices that could have been a flavorful sauce have been lost to the coals. For this reason, pan-fried steaks with a simple pan sauce are worth the time it takes to learn the technique, which is really très simple.

Serves 4

Hands-on time
20 minutes

Start to finish
20 minutes

4	8-oz (250 g) boneless beef top loin, strip loin or rib-eye steaks, about ¾ inch (2 cm) thick	4
	Salt and freshly ground black pepper	
2 tbsp	vegetable or olive oil	30 mL
1 tbsp	balsamic vinegar	15 mL
¼ cup	unsalted butter	60 mL

1. Remove steaks from refrigerator 30 minutes before you intend to cook them. Place on a plate or platter and let stand at room temperature. Pat steaks dry and salt and pepper liberally on both sides.

2. Heat a large skillet over medium-high heat and add oil. When the fat is hot, carefully arrange steaks in pan (they should sizzle) and fry for 4 minutes or until steaks have browned and no longer stick to pan. Flip steaks over and fry for 3 minutes for a medium-rare steak or 4 or 5 minutes for medium-well. (Adjust the heat if necessary while cooking so that the juices in the pan don't burn.) Remove pan from heat and transfer steaks to a clean plate. Cover loosely with foil to keep warm.

3. Let pan cool for about 3 minutes. In a small bowl, combine vinegar and 2 tbsp (30 mL) water and add to pan, scraping up browned bits on bottom of pan. The sauce should evaporate to about 1 tbsp (15 mL) because pan will still be very hot. If the liquid completely evaporates, add another 1 tbsp (15 mL) of water. Set aside.

4. Cut steak across the grain into strips and arrange on serving plates. Add butter to the slightly cooled pan and melt. (Cooling the pan slightly will ensure that the butter melts, but doesn't separate, which will create a greasy sauce. If you have to heat the pan briefly to melt the butter it's OK.) Pour sauce over steaks.

Steak with Red Wine Sauce and Mushrooms

Chances are, the last time you enjoyed a steak in a restaurant, it was cooked this way (1) because it is fast and renders a juicy steak and (2) saucewise, there's a world of flavor for you to discover in the browned bits stuck on the bottom of the pan. These bits give up an intense caramelized steak flavor that, when dissolved in red wine and reduced, makes one of the most recognized of the classic sauces. It's classic because that touch of acid in the wine makes a nice contrast to the juicy, fatty steak. In the preceding recipe, we used a touch of tart balsamic, so you see a bit of a trend here. Once you master this technique, all the many flavored reduction sauces will be at your fingertips, so heat up that sauté pan and get cooking. It really is pretty easy.

Serves 4

Hand- on time
20 minutes

Start to finish
25 minutes

4	8-oz (250 g) boneless beef top loin, strip loin or rib-eye steaks, about ¾ inch (2 cm) thick	4
	Salt and freshly ground black pepper	
2 tbsp	vegetable or olive oil	30 mL
6 tbsp	unsalted butter, divided	90 mL
1	shallot, minced	1
3 cups	thinly sliced shiitake mushroom caps	750 mL
¾ cup	dry red wine, such as Merlot, Pinot Noir or Zinfandel or a blend	175 mL
2 tbsp	minced fresh parsley, optional	30 mL

1. Remove steaks from refrigerator 30 minutes before you intend to cook them. Place on a plate or platter and let stand at room temperature. Pat steaks dry and salt and pepper liberally on both sides.

2. Heat a large skillet over medium-high heat and add oil. When the fat is hot, carefully arrange steaks in pan (they should sizzle) and fry for 4 minutes or until steaks have browned and no longer stick to pan. Flip steaks over and fry for 3 minutes for a medium-rare steak or 4 or 5 minutes for medium-well. (Adjust the heat if necessary while cooking so that the juices in the pan don't burn.) Remove pan from heat and transfer steaks to a clean plate. Cover loosely with foil to keep warm.

Continued on next page

3. Add 2 tbsp (30 mL) of the butter and shallot to pan and sauté for 30 seconds. Add mushrooms and sauté for about 3 minutes or until they begin to soften. Add wine, stirring up the browned bits by scraping the bottom of the pan with a spatula. Boil for about 3 minutes or until wine is reduced by half. Remove from heat. Taste for seasoning, adding more salt and or pepper, if desired. Add remaining 4 tbsp (60 mL) of butter and stir just until melted. Keep sauce warm.

4. Cut steaks across the grain into strips and arrange on serving plates. Pour sauce over steaks and garnish with parsley, if using.

THE DISH   **Room Temperature Steaks.** Allowing the steaks to come to room temperature 30 minutes before cooking is important because room temperature steaks will cook more evenly and much faster than a cold steak. But it's not all about speed here. A faster-cooking steak is also a juicier steak because it spends less time in the hot pan. It's almost too simple to be true, but it does make sense, doesn't it?

Fashion Plate

Add Gingered Carrot Purée (page 289) and Hazelnut Biscotti (page 336) with your best French press coffee and call it dinner.

Beef Stew

Every now and then we just need to eat something that is down to earth, with no fancy illusions to grandeur. Beef stew, with its rich gravy and tender vegetables, comforts like a warm hug, a good pair of boots in a snowstorm or a soft chenille robe after a hot shower. Beef stew is the warm winter coat of food. Are you hungry yet?

Serves 6

Hands-on time
30 minutes

Start to finish
2 hours

Make Ahead

The stew can be made up to 24 hours ahead and cooled, covered and refrigerated. Return to pot and reheat over medium heat, stirring often, until hot.

2 tbsp	olive oil, divided (approx.)	30 mL
2 lbs	boneless beef chuck, blade or cross-rib roast, cut into 1-inch (2.5 cm) cubes	1 kg
	Salt and freshly ground black pepper	
1	onion, chopped	1
2	carrots, peeled and cut into 1-inch (2.5 cm) slices	2
1	stalk celery, cut into 1-inch (2.5 cm) slices	1
1	parsnip, peeled and cut into 1-inch (2.5 cm) slices	2
1	turnip, peeled, quartered and cut into 1-inch (2.5 cm) slices	1
3	cloves garlic, minced	3
1 tsp	herbes de Provence or dried oregano or basil	5 mL
1	bay leaf	1
1¾ cups	Beef Stock (page 132) or ready-to-use beef broth	425 mL
1	can (14 oz/398 mL) diced tomatoes	1
	Cooked rice or noodles	
2 tbsp	chopped flat-leaf parsley	30 mL

1. Heat a large heavy pot over medium heat and add 1 tbsp (15 mL) of the olive oil to pan. When the oil is hot, add half the meat to pan. Don't crowd the pan or the meat won't brown. Depending on the size of the pan, you may want to brown the meat in two or three batches. Brown meat on one side before turning it. Salt and pepper the meat and brown the other side. Transfer meat to a large plate and repeat with remaining meat, adjusting heat and adding more oil between batches as necessary.

2. Add onion to pot and sauté for about 4 minutes or until it begins to soften. Add carrots, celery, parsnip, turnip, garlic and herbes de Provence and sauté for 5 minutes. Return meat and any accumulated juices to pot and add bay leaf, broth and tomatoes and bring to a boil, scraping bottom of pan so that all the brown pieces blend into the stew. Reduce heat to low, cover and simmer for 1 hour or until meat is tender. Simmer, uncovered, for another 30 minutes, until sauce is thickened and flavorful.

3. Taste stew and adjust seasoning with salt and pepper, if necessary. Ladle stew over rice or noodles and garnish with parsley.

THE DISH **Beef Chuck Roast for Stew.** Cutting up a roast for stew is one of the easiest ways to ensure that the stew meat will be tender when the cooking is done. The stew meat sold in the grocery store is usually cut too large to tenderize within 2 hours, and it is cheaper to cut a roast up yourself. So go ahead and use your savings to buy that nice bottle of red wine to go along with dinner. You deserve it, you thrifty wench, you.

Fashion Plate

We never tire of dinner in a bowl, but if you want to serve another dish with this entrée, rustle up Roasted Pear Salad with Gorgonzola Rounds (page 95) and for dessert, Chocolate Chip and Ice Cream Cookie-Wiches (page 368).

Beef Stew with Pearl Onions, Bacon and Mushrooms

OK, remember what we said about beef stew? Well, if the president and first lady of the United States (or the editor of Vogue) were coming to your house for dinner, you could serve them this version with no apologies. The additions of bacon, pearl onions, mushrooms and wine turn bourgeois beef stew into WOW. Just imagine how happy your ordinary (but special) family and friends will be to tuck in to this timeless classic from the Burgundy region of France.

Serves 6

Hands-on time
40 minutes

Start to finish
2 hours

Tip

By all means use a wine that you might be drinking with this dish to flavor it. Typically the French would use a Burgundy wine (Pinot Noir) for this stew, but feel free to use a Merlot, Zinfandel or Syrah (Shiraz). They will all work just fine.

Make Ahead

The stew can be made up to 24 hours ahead and cooled, covered and refrigerated. Return to pot and reheat over medium heat, stirring often, until hot.

- **6 heated serving bowls**

2 tbsp	olive oil, divided (approx.)	30 mL
8	thick slices bacon	8
2 lbs	boneless beef chuck, blade or cross-rib roast, cut into 1-inch (2.5 cm) cubes	1 kg
	Salt and freshly ground black pepper	
1	onion, chopped	1
2	carrots, peeled and cut into 1-inch (2.5 cm) slices	2
1	stalk celery, cut into 1-inch (2.5 cm) slices	1
3	cloves garlic, minced	3
1 tsp	herbes de Provence or dried oregano or marjoram	5 mL
2 cups	dry red wine, such as Pinot Noir, Merlot or Zinfandel (see Tip, left)	500 mL
1	bay leaf	1
2 cups	Beef Stock (page 132) or ready-to-use beef broth	500 mL
5 tbsp	unsalted butter, divided	75 mL
2 cups	frozen pearl onions, thawed	500 mL
8 oz	cremini or button mushrooms, quartered	250 g
1 tbsp	all-purpose flour	15 mL
	Cooked noodles or Spaetzle (page 278)	
2 tbsp	chopped flat-leaf parsley	30 mL

1. Heat a large heavy pot over medium heat and add 1 tbsp (15 mL) of the olive oil. When the oil is hot, add bacon and cook until crispy. Transfer to a paper towel–lined plate.

2. Add half the meat to pan. Don't crowd the pan or the meat won't brown. Depending on the size of the pan, you may want to brown the meat in 2 or 3 batches. Brown meat on one side before turning it. Salt and pepper the meat and brown the other side. Transfer meat to a large plate and repeat with remaining meat, adjusting heat and adding more oil between batches as necessary.

3. Add carrots, celery, garlic and herbes de Provence and sauté for about 4 minutes. Transfer vegetables to a bowl. Add wine to pan and bring to a boil. Scrape bottom of pan with a wooden spoon or spatula so that all the brown pieces blend into the stew. Boil for about 10 minutes or until reduced by half. Return meat and any accumulated juices and vegetables to pot. Add bay leaf and stock and bring to a boil. Reduce heat to low, cover and simmer for 1 hour or until meat is tender. Simmer, uncovered, for another 30 minutes.

4. Meanwhile, in a sauté pan, melt 3 tbsp (45 mL) of the butter over medium heat. Add pearl onions, a pinch of salt and pepper and brown onions, tossing occasionally to keep them from burning, for 5 minutes. Add mushrooms and sauté for 5 minutes or until mushrooms are soft. Set aside.

5. In a bowl, with the back of a fork, mix together flour and remaining 2 tbsp (30 mL) of butter. Whisk paste into simmering stew and simmer, stirring often, until sauce is thickened and velvety. Add mushroom mixture and crumbled bacon and simmer to reheat all the ingredients. Taste for seasoning and adjust with salt and pepper, if necessary.

6. Ladle stew over noodles or spaetzle in heated bowls and garnish with parsley.

THE DISH **Herbes de Provence.** A blend of dried herbs, such as basil, fennel, rosemary, sage, thyme, lavender and summer savory, commonly used in the south of France, herbes de Provence is one of our favorite herbal blends and can be used anytime you want something to taste fabulous.

Fashion Plate

This is really a meal in a bowl, but it would be nice to serve a light salad after the main course, as they do in Europe. Follow up with some cheese and fruit and call it a lovely dinner.

Grilled Veal Rolls with Arugula, Currants and Pine Nuts

Winter, spring, summer or fall, you're going to love these salty, sweet and peppery little veal rolls. They are just the thing when you're looking for a zippy new entrée. The filling is composed of nutty Parmesan cheese jazzed up with sweet currants, peppery arugula and crunchy pine nuts. It's a snap to pull them together, they cook in the blink of an eye and there's not even much in the way of cleanup, which stacks these neat little bundles of flavor firmly in our favorites column.

Serves 4

Hands-on time
20 minutes

Start to finish
30 minutes

Make Ahead

The veal rolls can be assembled up to 4 hours before serving and kept covered and refrigerated. Cook as directed.

- **Preheat barbecue grill or broiler to high**

¼ cup	currants	60 mL
¼ cup	warm water	60 mL
8	thin slices veal leg round (about 1½ lbs/750 g)	8
	Salt and freshly ground black pepper	
½ cup	freshly grated Parmesan cheese	125 mL
¼ cup	finely chopped arugula	60 mL
¼ cup	panko or dry bread crumbs (see The Dish, page 307)	60 mL
¼ cup	pine nuts, toasted	60 mL
2 tbsp	olive oil	30 mL

1. In a small bowl, combine currants and warm water and let stand for about 30 minutes. Drain, reserving water.

2. With a meat mallet, pound veal until it is very thin but not torn and place on a work surface. Lightly salt (the filling will be salty) and pepper the meat.

3. In a small bowl, stir together Parmesan, arugula, panko, pine nuts, currants and 2 tbsp (30 mL) of the currant water. Divide mixture among veal and spread out in a thin layer. Starting at the narrow end if there is one, roll up veal rolls and secure each with a toothpick. Drizzle rolls with olive oil and, using your fingers, rub all over to coat.

4. Arrange veal rolls at least 2 inches (5 cm) apart on hot grill or on a baking sheet under broiler with rack set on second-highest position. Grill or broil, turning 3 times, for 3 minutes per side for a total of about 10 minutes or until no longer pink inside. Remove picks and serve immediately.

Braised Veal Involtini with Tomatoes and Capers

As delicious as the previous recipe is, this dish definitely takes the flavor factor up a notch or two by combining the tart and tangy tomato, wine and capers to make a delicious sauce.

Serves 4

Hands-on time
40 minutes

Start to finish
1 hour 10 minutes

Make Ahead

The veal rolls can be assembled up to 4 hours before cooking and kept covered and refrigerated. The dish can be completed and kept warm for up to 1 hour.

1	recipe Grilled Veal Rolls with Arugula, Currants and Pine Nuts (page 190)	1
2 tbsp	olive oil	30 mL
1	onion, thinly sliced	1
	Salt and freshly ground black pepper	
3	cloves garlic, minced	3
1 cup	dry white wine	250 mL
1	can (14 oz/398 mL) diced tomatoes	1
2 tbsp	capers, rinsed	30 mL
2 tbsp	minced flat-leaf parsley, optional	30 mL

1. Assemble veal rolls as directed through Step 3 in previous recipe. Heat a large skillet over medium-high heat and sauté rolls, turning often, for about 8 minutes or until brown on all sides. Transfer to a plate.

2. Add olive oil, onion, $\frac{1}{4}$ tsp (1 mL) salt and pepper to taste to pan and sauté for about 6 minutes or until onions are softened. Add garlic and sauté for 1 minute longer or until fragrant.

3. Add wine and increase heat to high. Boil wine for about 5 minutes or until reduced by half. Add tomatoes and capers and bring to a simmer. Reduce heat and tuck veal rolls into sauce. Simmer for about 15 minutes or until rolls are cooked through. Remove rolls from pan and continue to cook tomato sauce, stirring occasionally, for 5 minutes more or until reduced and flavorful. Taste for seasoning and adjust with more salt or pepper, as desired.

4. Serve involtini napped with tomato sauce and garnish with parsley, if desired.

Fashion Plate

Pair with Roasted New Potatoes with Rosemary and Garlic (page 312), a simple tossed salad and Almond Cornmeal Cake with Balsamic Strawberries (page 332).

Braised Short Ribs

Think of this rich, intensely beefy dish as a more fashionable, even trendy, take on your mother's pot roast. Years ago, short ribs would have mostly been the domain of smart butcher's wives. Today they're found on the menus of smart restaurants everywhere from Los Angeles to Toronto. Their appeal is easy to see. Extremely flavorful, thick slabs of beef hold on to short, stout bones that are easily removed after a long bath in red wine, beef broth, Dijon mustard and tomatoes has rendered the meat to melt-in-your-mouth status.

Serves 6 to 8

Hands-on time
40 minutes

Start to finish
2 hours 40 minutes

Make Ahead

You can cook this dish up to 2 days ahead. Let cool, cover and refrigerate. Return to the pot and reheat slowly over low heat, stirring often, until hot and bubbly.

4 lbs	beef short ribs, cut into 1-rib pieces	2 kg
	Salt and freshly ground black pepper	
1 tbsp	olive oil (approx.)	15 mL
2	onions, chopped	2
4	cloves garlic, minced	4
1½ cups	dry red wine, such as Zinfandel	375 mL
1	can (28 to 32 oz/796 to 900 mL) whole tomatoes with juice, coarsely puréed in blender	1
1½ cups	Beef Stock (page 132) or ready-to-use beef broth	375 mL
3 tbsp	Dijon mustard (approx.)	45 mL

1. Pat short ribs dry and season with salt and pepper. In a large heavy Dutch oven, heat oil over medium-high heat. Working in three batches, brown ribs on all sides, about 10 minutes per batch. Make sure you don't overcrowd the pot or the ribs will not brown properly. Adjust the heat and add more oil as necessary between batches. Transfer ribs to a large plate.

2. Reduce heat to medium. Sauté onions for about 8 minutes or until they begin to brown. Add garlic and sauté for 1 minute. Add ribs and any accumulated juices, wine, tomatoes, stock, mustard, ½ tsp (2 mL) salt and ¼ tsp (1 mL) pepper and bring to a boil. Reduce heat and simmer, partially covered, for 2 to 2½ hours or until meat is very tender and falling off the bone. Taste and season with more salt, pepper and mustard to taste, if necessary.

THE DISH **A Good Bold Red Wine.** Don't anger the kitchen gods (or us) by using a wimpy red wine. This dish calls for a full-bodied red. We recommend a Zinfandel that has the cojones to stand up to the meaty short ribs.

Guinness-Braised Short Ribs with Horseradish Cream

Most people don't tend to think of braises or stews as elegant dishes, but this one is certainly an exception. We've taken our basic Braised Short Ribs, this time simmering them in a bath of deeply toasty Guinness stout, and topped them with the added element of a quick and easy Horseradish Cream. The result is perfection. There is no better dish to make when entertaining on a cold winter night. And when so little effort is required in the meal preparation, extra time can be allotted to more interesting endeavors, like a long, slow bath or a perhaps a pre-cocktail-hour cocktail. After all, relaxation is the key to a happy host or hostess.

Serves 6 to 8

Hands-on time
1 hour

Start to finish
3 hours

Make Ahead

You can cook this dish up to 2 days ahead. Let cool, cover and refrigerate. Return to the pot and reheat slowly over low heat, stirring often, until hot and bubbly.

- **6 to 8 heated serving plates**

4 lbs	beef short ribs, cut into 1-rib pieces	2 kg
	Salt and freshly ground black pepper	
1 tbsp	olive oil (approx.)	15 mL
2	onions, chopped	2
4	cloves garlic, minced	4
2	bottles (each 12 oz/341 mL) Guinness stout	2
1	can (28 to 32 oz/796 to 900 mL) whole tomatoes with juice, coarsely puréed in blender	1
1 cup	Beef Stock (page 132) or ready-to-use beef broth	375 mL
3 tbsp	Dijon mustard (approx.)	45 mL

Horseradish Cream

1 cup	sour cream	250 mL
2 tbsp	prepared horseradish	30 mL
2 tbsp	finely chopped chives	30 mL

1. Pat short ribs dry and season with salt and pepper. In a large heavy Dutch oven, heat oil over medium-high heat. Working in three batches, brown ribs on all sides, about 10 minutes per batch. Make sure you don't overcrowd the pot or the ribs will not brown properly. Adjust the heat and add more oil as necessary between batches. Transfer ribs to a large plate.

2. Reduce heat to medium. Sauté onions for about 8 minutes or until they begin to brown. Add garlic and sauté for 1 minute.

3. Add ribs and any accumulated juices, Guinness, tomatoes, stock, mustard, ½ tsp (2 mL) salt and ¼ tsp (1 mL) pepper and bring to a boil. Reduce heat and simmer, partially covered, for 2 to 2½ hours or until meat is tender and falling off the bone. Taste and season with more salt, pepper and mustard to taste, if necessary.

4. *Horseradish Cream:* Meanwhile, in a small bowl, combine sour cream and horseradish. Season with salt and pepper to taste.

5. *To serve:* Divide short ribs among heated serving plates and place a dollop of horseradish sour cream on top. Garnish with a sprinkling of chives.

DOUBLE DISH

Bone-In Short Ribs. When buying short ribs, be sure they are bone-in short ribs, not boneless. The bones are essential to the irresistible, velvety sauce. They contribute both body and flavor.

An Enameled Cast-Iron Dutch Oven. One of our most used and certainly best-loved pieces of kitchen equipment is our enameled cast-iron Dutch oven (we like Le Creuset). It's not only a thing of beauty but the perfect vessel for soups, stews or braises. Every cook should own at least one.

Fashion Plate

There is no better companion to this dish than a side of Crispy Potato Cakes with Pear Apple Salsa and Crème Fraîche (page 305). The combo of crispy cakes and the rich short rib gravy makes this meal one you won't soon forget. Start the night off with a Roasted Pear Salad with Gorgonzola Rounds (page 95) and end with Dark Chocolate Hazelnut Biscotti with Mexican Coffee (page 337). To die for!!

Beef Fajitas

Does anything in a Mexican restaurant smell better than one of those sizzling platters of beef and veggies as it wafts by your table? We think not. That's why we love this dish. Beef marinated in lime, garlic and cilantro and sautéed with onions and peppers makes for a nice little package of a meal, all wrapped up in a warm flour tortilla.

Serves 6

Hands-on time
50 minutes

Start to finish
50 minutes

Make Ahead
The beef can be marinated overnight and kept covered and refrigerated.

- **Blender**

5 tbsp	vegetable oil, divided	75 mL
1/3 cup	freshly squeezed lime juice	75 mL
1/4 cup	chopped fresh cilantro	60 mL
3	cloves garlic, minced	4
1	chipotle chile pepper in adobo sauce	1
1 tsp	ground cumin	5 mL
3/4 tsp	salt	3 mL
1/4 tsp	freshly ground black pepper	1 mL
2 lbs	boneless beef skirt or flank steak, trimmed and cut crosswise into 3 pieces	1 kg
1	large red onion, sliced into 1/4-inch (0.5 cm) wedges	1
2	poblano chile peppers, seeded and cut into 1/4-inch (0.5 cm) wide strips	2
1	large red bell pepper, cut into 1/4-inch (0.5 cm) wide strips	1
1	large yellow bell pepper, cut into 1/4-inch (0.5 cm) wide strips	1
	Salt and freshly ground black pepper	
12	6-inch (15 cm) flour tortillas, warmed	12
	Salsa	
	Sour cream	

1. In a blender, combine 2 tbsp (30 mL) of the oil, lime juice, cilantro, garlic, chipotle, cumin, salt and pepper and blend until smooth. Pour into a shallow baking dish. Add beef and turn to coat. Cover and refrigerate for 1 hour.

2. Remove beef from marinade and discard marinade. In a large heavy skillet, heat 1 tbsp (15 mL) of oil over medium-high heat. Add beef. (Do not crowd pan. This may have to be done in 2 batches.) Sauté beef for about 4 minutes per side for medium-rare or until desired doneness. Transfer to a cutting board and let stand for at least 10 minutes. Do not clean skillet.

3. Return skillet to medium-high heat and add 2 tbsp (30 mL) of oil. Add red onion and sauté for 3 minutes. Add poblano and red and yellow bell peppers and sauté for about 4 minutes or until vegetables are tender-crisp. Season with salt and pepper to taste. Transfer vegetables to a large serving platter.

4. Cut beef across the grain into ¼-inch (0.5 cm) wide strips and combine with vegetables on serving platter. Serve with tortillas, salsa and sour cream.

DOUBLE DISH

Poblano Pepper. If you've only experienced fajitas in one of those large, chain Mexican restaurants, you might think green bell peppers are an obligatory part of the dish. Not so (thank God!). Poblano chiles, which are a generally mild but extremely flavorful chile, will add the green note that you're looking for and so much more.

Lime Juice. Or lemon juice, for that matter, should never — and we repeat, never — come from a plastic fruit-shaped container or bottle. The lively character of citrus can only come from the fresh fruit itself. You'll get the most juice from warm or room temperature fruit.

Fashion Plate

One of the best things about this dish is it's a complete meal in itself, so no side dishes are necessary. We do like to frame it, though, with Pico de Gallo (page 38) and warm tortilla chips on one end and Tres Leches Cake (page 342) on the other.

Lime and Tequila–Marinated Flank Steak with Sweet-and-Sour Chipotle Sauce

A broken heart, an overdrawn checking account, a flank steak . . . is there anything tequila doesn't make better? Trust us, we've applied this salve on all kinds of wounds and it works for everything. This south-of-the-border dish just happens to be one of our favorite applications. Flank steak is marinated in lime juice, garlic, cilantro — and tequila. It's grilled to perfection and drizzled with a sweet, spicy, limey chipotle sauce that will no doubt become your favorite for all kinds of barbecue.

Serves 6

Hands-on time
50 minutes

Marinating time
1 hour

Start to finish
1 hour 50 minutes

Make Ahead

The beef can be marinated overnight and kept covered and refrigerated.

- **Blender**

1/3 cup	tequila	75 mL
1/4 cup	freshly squeezed lime juice	60 mL
2 tbsp	vegetable oil	30 mL
1/4 cup	chopped cilantro	60 mL
3	cloves garlic	3
1	chipotle chile pepper in adobo sauce	1
1 tsp	ground cumin	5 mL
3/4 tsp	salt	3 mL
1/4 tsp	freshly ground black pepper	1 mL
2 lbs	beef flank steak, trimmed	1 kg

Sweet-and-Sour Chipotle Sauce

1 1/2 cups	freshly squeezed orange juice	375 mL
1/4 cup	freshly squeezed lime juice	60 mL
3 tbsp	liquid honey	45 mL
2 tbsp	tomato paste	30 mL
1	chipotle chile pepper in adobo sauce, finely chopped	1
1	piece (4 inches/10 cm) cinnamon stick	1
2	whole cloves	2
1/2 tsp	salt	2 mL

1. In a blender, combine tequila, 1/4 cup (60 mL) of the lime juice, oil, cilantro, garlic, chipotle, cumin, salt and pepper and blend until smooth. Pour into a large resealable bag. Add beef and turn to coat. Cover and refrigerate for 1 hour.

2. *Sweet-and-Sour Chipotle Sauce:* Meanwhile, in a medium saucepan, combine orange juice, lime juice, honey, tomato paste, chipotle, cinnamon stick, cloves and salt and bring to a boil over medium heat. Reduce heat to low and simmer, stirring occasionally, for 30 minutes or until liquid is reduced by half. Discard cinnamon stick. Set aside.

3. Preheat barbecue grill to medium-high. Remove beef from marinade, discarding marinade. Place beef on barbecue grill and grill for 3 to 4 minutes per side for medium-rare. Transfer to a cutting board and let stand for 10 minutes.

4. Cut beef across the grain into $\frac{1}{4}$-inch (0.5 cm) wide strips. Drizzle with Sweet-and-Sour Chipotle Sauce and serve remaining sauce on the side.

THE DISH **A Wooden Cutting Board.** A wooden carving board with a trough around the edge to catch meat juices is a kitchen must have. There is also something about the way a knife grabs at the soft wooden surface that just feels right.

Fashion Plate

We think it would be nice to get some color on the plate by grilling the red onion and peppers in the previous recipe (page 196) and arranging them attractively on the plate. Place the flank steak slices partially across a mound of Buttermilk Mashed Potatoes (page 282).

Roasted Rack of Lamb

If you want to look like one of those hostesses who can pull off an elegant dinner party with one hand tied behind her back, or better yet holding a martini, try serving roasted rack of lamb. The whole thing can be assembled beforehand and popped into the oven as your guests are still swishing their first glass of wine, and then served without a moment of stress.

Serves 4 to 6

Hands-on time
15 minutes

Start to finish
40 minutes

- **Preheat oven to 450°F (230°C)**
- **Instant-read thermometer**

2	7- to 8-rib frenched racks of lamb (each about 1½ lbs/750 g)	2
	Salt and freshly ground black pepper	
1 tbsp	vegetable oil	15 mL
Crust		
2 cups	fresh bread crumbs	500 mL
¼ cup	finely chopped parsley	60 mL
2 tbsp	Dijon mustard	30 mL

1. Trim off all but a thin layer of fat from meat on lamb racks. Season lamb with salt and pepper. In a sauté pan or skillet, heat oil over high heat. Sear lamb, one rack at a time, on all sides for about 5 minutes for each rack or until nicely browned. Transfer lamb to a platter and let cool.

2. *Crust:* In a small bowl, mix together bread crumbs, parsley, ½ tsp (2 mL) salt and ¼ tsp (1 mL) pepper. When lamb is cool enough to handle, brush mustard on lamb and coat with crust mixture, pressing firmly to adhere.

3. Place lamb, bone side down, on a rimmed baking sheet and roast in preheated oven for 15 minutes. Remove from oven and insert an instant-read thermometer into one end of the meatiest part, not touching the bone. If it registers 125°F (52°C) or more, remove immediately. If it reads less, put lamb back into oven and continue roasting for 5 minutes or until temperature reaches 125°F (52°C). Transfer to a cutting board and let stand for 10 minutes. Separate the ribs by cutting down straight through them.

Fashion Plate

Start the meal off with a Winter Salad with Orange Vinaigrette (page 98) and serve with a Creamy Potato Gratin (page 308) on the side.

Pistachio-Crusted Rack of Lamb with Spiced Zinfandel Sauce

Although it's a special occasion anytime rack of lamb is on the table, the addition of a crunchy and vaguely exotic coating of pistachio nuts brings something different to the party. We dressed it up with a red wine sauce made with Zinfandel, a bold, slightly spicy varietal. Make sure that you dress up too.

Serves 4 to 6

Hands-on time
30 minutes

Start to finish
40 minutes

- **Preheat oven to 450°F (230°C)**
- **Rimmed baking sheet**
- **Instant-read thermometer**

Lamb

2	8-rib frenched racks of lamb (each about 1½ lbs/750 g)	2
	Salt and freshly ground black pepper	
1 tbsp	olive oil	15 mL

Crust

1 cup	finely chopped unsalted natural pistachios	250 mL
1 cup	fresh bread crumbs	250 mL
¼ cup	finely chopped parsley	60 mL
½ tsp	salt	2 mL
¼ tsp	freshly ground black pepper	1 mL
2 tbsp	Dijon mustard	30 mL

Spiced Zinfandel Sauce

1 tbsp	olive oil	15 mL
3 tbsp	finely chopped shallot	45 mL
¼ tsp	ground allspice	1 mL
¼ tsp	ground cinnamon	1 mL
1 cup	Zinfandel wine	250 mL
1 cup	Beef Stock (page 132) or reduced-sodium ready-to-use beef broth	250 mL
¼ cup	unsalted butter	60 mL
1 tbsp	balsamic vinegar	15 mL
	Salt and freshly ground black pepper	

1. *Lamb:* Trim off all but a thin layer of fat from meat on lamb racks. Season lamb with salt and pepper. In a sauté pan or skillet, heat oil over high heat. Sear lamb, one rack at a time, on all sides for about 5 minutes total or until nicely browned. Transfer lamb to a platter and let cool. Do not wash pan.

2. *Crust:* In a small bowl, mix together pistachios, bread crumbs, parsley, salt and pepper. When lamb is cool enough to handle, brush mustard on lamb and coat with crust mixture, pressing firmly to adhere.

3. Place lamb, bone side down, on baking sheet and roast in preheated oven for 15 minutes. Remove from oven and insert an instant-read thermometer into one end of the meatiest part, not touching the bone. If it registers 125°F (52°C) or more, remove immediately. If it reads less, put lamb back into oven and continue roasting for 5 minutes or until temperature reaches 125°F (52°C). Transfer to a cutting board and let stand for 10 minutes.

4. *Spiced Zinfandel Sauce:* While lamb is resting, make sauce. In the pan that you seared the lamb in, pour off all the fat. Heat olive oil over medium heat. Add shallot and sauté for 3 to 4 minutes or until softened. Add allspice and cinnamon and sauté for 1 minute more. Add wine and boil, stirring and scraping, for about 5 minutes or until most of the wine has evaporated.

5. Add stock and continue to boil for 3 to 4 minutes or until about ½ cup (125 mL) of liquid remains. Remove from heat and whisk in butter, 1 tbsp (15 mL) at a time. Add balsamic vinegar and season with salt and pepper to taste.

6. Separate the ribs by cutting down straight through them. Spoon sauce on warmed plates and lay chops over sauce.

THE DISH **Shelled Natural Pistachio Nuts.** Why? Your manicure won't last through an hour's worth of pistachio shelling.

Fashion Plate

The flavors in the sauce marry beautifully with the elegant Potato Galette with Celery Root (page 296). Top the meal off with a slice of Almond Cornmeal Cake with Balsamic Strawberries (page 332).

Pork Chops with Sweet Potatoes, Apples and Walnuts in Cider Sauce

This never-fail recipe has gotten us through more dinners than we dare confess. It resonates, first, because it is delicious, second because it is a one-dish meal and last because it has a great sauce to moisten what can sometimes be a dry cut of meat. It's sure to become one of your family's favorites.

Serves 4

Hands-on time
30 minutes

Start to finish
1 hour

Make Ahead

The pork doesn't really reheat well, so make this dish when you plan to eat it right away.

- **4 heated serving plates**

2 tbsp	vegetable oil	30 mL
4	boneless center-cut pork loin chops, 1 inch (2.5 cm) thick	4
	Salt and freshly ground black pepper	
2	large sweet potatoes, peeled and thinly sliced (about 1 lb/500 g total)	2
2	apples, such as Crispin (Mutsu) or Braeburn, peeled and cut into 8 sections	2
1 cup	unsweetened apple cider	250 mL
1/4 tsp	ground cinnamon	1 mL
2 tsp	Dijon mustard	10 mL
1/3 cup	toasted walnut halves	75 mL
2 tbsp	minced parsley, optional	30 mL

1. Heat a large sauté pan over medium-high heat and add the vegetable oil. Season pork chops with salt and pepper and cook for 3 minutes or until a crust forms and chops are browned. (Do not try to move them at this stage.) Turn chops and cook for about 2 minutes. They will not be cooked through at this point. Transfer pork chops to a plate.

2. Add sweet potatoes, apples, cider and cinnamon to pan. Sprinkle 1/4 tsp (1 mL) salt over top and bring to a simmer. Cover pan, reduce heat to medium and boil for about 10 minutes or until almost tender.

3. Return pork chops to pan, nestling them into potatoes. Reduce heat to low, cover and cook for about 10 minutes or until a hint of pink remains in pork and potatoes are tender.

4. Transfer pork chops, potatoes and apples to a large platter and cover with foil, leaving liquid in pan. Increase heat to high and boil for about 3 minutes to reduce sauce. Whisk in mustard and taste for seasoning, adding more salt or pepper to taste, if necessary.

5. Divide meat and vegetables among 4 heated plates and ladle over cider sauce. Garnish with walnuts and parsley, if desired.

DOUBLE DISH

Saucy Apples. The Braeburn and Crispin apples that are recommended in the recipe will result in a chunky applesauce with distinct pieces of apples that have maintained their shape. If you like a more "saucy" applesauce where the apples are more broken down, try using Golden Delicious, McIntosh or Gala.

Thick Pork Chops. By using a thicker than usual cut (1 inch/2.5 cm), we have a better chance of ending up with a juicy cut of meat. The pork of yesteryear contained more marbling and could withstand a sustained blazing heat. But today's pork is much leaner, so if your chops are a little on the thin side, cook them for less time than we call for here.

Fashion Plate

This recipe is a meal in a pan, but if you want something else, go ahead and add a salad like the Winter Salad with Orange Vinaigrette (page 98) and finish with Baked Pears with Mascarpone Cream (page 354).

Maple-Brined Pork Chops with Mustard Sauce and Sweet Potato–Apple Gratins

As the previous recipe demonstrates, pork chops go especially well with sweet potatoes, apples, mustard and cinnamon. This dressed-up version features a nifty brining solution to assure delectable, juicy meat, along with a velvety sweet potato and apple custard that launches this plate from casual to evening wear.

Serves 4

Hands-on time
40 minutes

Marinating time
2 hours

Start to finish
3 hours

Make Ahead

The pork can brine for up to 24 hours. The custards can be assembled unbaked up to 24 hours ahead, but the pork must be cooked and eaten right away.

- **Four ¹/₂-cup (125 mL) ramekins, greased**
- **4 heated serving plates**

¹/₄ cup	kosher salt	60 mL
¹/₄ cup	granulated sugar	60 mL
¹/₄ cup	pure maple syrup	60 mL
3	cloves garlic, smashed	3
2 tsp	dried rosemary	10 mL
1 tsp	dried thyme	5 mL
¹/₄ tsp	hot pepper flakes	1 mL
2 cups	ice	500 mL
4	boneless center-cut pork loin chops, 1¹/₂ inches (4 cm) thick	4
1	large sweet potato, peeled and thinly sliced (11 oz/340 g)	1
1	apple, such as Crispin (Mutsu) or Braeburn, peeled and cut into 8 sections	1
1 cup	apple cider or apple juice	250 mL
¹/₂ tsp	ground cinnamon	2 mL
¹/₄ tsp	salt	1 mL
2	large egg yolks, beaten	2
¹/₂ cup	heavy or whipping (35%) cream	125 mL
2 tbsp	minced parsley	30 mL
Pinch	freshly grated nutmeg	Pinch
	Freshly ground black pepper	
2 tbsp	vegetable oil	30 mL
¹/₂ cup	dry white wine	125 mL
2 tbsp	unsalted butter, divided	30 mL
2 tsp	Dijon mustard	10 mL
¹/₃ cup	toasted walnut halves	75 mL

1. In a large pot, combine $\frac{1}{2}$ cup (60 mL) water, kosher salt, sugar, maple syrup, garlic, rosemary, thyme and hot pepper flakes. Heat over medium-high heat, stirring, until sugar and salt have dissolved. Pour mixture into a heatproof bowl and add ice. Stir until dissolved. Add pork chops to brine, cover and refrigerate for at least 2 hours or for up to 24 hours.

2. When pork is nearly finished brining, in a large skillet, combine sweet potatoes, apple, cider, cinnamon and salt and bring to a simmer over medium-high heat. Cover, reduce heat to low and simmer for about 10 minutes or until potatoes are tender.

3. Meanwhile, preheat oven to 350°F (180°C).

4. In a large bowl, whisk together egg yolks, cream, parsley and nutmeg. Strain vegetables, reserving cooking liquid, and add to bowl of custard. Set cooking liquid aside.

5. Divide custard mixture equally among prepared ramekins. Arrange cups on a baking sheet and bake in preheated oven for 25 minutes or until custard is set.

6. Meanwhile, remove pork chops from brine and pat dry. Discard brine. Season chops with pepper (no need for salt).

7. Heat a large sauté pan over medium-high heat and add the oil. Add pork chops and cook for 5 minutes or until a crust forms and chops are browned. (Do not try to move them at this stage.) Turn chops and cook for about 5 minutes. Add reserved cider cooking liquid and wine. Cover, reduce heat to low and simmer chops for 5 minutes or until just a hint of pink remains.

8. Transfer pork chops to a large platter and cover with foil, leaving liquid in pan. Increase heat to high and cook for about 2 minutes to reduce sauce. Whisk in butter and mustard. Taste sauce for seasoning, adding more salt or pepper, as desired.

9. Run a thin knife around perimeter of the ramekins and invert custard onto 4 heated plates. Arrange a pork chop on each plate and ladle sauce over top. Garnish with walnuts.

THE DISH **Brining Solution.** Primarily a salty flavoring solution, brines can give lean meats such as pork chops, chicken breasts, veal chops and pork tenderloins a more juicy and flavorful character after resting in this salty, sweet and aromatic liquid. You don't have to brine the chops in this recipe, but if you have the time, try it. You'll be amazed at how juicy and delicious a pork chop can be.

Mustard and Garlic–Roasted Pork Loin

We can't help but like a dish that's easy and goes with everything (just like our favorite black dress, only more delicious), and there's no better way to sum up this simple but flavorful roast pork loin. Slathered in a mixture of garlic, herbs and mustard and roasted just until it's slightly pink but still moist and juicy, this roast is a go-to recipe for either a family or fancy dinner.

Serves 8

Hands-on time
10 minutes

Start to finish
1 hour

Make Ahead

The roast can be prepared and kept overnight, uncooked, in the refrigerator.

- **Preheat oven to 375°F (190°C)**
- **Instant-read thermometer**

4	cloves garlic	4
2 tsp	fresh thyme leaves	10 mL
3 tbsp	Dijon mustard	45 mL
2 tbsp	olive oil	30 mL
1 tsp	salt	5 mL
1/4 tsp	freshly ground black pepper	1 mL
1	3½-lb (1.75 kg) boneless center-cut pork loin roast	1

1. Finely chop garlic together with thyme and transfer to a small bowl. Whisk in mustard, olive oil, salt and pepper.

2. Brush roast with mustard mixture. Transfer to a roasting pan and roast for 40 to 50 minutes or until an instant-read thermometer inserted in the center registers 150°F (65°C). Transfer to a cutting board and let stand for 10 minutes. Cut crosswise into ¾-inch (2 cm) slices and serve.

THE DISH **Good Dijon Mustard.** If you think you don't like Dijon mustard, try a good-quality brand imported from France. Our favorite is Maille. Good Dijon mustard should be assertive without being too sharp and will add just the right note to almost any recipe.

Fashion Plate

A simple roast like this stands up well to bold sides like Southern Corn Spoonbread (page 302) and Green Beans with Bacon, Pecans and Pearl Onions (page 287).

Glazed Pork Loin Stuffed with Apricots and Figs

How do you dress up something as inherently elegant as a simple roasted pork loin? We've decided to create a little more inner beauty by stuffing it with an exotic array of dried fruits like figs and apricots and brushing it with a sweet-and-sour balsamic-honey glaze. Et voila . . . you have perfection.

Serves 8

Hands-on time
20 minutes

Start to finish
1 hour 30 minutes

- **Preheat oven to 375°F (190°C)**
- **Long thin boning knife**
- **Instant-read thermometer**

4 oz	dried apricot halves, finely chopped	125 g
4 oz	dried figs, finely chopped	125 g
⅓ cup	golden raisins	75 mL
1 cup	Brown or Quick Chicken Stock (pages 110 and 119) or ready-to-use chicken broth	250 mL
¼ cup	balsamic vinegar	60 mL
2 tbsp	liquid honey	30 mL
4 tbsp	olive oil, divided	60 mL
5 tbsp	Dijon mustard, divided	75 mL
1	3½-lb (1.75 kg) boneless center-cut pork loin roast	1
4	cloves garlic	4
2 tsp	fresh thyme leaves	10 mL
1 tsp	salt	5 mL
¼ tsp	freshly ground black pepper	1 mL

1. In a small saucepan, combine apricots, figs, raisins and chicken stock and bring to a boil over medium heat. Reduce heat and simmer for 10 minutes or until liquid is evaporated and fruit is plump. Set stuffing aside.

2. In a small bowl, whisk together balsamic vinegar, honey, 2 tbsp (30 mL) of the olive oil and 2 tbsp (30 mL) of the Dijon mustard. Divide equally between two small bowls and set aside.

3. Beginning in middle of one end of pork roast, insert a sharp long thin boning knife lengthwise and cut toward center of loin. Then repeat at opposite end of loin to complete incision running through middle. Open up incision with your fingers, working from both ends, to create a 1-inch (2.5 cm) wide opening. Pack opening with all of the stuffing, pushing from both ends toward center. Pat pork roast dry.

4. Finely chop garlic together with thyme and transfer to a small bowl. Whisk in remaining 2 tbsp (30 mL) of olive oil, remaining 3 tbsp (45 mL) of mustard, salt and pepper. Brush roast with mustard mixture. Transfer to a roasting pan and roast in preheated oven for 25 minutes. Brush with half the balsamic glaze and roast for about 20 minutes or until an instant-read thermometer inserted in the center of meat (avoiding stuffing) registers 150°F (70°C). Transfer to a cutting board and let stand for 20 minutes. Cut crosswise into ¾-inch (2 cm) thick slices.

5. Dip a clean brush into remaining bowl of glaze and brush it decoratively onto one side of each serving dish. Lay two slices, slightly overlapping, along side of plate with glaze, not covering glaze completely.

THE DISH **A Long Thin Boning Knife.** For this dish, you will need a long thin knife to make the right size hole in the middle of the pork roast for stuffing. But even if that wasn't the case, a sharp boning knife is a The Dish for any number of tasks, like trying to deftly remove a chicken breast off the bone or a fillet off a salmon.

Fashion Plate

This dish looks good on a plate with the Creamy White Winter Gratin with Caramelized Onions (page 310). Start out this stunning entrée with Winter Salad with Orange Vinaigrette (page 98) and end with Dark Chocolate Hazelnut Biscotti with Mexican Coffee (page 337). Oh, and make sure to let us know what time dinner is being served!

Grilled Herbed Pork Tenderloin

Anyone who is big on the pig will love this simple, lean cut cooked in this simple, straightforward way. Pork tenderloin is a flavorful, fast and easy answer to what's for dinner on a Wednesday night. Rubbing the meat with olive oil and dried herbs means it picks up a protective layer that keeps the cut juicy. Sometimes simple really is best.

Serves 6

Hands-on time
20 minutes

Start to finish
1 hour

Tip

Instead of herbes de Provence, you could use an Italian herb mix or a combination of dried thyme, oregano and marjoram.

Variation

If cooking on a grill pan, turn as tenderloins brown, and once browned on 3 sides, after about 10 minutes, pop in preheated oven and roast for 10 minutes or until an instant-read thermometer registers 140°F (60°C). Let stand for 5 minutes.

Make Ahead

The tenderloins can be rubbed with the herbs up to 24 hours ahead and kept covered and refrigerated.

• **Instant-read thermometer**

2	pork tenderloins, (each about 1 lb/500 g), silverskin removed	2
2 tbsp	olive oil	30 mL
1 tbsp	herbes de Provence (see Tip, left)	15 mL
	Salt and freshly ground black pepper	

1. Fold up thin tails over top of tenderloin and tie so they are an even thickness.

2. Rub tenderloins with oil and sprinkle with herbes de Provence, salt and pepper. Let stand at room temperature for about 20 minutes so that they will cook more evenly. Preheat barbecue grill to medium-high heat or preheat oven to 425°F (220°C).

3. Place tenderloins on barbecue grill and grill for 5 minutes. Turn and grill second side for 5 minutes and third side for 5 minutes. Close barbecue lid and cook for 5 minutes more or until an instant-read thermometer registers 140°F (60°C) for medium or until desired doneness. Tent with foil and let stand for about 10 minutes (the temperature will rise as meat rests).

4. To serve, cut tenderloins crosswise on the diagonal into slices about ¾ inch (2 cm) thick.

Instant-Read Thermometer.
Instant-read thermometers make it easy
for you to know when meat is done. Just take the meat
off the grill or out of the oven and insert the thermometer
into the thickest part of the tenderloin for the most accurate
read. Remember that the meat will continue to cook for
a few minutes after being removed from the grill. So we
recommend that you remove the meat when it registers
140°F (60°C). It will climb to close to 150°F (65°C) before
you are ready to slice it.

Smart Oven. If you have one of the newer ovens, more
likely than not it came equipped with a temperature probe. It's
worth the time to dig this thingamajig out of the "I don't know
what the hell this is" drawer and read the instructions on how
to use it. It actually does all the thinking for you (something we
always love). When inserted into a piece of meat, this gadget
keeps track of the temperature as your meat cooks and lets
you know exactly when to remove it.

Fashion Plate

Try serving this pork tenderloin with the Butternut Squash
Gratin with Caramelized Onions (page 318) or Maple-Glazed
Carrots (page 288) and Individual Chocolate and Almond
Bread Puddings (page 329).

Grilled Pork Tenderloin with Berry Sauce

Pork is a lean cut that benefits from a good sit in a flavorful marinade — especially when the marinade is a tart fruit concoction that ends up serving as a zesty sauce. This recipe's roots go back to Italy, believe it or not, where the inventive use of whatever foods the cook had on hand surely got its start. Just imagine a warm spring day and more fresh berries than you could use in a dessert tart. The rest, as they say, is history.

Serves 6

Hands-on time
30 minutes

Marinating time
4 hours

Start to finish
5 hours 30 minutes

Make Ahead

The pork can be kept in the marinade, covered and refrigerated, for up to 24 hours.

2	pork tenderloins, (each about 1 lb/500 g), silverskin removed	2
½ cup	red wine vinegar	125 mL
½ cup	dry red wine	125 mL
¾ cup	granulated sugar	175 mL
	Grated zest of 1 lemon	
2 cups	frozen mixed berries (12 oz/375 g)	500 mL
	Salt and freshly ground black pepper	

1. Fold up tails over top of tenderloin and tie so they are an even thickness.

2. In a medium saucepan, combine vinegar, wine, sugar, lemon zest and berries and bring to a boil over medium-high heat. Let cool to room temperature, about 1 hour.

3. Pour marinade into a large resealable bag and add tenderloins. Seal and refrigerate for at least 4 hours or for up to 24 hours.

4. When ready to cook, remove tenderloins from marinade and pat dry. Set pork aside. Transfer marinade to a medium saucepan and bring to a boil over medium-high heat. Reduce heat and simmer, stirring often, for about 30 minutes or until reduced to a thick sauce (be careful not to let it burn on the bottom of the pan). Remove from heat and keep warm.

5. Meanwhile, preheat barbecue grill to medium-high heat. Season tenderloins with salt and pepper. Place on barbecue grill and grill for 5 minutes. Turn and grill second side for 5 minutes and third side for 5 minutes. Close barbecue lid and cook for 5 minutes more or until an instant-read thermometer registers 140°F (60°C) for medium or until desired doneness. Let stand for about 5 minutes (the temperature will rise as meat rests).

6. To serve, cut tenderloins crosswise on the diagonal into slices about ¾ inch (2 cm) thick, place on serving plates and nap with sauce.

DOUBLE DISH **Frozen Mixed Berries.** Save your fresh berries for the Vanilla Gelato with Summer Berries and Limoncello (page 350) and pull out a bag of frozen berries for the marinade. It will be much cheaper than using fresh and the flavor will still be to die for.

Butcher's Twine. Buying a roll of waxed butcher's twine is worth the investment. The wax on the twine renders it more rigid, making it much easier for those of us with less than nimble fingers to tie the knots.

Fashion Plate

We love to pair this zesty pork dish with Creamy White Winter Gratin with Caramelized Onions (page 310) and finish the meal with Chocolate Mousse–Filled Profiteroles (page 340).

The Hen House
Poultry

Stuffed Chicken Thighs with Escarole and Barley Risotto

Dark meat is moister and tends to be more flavorful than white meat, but if you don't enjoy gnawing your protein off a bone, what's a girl to do? How about boneless skinless chicken thighs? And now that we can find them in almost any grocery store, they are one of our favorite cuts for quick weeknight meals. You're going to love this unusual one-dish meal of juicy chicken, figs, bacon and barley.

Serves 4

Hands-on time
30 minutes

Start to finish
50 minutes

Make Ahead

The chicken and barley can be made up to 30 minutes ahead and kept warm in a 200°F (100°C) oven.

- **Skillet with lid**

½ cup	sherry or dry white wine	125 mL
12	dried black Mission figs, stemmed and cut in half	12
8	boneless skinless chicken thighs, trimmed of fat	8
	Salt and freshly ground black pepper	
8	slices bacon	8
2 tbsp	olive oil	30 mL
1	onion, chopped	1
1	head escarole, chopped	1
1	clove garlic, minced	1
1½ cups	pearl barley	375 mL
2 cups	Quick Chicken Stock (page 119) or ready-to-use chicken broth	500 mL
½ tsp	salt	2 mL
2 tbsp	heavy or whipping (35%) cream	30 mL
2 tbsp	minced fresh chives	30 mL
	Zest of 1 lemon	

1. In a saucepan, heat sherry over medium heat. Bring to a boil and add figs (be careful, it might flame up. Just remove it from the heat). Let stand for 20 minutes. Remove figs and set aside, reserving sherry.

2. Lay chicken thighs skinned side down and season with salt and pepper. (Even though there is no skin here, the skinned side will be the most attractive side to present on the plate.) Divide figs evenly among chicken and roll thighs up to enclose filling. Wrap chicken in bacon and secure with a toothpick.

3. In a skillet with lid, heat oil over medium heat. Add chicken rolls and brown on all sides, about 5 minutes total. Remove chicken and pour off all but 2 tbsp (30 mL) fat from pan. Add onion and escarole and sauté for 3 minutes or until escarole is wilted. Add garlic and sauté for 1 to 2 minutes or until garlic is fragrant. Add reserved sherry, stirring, for about 3 minutes or until liquid is reduced. Add barley, stock and salt and bring to a boil. Reduce heat and tuck chicken into barley. Cover and cook for 20 minutes or until chicken juices run clear and barley is tender.

4. Transfer chicken to a heated platter and remove toothpicks. Stir cream and chives into the barley. Taste for seasoning and add more salt and pepper as desired.

5. Mound barley risotto onto a platter and top with chicken thighs. Garnish with lemon zest.

THE DISH **Escarole.** One of the most versatile of greens, escarole, a type of endive, is good in a tossed salad or as a sautéed vegetable. With its chewy texture and slightly bitter edge, this is one green with attitude. It is available year-round, but we really appreciate it in the fall when added raw to salads with apples or pears or when we sauté it up and add it to soups or casseroles.

Fashion Plate

Pair this weeknight favorite with Arugula Salad with Grape Tomatoes and Shallot Vinaigrette (page 86) and Hazelnut Biscotti (page 336).

Fig and Escarole–Stuffed Chicken Thighs with Sherry Cream Sauce

We've taken the stuffed chicken from the previous recipe and turned it into a special occasion entrée with the addition of a creamy sherry sauce. The fig and escarole stuffing, with its blend of sweet and bitter, is a pleasant surprise stuffed in the center of a juicy chicken thigh.

Serves 4

Hands-on time
30 minutes

Start to finish
1 hour

Make Ahead

The chicken can be assembled up to 4 hours ahead and kept covered and refrigerated. The finished dish can be made up to 1 hour ahead and kept warm in a 200°F (100°C) oven.

- **Skillet with lid**

½ cup	sherry or dry white wine	125 mL
8	dried black mission figs, stemmed and cut in half	8
2 tbsp	olive oil, divided	30 mL
1	onion, chopped, divided	1
1	head escarole, chopped	1
1	clove garlic, minced	1
8	boneless skinless chicken thighs, trimmed of fat	8
	Salt and freshly ground black pepper	
8	slices bacon	8
2 cups	Quick Chicken Stock (page 119) or ready-to-use chicken broth	500 mL
½ cup	heavy or whipping (35%) cream	125 mL
2 tbsp	minced fresh chives, divided	30 mL
	Zest of 1 lemon	

1. In a saucepan, heat sherry over medium heat. Bring to a boil and add figs (be careful, it might flame up. Just remove it from the heat). Let stand for 20 minutes. Remove figs and chop them roughly. Reserve sherry.

2. In a skillet, heat 1 tbsp (15 mL) of the oil over medium-high heat. Sauté half the onion for 3 minutes or until it begins to soften. Add escarole and sauté for 3 minutes or until escarole is wilted. Add garlic and sauté for 1 to 2 minutes or until garlic is fragrant. Let cool.

3. Lay chicken thighs skinned side down and season with salt and pepper. (Even though there is no skin here, the skinned side will be the most attractive side to present on the plate.) Divide greens mixture and figs evenly among chicken and roll thighs up to enclose filling. Wrap chicken in bacon and secure with a toothpick.

4. In a skillet with lid, heat remaining oil over medium heat. Add chicken rolls and brown on all sides, about 5 minutes total. Remove chicken and pour off all but 2 tbsp (30 mL) fat from pan. Add remaining onion and sauté for about 6 minutes or until it begins to soften. Add reserved sherry and stock. Nestle chicken rolls back into pan and bring to a simmer. Cover, reduce heat and simmer rolls for about 20 minutes or until juices run clear.

5. Transfer rolls to a heated platter and remove toothpicks.

6. Increase heat and reduce liquid in pan until halved, about 5 minutes. Add cream and bring to a boil and cook for 5 minutes or until sauce is thickened. Taste for seasoning and adjust with salt and pepper, if necessary.

7. Stir in half the chives and lemon zest. Arrange chicken on a platter or on individual plates and nap with sauce. Garnish with remaining chives and lemon zest.

THE DISH **Sauté Pan.** A heavy-bottomed sauté pan with a lid is similar to a frying pan, but instead of sloping sides, the sides of the pan are straight up and down. You will want a pan at least 12 inches (30 cm) in diameter with a tight-fitting lid.

Fashion Plate

Pair this classic with Gingered Carrot Purée (page 289), Potato Haystacks with Gruyère (page 283) and Fudgy Chocolate Babycakes with Peanut Buttercream (page 360).

White Wine Braised Chicken

Delicious and impressive, this dish is deceptively simple and easy to pull together. The orange zest added at the end gives this chicken-in-a-pot a bright citrusy note that we find particularly compelling. This cozy staple comforts like a cashmere scarf on a blustery day. Serve with cooked rice, noodles, spaetzle or toasted bread.

Serves 6

Hands-on time
20 minutes

Total cooking time
1 hour 30 minutes

Tip

Removing the skin before cooking is a time saver because it reduces the amount of fat that must be skimmed from the top of the sauce at the end of cooking. You can definitely use a cut-up whole chicken in this dish, but the breast meat ends up flavorless and tough unless you remove it halfway through the cooking process.

Make Ahead

The dish can be made, cooled, covered and refrigerated for up to 2 days before serving. Just reheat over medium-low heat and serve.

• 6 heated shallow serving bowls

2 tbsp	olive oil	30 mL
1	onion, diced	1
2	carrots, sliced	2
1	stalk celery, sliced	1
1 tsp	dried thyme	5 mL
	Salt and freshly ground black pepper	
12	large bone-in skinless chicken thighs (about 3 lbs/1.5 kg) (see Tip, left)	12
3	cloves garlic, minced	3
1 cup	dry white wine	250 mL
1	bay leaf	1
1	can (14 oz/398 mL) diced tomatoes	1
	Salt and freshly ground black pepper	
1/4 cup	minced flat-leaf parsley	60 mL
	Zest of 1 orange	

1. In a large heavy pot, heat oil over medium heat. Sauté onion for 6 minutes or until softened. Add carrots, celery and thyme and sauté for 5 minutes or until vegetables begin to soften.

2. Salt and pepper chicken. Add chicken to pan in 2 batches until browned, about 5 minutes per side. Return all chicken to pan and add garlic, wine, bay leaf and tomatoes and bring to a simmer. Reduce heat to low, cover and simmer chicken for 1 hour or until juices run clear and chicken is tender. Remove chicken from pot and let cool.

3. If desired, degrease liquid in pot with a large spoon and discard fat. Increase heat to medium-high and boil for about 4 minutes or until sauce reduces somewhat and flavor intensifies. Season with salt and pepper to taste.

4. Separate chicken from bones and return to pot. Discard bones.

5. Serve chicken stew in shallow heated bowls with rice, noodles, spaetzle or toasted bread. Garnish top with parsley and orange zest.

DOUBLE DISH

Braising. Braising is a cooking technique in which tough cuts of meat are first browned in fat, then cooked with a small amount of liquid over low heat until tender. In braising, the sauce surrounding the meat is the focus and when it comes to creating a sauce rich with chicken flavor, chicken thighs reign supreme. The bones give a delicious velvety texture and body to the sauce, while the slow cook in wine renders the sometimes tough meat tender, juicy and full of flavor.

White Wine. Choose a food-friendly wine, such as a Sauvignon Blanc, Pinot Grigio or a non-oaky Chardonnay, when cooking with wine, and by all means pour yourself a little glass to sip while pulling dinner together. You will immediately be transformed into the ravishing Doris Day, wearing one of those cute little aprons from the '60s as she waits for David Niven in *Please Don't Eat the Daisies* to return home from a hard day at the office.

Fashion Plate

Begin this meal with Baby Greens Salad with Goat Cheese and Balsamic Vinaigrette (page 62) and finish with Chocolate Chip Bread Pudding (page 328).

Coq au Vin with Mushrooms, Bacon and Pearl Onions

Coq au vin (rooster in wine) is White Wine Braised Chicken's city cousin. This uptown version of a country classic adds bacon, mushrooms and pearl onions to meltingly tender chicken in a rich, gratifying sauce. This dish never goes out of style and is as appropriate served at a formal dinner with the boss as it is shuttled to a friend who has just had a baby and could use some coddling.

Serves 6

Hands-on time
40 minutes

Start to finish
1 hour 40 minutes

Make Ahead

The dish can be made, cooled, covered and refrigerated for up to 2 days before serving. Just reheat over medium-low heat and serve.

- **6 heated serving bowls**

1	recipe White Wine Braised Chicken (page 222)	1
4	slices bacon	4
2 cups	frozen pearl onions, thawed	500 mL
8 oz	mushrooms, halved	250 g
3	cloves garlic, minced	3
	Salt and freshly ground black pepper	
¼ cup	minced flat-leaf parsley	60 mL

1. Make White Wine Braised Chicken. While chicken is cooking, in a large skillet over medium heat, fry bacon on both sides for 3 minutes or until crispy. Transfer to a large paper towel–lined plate. When cool enough to handle, crumble bacon.

2. Add onions to fat in skillet and brown over medium heat, shaking occasionally, about 10 minutes. Transfer onions to a bowl. Add mushrooms to remaining fat and sauté for 5 minutes or until they begin to give off their liquid. Add garlic and sauté for about 4 minutes or until mushrooms are soft.

3. About 10 minutes before serving, stir crumbled bacon, onions and mushrooms into chicken. Taste and adjust seasoning with extra salt and pepper, if desired.

4. Add coq au vin to 6 heated bowls. Garnish with parsley.

Fashion Plate

Begin with the Arugula Salad with Shaved Fennel and Prosciutto (page 87) and Wild Mushroom Risotto (page 306) and for dessert White Wine Poached Pears with Rosemary Syrup and Triple Crème Cheese (page 324).

Sautéed Chicken Breasts with Lemon Sauce

The true beauty of this dish is a perfectly cooked, juicy chicken breast. No more overcooked, cardboard-tasting, tough, dry chicken for you. And the sauce is like a little exclamation point — just a small, bright note that turns this simple chicken sauté into a red carpet knockout.

Serves 4

Hands-on time
20 minutes

Start to finish
20 minutes

Tips

To pound out the breasts, arrange the chicken breasts side by side on a cutting board and lay a piece of plastic wrap over them. Pound with a flat meat mallet until they are about 1/4 inch (0.5 cm) thick. Remove the plastic wrap and continue with the recipe.

Chicken breasts may be sold as whole breasts (2 single breasts attached at the center) or as chicken breast halves (each a single breast). For this recipe, purchase 2 whole breasts or 4 single breasts. If you purchase whole breasts, separate the two at the thin, center joining area, trimming off excess connective tissue.

2 tbsp	olive oil	30 mL
4	boneless skinless chicken breast halves, pounded to 1/2-inch (1 cm) thickness (see Tips, left)	4
	Salt and freshly ground black pepper	
	Zest and juice of 1 lemon	
1/3 cup	dry white wine	75 mL
2 tbsp	capers, rinsed if packed in salt	30 mL
2 tbsp	unsalted butter	30 mL
2 tbsp	minced flat-leaf parsley, optional	30 mL

1. In a heavy frying or sauté pan, heat oil over medium-high heat. While pan is heating, salt and pepper chicken breast halves. Add chicken, skinned side down, to pan. (Even though there is no skin here, the skin side will be the most attractive side to present on the plate.) Do not attempt to move chicken once in pan for at least 3 minutes. Watch surface of chicken as it begins to look wet and small puddles of moisture begin to form. At this point, turn chicken over. It should be nicely browned. If it still sticks to pan, give it another minute before attempting to turn again. Cook on second side for only 2 minutes and remove pan from heat. Transfer chicken to a warm platter and cover with foil while you make sauce.

2. Return hot sauté pan to medium heat. Add lemon juice and let boil down for 2 minutes or until only 1 tsp (5 mL) or so remains. The lemon juice will pick up lots of the brown chicken flavor from the pan. Add wine and cook for 3 minutes or until reduced by half. Add capers and butter and remove pan from heat. Taste for seasoning, it might need a little salt and pepper. If sauce is too sharp, add 1 tbsp (15 mL) more or so of butter.

3. Arrange chicken on dinner plates or a serving platter and make diagonal cuts into chicken breasts, about ¼ inch (0.5 cm) deep, so the sauce can better penetrate the meat. Top each breast with about 1 tbsp (15 mL) of sauce. Garnish with lemon zest and parsley, if desired. Serve immediately.

THE DISH

Capers. Plucked from low-lying bushes found in the Mediterranean, capers are the pickled buds of unopened flowers. They arrive in one of two ways — packed in brine or in salt. If packed in salt, they must be rinsed and then soaked in a few changes of water to remove some of the saltiness. If you purchase them in the brine, they can be used as is.

Once discovered, capers will have a way of creeping into many dishes, such as olive spreads or salads, or just sprinkled over a grilled steak. We have a slight preference for the capers packed in salt, as they have a more pronounced texture.

Tip

The sauce will evaporate if you let it sit for very long. Just add a little water, 1 tbsp (15 mL) at a time, to bring it back.

Make Ahead

There is really no need to make this dish ahead since it only takes a few moments to pull together. The chicken doesn't reheat well and will become tough and dry if held over for too long.

Fashion Plate

Turkish Spiced Rice Pilaf (page 281) will accompany this deliciously sauced chicken very nicely. Top this simple but impressive meal with Almond Cornmeal Cake with Balsamic Strawberries (page 332).

Sautéed Chicken with Lemon Beurre Blanc and Liquid Rubies

It is just a small step from the lemon deglazing sauce in the previous recipe to the lemon beurre blanc (white butter) here. This sauce is rich, velvety and luscious, and makes plenty, so feel free to slather it over any vegetables or potatoes sharing space on the plate.

Serves 4

Hands-on time
30 minutes

Start to finish
30 minutes

Tips

If the beurre blanc becomes too warm, the butter will melt out of the sauce and become greasy-looking (this phenomenon is called breaking). Be sure to keep the sauce from any high heat source that might break it. If it does break, try whisking in 1 tbsp (15 mL) more or so of whipping (35%) cream to cool it and bring it back together.

Use the extra pomegranate syrup over ice cream or fruit, or add it to cocktails.

Make Ahead

The pomegranate syrup can be made up to 1 week ahead and kept covered and refrigerated.

2 cups	pomegranate juice	500 mL
¼ cup	granulated sugar	60 mL
2 tbsp	olive oil	30 mL
4	boneless skinless chicken breast halves, pounded to ½-inch (1 cm) thickness	4
	Salt and freshly ground black pepper	
2 tbsp	freshly squeezed lemon juice	30 mL
⅓ cup	dry white wine	75 mL
1 tbsp	minced shallot	15 mL
2 tbsp	heavy or whipping (35%) cream	30 mL
8 tbsp	cold unsalted butter, cut into 8 pieces	125 mL
Pinch	each ground white pepper and cayenne	Pinch
	Zest of 1 lemon	

1. In a large saucepan, heat pomegranate juice and sugar over medium-high heat until sugar has dissolved and juice simmers. Reduce heat to maintain a simmer. After 20 minutes, it should be very bubbly. Watch for next 10 minutes or so. When it looks syrupy when you swirl pan, remove from heat. It will thicken as it cools. You will have more than you need for this dish. Store in a jar, covered and refrigerated, for up to 2 months. It will thicken in refrigerator and should be warmed up in a microwave in order to drizzle.

2. In a heavy frying or sauté pan, heat oil over medium-high heat. While pan is heating, salt and pepper chicken breast halves. Add chicken, skinned side down, to pan. (Even though there is no skin here, the skin side will be the most attractive side to present on the plate.) Do not attempt to move chicken once in pan for at least 3 minutes. Watch surface of chicken as it begins to look wet and small puddles of moisture begin to form. At this point, turn chicken over. It should be nicely browned. If it still sticks to pan, give it another minute before attempting to turn again. Cook on second side for only 2 minutes and remove pan from heat. Transfer chicken to a warm platter and cover with foil while you make sauce.

3. Add lemon juice, wine and shallot to pan and cook over medium-high heat for 5 minutes or until liquid is reduced to about 1 tbsp (15 mL). Add cream and remove pan from heat.

4. Add butter to pan, one piece at a time, and whisk until melted. Add another piece of butter, whisking until all butter is absorbed. If butter stops melting, place skillet back over low heat just until mixture is hot enough to melt butter, but not break the sauce (see Tips, page 228). It should take about 3 minutes to get all the butter into the sauce. Taste sauce. If it is too sharp, add another 1 tbsp (15 mL) or so of butter. Season sauce with salt, white pepper and cayenne pepper to taste, if necessary.

5. Drizzle plate with drops of pomegranate reduction. Place a chicken breast slightly off center on the plate and nap chicken with the beurre blanc. Sprinkle lemon zest over all.

THE DISH **Pomegranate Juice.** When sweet-tart pomegranate juice is reduced, it becomes a thick, luscious, deep ruby-colored syrup (liquid rubies). In the same way that a pair of red shoes can make a black dress sing, this avant-garde syrup ramps up the swank factor on this plate of juicy chicken draped in rich butter sauce. Pomegranate juice is widely available in most grocery stores. Look for it in the refrigerated juice section.

Fashion Plate

Roasted Asparagus (page 290) would make a nice accessory to this savory plate. The green color will give the dish a visual boost.

Chicken Breasts Stuffed with Goat Cheese

It is important to have a repertoire of chicken dishes in one's culinary arsenal, and this one is too simple not to overlook. Even bland chicken breast can taste exotic and robust when combined with creamy goat cheese, flavor-packed sun-dried tomatoes and vinaigrette-seasoned artichokes. It's like a delicious salad tucked inside a chicken breast.

Serves 4

Hands-on time
20 minutes

Start to finish
30 minutes

Tip

To seal the opening on the chicken breasts, close them with a few wooden toothpicks and then break off the extraneous bits so the breast will cook flat. Remember to remove the picks before serving.

Make Ahead

The chicken can be stuffed and held, uncooked, in the refrigerator for up to 24 hours in advance.

- **Preheat oven to 375°F (190°C)**
- **Large ovenproof skillet**

¾ cup	drained chopped marinated artichoke hearts	175 mL
½ cup	oil-packed sun-dried tomatoes, drained and chopped	125 mL
4 oz	goat cheese, softened	125 g
½ tsp	dried basil	2 mL
4	boneless skinless chicken breast halves (see Tips, page 226)	4
	Salt and freshly ground black pepper	
3 tbsp	olive oil	45 mL
2 tbsp	minced flat-leaf parsley	30 mL

1. In a medium bowl, combine artichokes, sun-dried tomatoes, goat cheese and basil.

2. With a small sharp knife, make a horizontal pocket in the thick side of each of the chicken breasts. Slide the knife back and forth inside the pocket to make the pocket larger than the hole. Stuff each breast with artichoke mixture (there may be some stuffing left over. Refrigerate and use as a spread or in the following recipe). Using toothpicks, seal the opening closed. Season breasts with salt and pepper.

3. In a large ovenproof skillet, heat oil over medium-high heat. Add chicken, skinned side down (even though they are skinless, this side should be cooked first), and cook chicken for 3 minutes or until browned. Turn chicken and transfer skillet to preheated oven. Bake chicken for 10 minutes or until firm. Remove toothpicks and discard.

4. Transfer chicken to serving plates and garnish with parsley.

Stuffed Chicken Breasts with Olives and White Wine Sauce

The white wine sauce comes together effortlessly and makes this dish a stunner. It's amazing how easy it is to make a delicious dish by taking advantage of a little white wine (ahh, the glories of wine) and the olive bar at your local grocery. We love how this dish looks on a plain white platter . . . very Provençal. All that's missing is a little table under an arbor of grapes and two chairs.

Serves 4

Hands-on time
30 minutes

Start to finish
40 minutes

Tip

Basil is a tender herb that doesn't hold up to repeated chopping. We like to pile the leaves, roll them and then slice thinly. This technique is called chiffonade, and it's the best way to chop basil.

Make Ahead

The chicken can be stuffed and held, uncooked, in the refrigerator for up to 24 hours in advance.

1	recipe Chicken Breasts Stuffed with Goat Cheese (page 230)	1
½ cup	pitted mixed olives	125 mL
⅔ cup	dry white wine	150 mL
3 tbsp	fresh basil, cut into chiffonnade (see Tip, left)	45 mL

1. Make Chicken Breasts Stuffed with Goat Cheese. Transfer chicken to a platter and tent with foil to keep warm.

2. Return skillet to medium-high heat. Sauté olives and wine, stirring up the browned bits, about 3 minutes or until wine has reduced by half. Remove pan from heat and whisk in remaining stuffing from previous recipe to create a creamy sauce.

3. Slice chicken and arrange on a heated serving platter. Pour sauce over top. Garnish with basil.

THE DISH **Mixed Olives.** The olives provide a briny note, and we especially like their shades of green, brown and black next to the golden chicken breasts. Most grocery stores carry a selection of mixed olives at the olive bar. If not, just make a mixture of your own. The previous recipe was delicious, but the dish is elevated to the chef's table here thanks to the sauce.

Fashion Plate

We especially like the way the sauce adds extra flavor to Pommes Anna (page 294) and Roasted Asparagus (page 290). For dessert, Chocolate Mousse–Filled Profiteroles (page 340).

Grilled Chicken Breasts with Mango Salsa

Savvy cooks turn to the grill two or three times a week. Not only is the cleanup reduced, but the taste of food cooked outdoors almost always trumps oven cooking. Once you've mastered the art of grilling a chicken breast to juicy perfection, you can match it with countless fruit and vegetable salsa variations.

Serves 6

Hands-on time
20 minutes

Start to finish
1 hour

Tip

Mangos have a flat, wide pit that must be cut away. Look at the mango. It will be flatter on two sides. We like to cut through the flesh to the pit in quarters and then position the knife between the pit and the flesh, severing the flesh from the pit. Then all you have to do is peel the mango and cut it into cubes.

Make Ahead

The salsa can be made up to 4 hours in advance and kept covered and refrigerated.

• **Preheat broiler or barbecue grill to medium-high**

2	ripe mangos, diced into $\frac{1}{2}$-inch (1 cm) cubes (see Tip, left)	2
$\frac{1}{4}$ cup	diced red bell pepper	60 mL
$\frac{1}{4}$ cup	diced red onion	60 mL
2 tbsp	minced fresh cilantro	30 mL
2 tbsp	minced pickled jalapeño, or more to taste	30 mL
2 tbsp	freshly squeezed lime juice	30 mL
6	boneless skinless chicken breast halves (see Tips, page 226)	6
1 tbsp	olive oil	15 mL
	Salt and freshly ground black pepper	

1. In a large bowl, combine mango, bell pepper, red onion, cilantro, jalapeño, lime juice and $\frac{1}{2}$ tsp (2 mL) salt. Let stand at room temperature if cooking chicken right away. If making ahead, refrigerate for up to 4 hours.

2. Drizzle chicken breasts with olive oil and season with salt and pepper. Grill chicken for about 10 minutes. Turn and cook for 7 minutes more or until chicken is no longer pink inside. Transfer chicken to a baking sheet and let stand for 3 minutes to allow juices to settle. (If cooking in oven, place a rack on the second to the top setting and broil chicken for about 10 minutes or until golden. Turn and cook for 7 or 8 minutes more or until no longer pink inside.)

3. Cut chicken on the diagonal and serve with salsa piled over top. Eat and smile.

Fashion Plate

Complete the plate with Southern Corn Spoonbread (page 302) and finish with Fudgy Brownie Cake (page 358).

Tequila-Marinated Chicken Breasts with Mango Citrus Salsa

Chicken really benefits from even a short marinating. As it sits in a flavorful marinade, the chicken breast picks up flavor, moisture and a bit of fat that helps the meat stay moist when cooking. You owe it to yourself to whisk up this citrusy and potent potion, guaranteed to spice up even the most humdrum poultry.

Serves 6

Hands-on time
30 minutes

Marinating time
4 hours

Start to finish
4 hours 30 minutes

Tip

The avocado has a round pit in the center of the fruit. Cut around the pit from the top of the avocado to the bottom. Twist the two halves apart. Hold the half with the pit in one hand and hit the pit with the sharp blade of a large knife. The knife will be stuck in the pit. Twist the knife and the pit will pop out of the avocado. Scrape the knife against the edge of your sink to release the pit. If this sounds too scary, just scoop it out with a spoon, but you will lose more of the flesh this way.

¼ cup	tequila	60 mL
¼ cup	freshly squeezed lime juice	60 mL
2 tbsp	olive oil	30 mL
1 tbsp	brown sugar	15 mL
2 tsp	ground cumin	10 mL
3	cloves garlic, minced	3
1 tsp	salt	5 mL
6	boneless skinless chicken breast halves (see Tips, page 226)	6

Mango Citrus Salsa

2	ripe mangos, diced into ½-inch (1 cm) cubes (see Tip, page 232)	2
1	ripe avocado, diced (see Tip, left)	1
¼ cup	diced red bell pepper	60 mL
¼ cup	diced red onion	60 mL
3 tbsp	freshly squeezed lime juice	45 mL
2 tbsp	minced fresh cilantro	30 mL
2 tbsp	minced pickled jalapeño, or more to taste	30 mL
1 tbsp	olive oil	15 mL
½ tsp	salt	2 mL
	Salt and freshly ground black pepper	

1. In a nonreactive bowl or plastic resealable bag, whisk together tequila, lime juice, olive oil, brown sugar, cumin, garlic and salt. Add chicken breasts to marinade, coating evenly, and refrigerate for 4 hours or for up to 24 hours.

2. *Mango Citrus Salsa:* Meanwhile, in a large bowl, combine mangos, avocado, bell pepper, red onion, lime juice, cilantro, jalapeño, olive oil and salt. Taste and correct seasoning with more lime, salt, pepper or jalapeño, if necessary.

3. Preheat barbecue grill to medium-high or oven to broil. Remove chicken from marinade, pat dry and season with salt and pepper. Grill for about 10 minutes. Turn and cook for 7 minutes more or until chicken is no longer pink inside. Transfer chicken to a baking sheet and let stand for 3 minutes so that juices can settle. (If cooking in the oven, place a rack on the second to the top setting and broil chicken for about 10 minutes or until golden. Turn and cook for 7 or 8 minutes more or until no longer pink inside.)

4. Serve chicken with salsa piled on top or on the side.

Make Ahead

The chicken can marinate for up to 24 hours. The salsa can be made up to 4 hours in advance and kept covered and refrigerated.

DOUBLE DISH

Tequila. If anything can get you to take your clothes off faster than tequila, we'd like to know about it.

Seriously, though, tequila makes a great marinade ingredient because that distinctive flavor penetrates the meat and tenderizes it as well. Of course, the better the tequila, the better.

Pickled Jalapeños. They sit in your refrigerator just waiting in the wings for when you need a bit of predictable heat and, lo and behold, your fresh jalapeños taste more like a green bell pepper. The vinegary spice of the pickled version is a welcome addition to most salsas and other Latin-inspired dishes.

Fashion Plate

Serve this Caribbean classic with Crispy Potato Cakes (page 304) and Vanilla Gelato with Summer Berries and Limoncello (page 350).

Butterflied Herb-Roasted Chicken

Roasted chicken, if done well, can come to the culinary rescue for you time and time again. Everyone loves it, from children to grownups, and it's perfect for practically every occasion. The good news is that it's not difficult to do well, especially if you use our butterflying technique. Butterflying, which means removing the backbone and laying the chicken out flat, ensures a more even cooking process so everything comes out perfectly cooked at the same time.

Serves 4 to 6

Hands-on time
20 minutes

Start to finish
1 hour 20 minutes

- **Preheat oven to 425°F (220°C)**
- **Instant-read thermometer**

1	whole chicken, about 4 to 5 lbs (2 to 2.5 kg)	1
¼ cup plus 1 tbsp	unsalted butter, at room temperature, divided	75 mL
2 tbsp	chopped fresh parsley	30 mL
3	cloves garlic, minced	3
2 tsp	chopped fresh thyme	10 mL
2 tsp	chopped fresh rosemary	10 mL
¼ tsp	freshly ground black pepper	1 mL
	Salt	

1. To butterfly chicken, place whole chicken, breast side down, with drumsticks pointing toward you. The backbone is now on top. Holding the tail (that is pointing toward you), cut along each side of the backbone with a pair of kitchen shears. Cut all the way through on each side and remove entire backbone. Once backbone is removed, you will be able to lay the chicken out flat and flatten it on both sides. (Or have your butcher do this step for you.)

2. In a medium bowl, combine ¼ cup (60 mL) of the butter, parsley, garlic, thyme, rosemary and pepper.

3. Rinse chicken inside and out and thoroughly pat dry with paper towels. Slide your hand between skin and breast meat to loosen skin. Spread with half of the seasoned butter over breast meat under skin. Repeat process using remaining seasoned butter over both thighs. Rub remaining 1 tbsp (15 mL) of butter all over skin. Sprinkle chicken inside and out with salt. Tuck wing tips under chicken.

4. Place chicken on a baking sheet, skin side up, and roast in preheated oven for 15 minutes. Reduce temperature to 375°F (190°C) and cook for 30 to 45 minutes more or until an instant-read thermometer registers 160°F (71°C). Let chicken stand for at least 10 to 15 minutes before carving.

THE DISH **Fresh Herbs.** Although dried herbs can be used successfully in many recipes, for this one we suggest you use fresh herbs. The herbs are combined with butter and garlic and stuffed underneath the chicken's skin to give flavor and moisture to the bird. Dried herbs tend to have a sticks and twigs texture after the roasting process and they never really tenderize.

Fashion Plate

We love this dish as the centerpiece of a Sunday meal. Try starting with the Roasted Cherry Tomato Soup with Basil Cream (page 118). Buttermilk Mashed Potatoes (page 282) and Maple-Glazed Carrots (page 288) make the perfect accompaniments. End this family dinner with Chocolate Chip Bread Pudding (page 328).

Herb-Roasted Chicken with Oranges, Olives and Fennel

Oranges infuse their flavor and scent throughout this upscale version of our basic roasted chicken. The combination of the citrus, roasted olives and fennel give this dish a decidedly Mediterranean flair, and the addition of roasted potatoes makes it a one-pan meal.

Serves 4 to 6

Hands-on time
40 minutes

Start to finish
1 hour 40 minutes

- **Preheat oven to 425°F (220°C)**
- **Instant-read thermometer**

1	whole chicken, about 4 to 5 lbs (2 to 2.5 kg)	1
¼ cup plus 1 tbsp	unsalted butter, at room temperature, divided	75 mL
2 tbsp	chopped fresh parsley	30 mL
2 tsp	chopped fresh rosemary	10 mL
2 tsp	chopped fresh thyme	10 mL
	Zest of 1 orange	
	Salt and freshly ground black pepper	
1	orange, cut into 8 wedges	1
2	small fennel bulbs (about 3 inches/7.5 cm in diameter)	2
4	medium Yukon Gold potatoes, cut into ½-inch (1 cm) wedges	4
1	large head garlic, separated into individual cloves and peeled	1
2 tbsp	olive oil	30 mL
½ cup	kalamata olives, pitted	125 mL

1. To butterfly chicken, place whole chicken, breast side down, with drumsticks pointing towards you. The backbone is now on top. Holding the tail (that is pointing towards you), cut along each side of the backbone with a pair of kitchen shears. Cut all the way through on each side and remove entire backbone. Once backbone is removed, you will be able to lay the chicken out flat and flatten it on both sides. (Or have your butcher do this step for you.)

2. In a medium bowl, combine ¼ cup (60 mL) of the butter, parsley, rosemary, thyme, orange zest and ¼ tsp (1 mL) black pepper.

3. Rinse chicken inside and out and thoroughly pat dry with paper towels. Slide your hand between skin and breast meat to loosen skin. Spread with half of the seasoned butter over breast meat under skin. Repeat the process using remaining seasoned butter over both thighs. Rub remaining 1 tbsp (15 mL) of butter all over skin. Sprinkle chicken inside and out with salt. Tuck wing tips under chicken.

4. Place orange wedges in a pile in center of a large baking sheet. Place chicken on top, skin side up, and roast in preheated oven for 15 minutes.

5. Meanwhile, trim fennel and cut each bulb vertically into 8 wedges with core attached to each wedge. In a medium bowl, combine fennel, potatoes, garlic, olive oil, $\frac{1}{2}$ tsp (2 mL) salt and $\frac{1}{4}$ tsp (1 mL) pepper. Toss to coat.

6. Reduce temperature to 375°F (190°F). Scatter vegetables around chicken and cook for 30 to 45 minutes more or until an instant-read thermometer registers 160°F (71°C). Transfer chicken to a cutting board. Let stand for 15 minutes before carving.

7. While chicken is resting, return oven temperature to 425°F (220°C). Add olives to vegetables in roasting pan, stirring to redistribute vegetables, and cook for 10 to 15 minutes more or until vegetables are browned.

8. Carve chicken as desired and serve with vegetables on the side.

THE DISH **Kitchen Shears.** There is no end to the culinary tasks that kitchen shears can accomplish. In this recipe and the previous recipe, we use them to remove the backbone of the chicken, which is way easier than using a knife. But we are also likely to use them to cut herbs from the garden and cut dried fruit into smaller pieces.

Fashion Plate

This one-pan meal only needs a starter of Roasted Tomato, Mozzarella and Pesto Bruschettas (page 23) to make it shine.

Arroz con Pollo

Classic, stylish and versatile are the perfect adjectives to describe this easy-to-do chicken and rice dish. The fact that it's all done in one pan only makes us love it more. This dish is Latin comfort food at its finest.

Serves 4 to 6

Hands-on time
35 minutes

Start to finish
1 hour 10 minutes

- **Preheat oven to 400°F (200°C)**
- **Large ovenproof skillet**

2 tbsp	olive oil, divided	30 mL
4	chicken thighs	4
4	chicken legs	4
	Salt and freshly ground black pepper	
1	onion, diced	1
1	red bell pepper, diced	1
4	cloves garlic, minced	4
2 cups	medium-grain rice, such as Arborio	500 mL
¾ tsp	ground cumin	3 mL
½ tsp	salt	2 mL
2	bay leaves	2
4 cups	Quick Chicken Stock (page 119) or ready-to-use chicken broth	1 L
1 cup	chopped seeded tomato	250 mL
½ cup	frozen peas	125 mL

1. In a large ovenproof skillet, heat 1 tbsp (15 mL) of the oil over medium-high heat. Season chicken thighs and legs with salt and pepper. Add chicken to pan, in batches if necessary, and cook for about 5 minutes per side or until well browned. Do not crowd chicken or it will not brown properly. Transfer to a plate.

2. Reduce heat to medium. Add remaining oil to pan with onion and bell pepper. Cook, stirring occasionally, for about 6 minutes or until vegetables are tender. Add garlic and sauté for 1 minute. Add rice, cumin, salt and bay leaves, stirring to coat rice with oil. Sauté for about 1 minute or until rice is opaque.

3. Stir in chicken stock and tomato and bring to a boil. Arrange chicken in pan and transfer skillet to oven. Cook in preheated oven for 25 minutes. Add peas and cook for 10 minutes or until liquid has been absorbed. Let dish stand for 10 minutes before serving.

Chicken, Sausage and Seafood Paella

Once you have a handle on Arroz con Pollo, you only need a pinch of saffron and some fresh seafood to bring you right to paella's door. Paella is a show-stopping dish that is easy to make your own. In our version, we add the smoked and cured variety of chorizo, so common in Spanish dishes, along with some clams, mussels and shrimp, but if you have a few lobster tails or scallops on hand, all the better.

Serves 4 to 6

Hands-on time
35 minutes

Start to finish
1 hour 20 minutes

- **Preheat oven to 400°F (200°C)**

2 tbsp	olive oil, divided	30 mL
4	chicken thighs	4
4	chicken legs	4
	Salt and freshly ground black pepper	
12 oz	cured chorizo sausage, sliced	375 g
1	onion, diced	1
1	red bell pepper, diced	1
2	cloves garlic, minced	2
2 cups	medium-grain rice, such as Arborio	500 mL
½ tsp	ground cumin	2 mL
½ tsp	salt	2 mL
Pinch	saffron	Pinch
2	bay leaves	2
4 cups	Quick Chicken Stock (page 119) or ready-to-use broth	1 L
12	littleneck clams, scrubbed	12
12	mussels, scrubbed and debearded	12
1 lb	jumbo shrimp, peeled and deveined	500 g
1 cup	chopped seeded tomato	250 mL
½ cup	frozen peas	125 mL

1. In a large ovenproof skillet or paella pan (one that can be used on both a stovetop or in the oven), heat 1 tbsp (15 mL) of the oil over medium-high. Season chicken thighs and legs with salt and pepper. Add chicken to pan, in batches if necessary, and cook for about 5 minutes per side or until well browned. Do not crowd chicken or it will not brown properly. Transfer to a plate. Add sausage and sauté until lightly browned. Transfer to plate with chicken.

2. Reduce heat to medium. Add remaining oil to pan with onion and bell pepper. Cook, stirring occasionally, for about 6 minutes or until vegetables are tender. Add garlic and sauté for 1 minute. Add rice, cumin, salt, saffron and bay leaves, stirring to coat rice with the oil. Cook for about 1 minute or until rice is opaque.

3. Stir in chicken stock and bring to a boil. Arrange chicken in pan and transfer skillet to oven. Cook in preheated oven for 25 minutes. Add clams and mussels, hinge side down, and shrimp, tomato and peas. Cook for 10 to 15 minutes or until clams and mussels have opened and liquid has been absorbed. Discard any clams or mussels that do not open. Let paella stand for 10 minutes before serving.

DOUBLE DISH

Paella Pan. Paella pans are large, shallow circular pans that resemble skillets with two handgrips on either side. They are meant to go from oven to table for a spectacular presentation. You can absolutely make this in a large skillet. You'll lose points on presentation, but it will taste just as good.

The Right Rice. In our Goldilocks style of culinary investigation, we've tried all types of rice, from long-grain to short-grain, for this dish. And, just like Goldilocks, we've found that the medium-grain works best. Medium-grain rice, like the Arborio that's traditionally used for risotto, maintains its shape and resists the urge to get mushy or gummy.

Fashion Plate

Gazpacho (page 104) makes a light and refreshing beginning to the traditional Spanish meal. End with the Navel Oranges with Caramel (page 372).

Soft Chicken Tacos with Tomatillo Salsa

For many people, salsa comes in one color — red. To that select group of Mexican food novices, we have a treat for you. Our bright green salsa uses tart tomatillos as the base and has a completely different flavor from that of red salsa. It's alive with the bright notes of lime, cilantro and, of course, the unique tomatillo. This salsa recipe makes more than you may need for these simple chicken tacos, but no worries. You'll pull it out of the fridge time and time again to slather on scrambled eggs, spoon over grilled steak or just eat with a handful (or two) of tortilla chips.

Serves 4 to 6

Hands-on time
45 minutes

Start to finish
45 minutes

Make Ahead

The salsa can be made up to 4 weeks ahead and kept, frozen, in a covered container.

- **Baking sheet, lined with foil**
- **Preheat broiler**
- **Blender**

Tomatillo Salsa

2 lbs	tomatillos, paper-thin husk removed	1 kg
2	serrano chile peppers	2
1 tbsp	vegetable oil	15 mL
1 cup	chopped onion	250 mL
¼ cup	freshly squeezed lime juice	60 mL
4	cloves garlic, chopped	4
6 tbsp	chopped fresh cilantro	90 mL
1½ tsp	granulated sugar	7 mL
1 tsp	ground cumin	5 mL
1 tsp	salt	5 mL

Tacos

3 cups	shredded cooked chicken (rotisserie is fine)	750 mL
12	6-inch (15 cm) flour tortillas, warmed	12
	Sour cream	
	Shredded Monterey Jack cheese	

1. *Tomatillo Salsa:* Rinse tomatillos under warm water to remove any stickiness and dirt. Place tomatillos and chiles on prepared baking sheet and broil 1 to 2 inches (2.5 to 5 cm) from heat, turning once, for about 7 minutes or until tomatillos are softened and slightly charred.

2. In a large skillet, heat oil over medium heat. Sauté onion for about 5 minutes or until golden brown.

3. Transfer tomatillos, chiles, sautéed onions, lime juice, garlic, cilantro, sugar, cumin and salt to a blender and purée until smooth.

4. Return tomatillo sauce to skillet over medium heat and cook, stirring frequently to prevent sticking, for about 5 minutes or until thickened. Set aside and let cool.

5. In a medium bowl, mix together $\frac{1}{2}$ cup (125 mL) of the salsa and shredded chicken.

6. To assemble tacos, place $\frac{1}{4}$ cup (60 mL) of the chicken filling into each flour tortilla. Top as desired with sour cream, cheese and remaining salsa.

DOUBLE DISH

Fresh Tomatillos. Tomatillos are small green tomato-like fruits, covered in a papery husk. They have a tart flavor and are the key ingredient in many Latin American sauces. They can be found in the produce section of almost any grocery store. Look for fruit that is firm and bright green.

Rotisserie Chicken. Roasting your own whole chicken to use in this salad, or any dish that calls for precooked chicken, is, as our TV pal would tell you, "a good thing." But, just like stenciling your driveway or personalizing your tissue boxes, it's not always in the cards. When that's the case, we turn to the store-bought rotisserie chickens. They can be hugely helpful on hectic nights when dinner needs to be on the table quick and you've just walked in the door.

Fashion Plate

Pair these flavorful tacos with Pico de Gallo (page 38), which can be served as a starter with warm tortilla chips and also alongside the Tomatillo Salsa as another topping for the tacos.

Chicken Chorizo Enchiladas with Creamy Tomatillo Sauce

A batch of homemade salsa can make impressing your friends and family at the dinner table a much easier task. All we've done for this dish is splash around a little cream and chicken broth and our simple salsa is now an elegant sauce for these cheesy chicken- and chorizo-filled enchiladas.

Serves 6 to 8

Hands-on time
1 hour

Start to finish
1 hour 30 minutes

- **Preheat oven to 375°F (190°C)**
- **13- by 9-inch (33 by 23 cm) baking pan (see The Dish, right)**

Creamy Tomatillo Sauce

1	recipe Tomatillo Salsa (page 244)	1
½ cup	Quick Chicken Stock (page 119) or ready-to-use chicken broth	125 mL
¾ cup	heavy or whipping (35%) cream Salt, optional	175 mL

Enchiladas

3 tbsp	vegetable oil, divided	45 mL
1 lb	fresh chorizo sausage, removed from casings	500 g
1	onion, finely chopped	1
12	6-inch (15 cm) corn tortillas	12
3 cups	shredded cooked chicken (rotisserie is fine)	750 mL
1½ cups	shredded mild Cheddar cheese, divided	375 mL
1½ cups	shredded Monterey Jack cheese, divided	375 mL
½ tsp	salt	2 mL

1. *Creamy Tomatillo Sauce:* Reserve ½ cup (125 mL) of the tomatillo salsa and set aside. Pour remaining salsa into a saucepan and add broth and cream. Cook over medium heat for 5 minutes or until slightly thickened and not watery at all. Taste and add salt, if necessary.

2. *Enchiladas:* In a large skillet, heat 1 tbsp (15 mL) of the oil over medium heat. Add chorizo and sauté for 5 minutes. Add onion and sauté for about 5 minutes or until onion is softened and sausage is cooked through. Set aside and let cool.

3. Brush both sides of tortillas lightly with remaining oil. Place on a baking sheet in stacks of two. Heat in preheated oven for about 3 minutes or just until soft and pliable.

4. In a large bowl, combine chorizo mixture with chicken, ¾ cup (175 mL) of the Cheddar cheese, ¾ cup (175 mL) of the Monterey Jack cheese and salt. Add reserved ½ cup (125 mL) of salsa and toss to combine.

5. Spread one-third of the sauce in bottom of baking pan. Place ¼ cup (60 mL) of filling in center of 1 tortilla. Roll up tortilla. Place, seam side down, in baking dish. Repeat with remaining tortillas. Pour remaining sauce over enchiladas. Sprinkle with reserved ¾ cup (175 mL) of Cheddar and Monterey Jack cheeses. Bake for about 20 minutes or until cheese melts and enchiladas are heated through.

THE DISH **Colorful Baking or Lasagna Pan.**
Whenever you can serve a dish right out of the pan, the pan itself becomes part of the show. For that reason, we always try to make dishes like this one in a lovely baking pan. Look for the ceramic variety, often labeled "lasagna pan." These are not only great to have at home, but also nice when you have to transport your dish to someone else's table.

Fashion Plate

To start this fiesta off with a bang, serve Tequila Bloody Mary Shrimp Cocktails (page 42). The Mango, Jicama and Red Onion Salad (page 70) makes the perfect foil for these rich enchiladas. If you have some room left for dessert, Tres Leches Cakes (page 342) would be a delicious ending to this memorable meal.

Bathing Beauties
Fish and Seafood

Ahi Tuna Burgers

Tuna burgers are the ultimate in clean, fresh tastes. Perfumed with the scents and flavors of ginger, lemon and garlic, this protein-packed burger is just the ticket when you crave something exotic but not too chi-chi to pull together quickly.

Serves 6

Hands-on time
40 minutes

Start to finish
40 minutes

Make Ahead

The burgers can be assembled up to 4 hours ahead and kept covered and refrigerated. Coat with panko just before cooking.

- **Food grinder or food processor**

1½ lbs	ahi tuna steak, cut into 2-inch (5 cm) cubes	750 g
1	large egg	1
1	large egg white	1
1½ cups	panko bread crumbs or dry medium-size bread crumbs, divided	375 mL
⅓ cup	finely diced celery	75 mL
⅓ cup	finely diced red bell pepper	75 mL
1 tbsp	fresh grated gingerroot	15 mL
	Zest of 1 lemon	
1 tbsp	freshly squeezed lemon juice	15 mL
2 tsp	finely minced garlic	10 mL
1½ tsp	salt	7 mL
¼ tsp	freshly ground black pepper	1 mL
Pinch	cayenne pepper	Pinch
¼ cup	vegetable oil	60 mL
6	hamburger buns, toasted, if desired	6
	Mayonnaise	
	Lettuce	

1. In a food grinder or food processor, grind or pulse tuna in 2 batches (pulsing about 8 to 10 times) until it comes together in a mass.

2. In a medium bowl, combine tuna, egg, egg white, ½ cup (125 mL) of the bread crumbs, celery, bell pepper, ginger, lemon zest, lemon juice, garlic, salt, pepper and cayenne. Shape tuna into 6 burgers, about 1 inch (2.5 cm) thick.

3. Place 1 cup (250 mL) of bread crumbs on a plate. Gently press burgers into crumbs on both sides so that they adhere.

4. In a skillet, heat vegetable oil over medium-high heat. Cook burgers for about 4 minutes on one side or until crispy and brown. Turn burgers and cook for 3 to 4 minutes or until cooked through.

5. Serve burgers on buns with mayonnaise and lettuce.

DOUBLE DISH

The Fish. It's always better to buy fish at a store that specializes in fish. Your fishmonger should be able to tell you where it's from, when it was caught and how long it's been sitting on ice in the case. Don't be afraid to ask to smell the fish, and if your fish guy says no, find a new place to shop. The fish should smell clean, like the ocean, and not at all fishy.

We're pretty sure you could get the fish guy to grind the tuna for you, but if he balks, the food processor will do a great job.

Panko Bread Crumbs. Japan's gift to the world. These flaky, light crumbs are crispier and crunchier than the typical dried bread crumbs and give these burgers a delightful crust.

Fashion Plate

Pair this burger with Yukon Gold Salad with green beans (page 100).

Ahi Tuna Cakes with Asian Coleslaw and Wasabi Mayonnaise

If you thought crab had the market for seafood cakes cornered, think again. Tuna makes a wonderfully meaty and unique version of this coastal classic. And the crunchy cabbage, carrot and peppers with a hint of spice and sesame oil are just the foil for these toothsome tuna cakes.

Serves 6

Hands-on time
1 hour

Start to finish
1 hour

Make Ahead

The slaw can be made up to 8 hours ahead and kept covered and refrigerated. The burgers can be assembled up to 4 hours ahead and kept covered and refrigerated. Coat with panko just before cooking.

Asian Coleslaw

3 tbsp	rice wine vinegar or apple cider vinegar	45 mL
3 tbsp	vegetable oil	45 mL
2 tsp	liquid honey	10 mL
2 tsp	dark sesame oil	10 mL
1/2 tsp	salt	2 mL
1/4 tsp	freshly ground black pepper	1 mL
4 cups	very thinly sliced napa cabbage, Chinese cabbage or snow cabbage	1 L
1	carrot, peeled and grated	1
1/2 cup	red bell pepper, thinly sliced	125 mL
1/3 cup	thinly sliced red onion	75 mL
1/3 cup	finely chopped fresh cilantro	60 mL
1	serrano or jalapeño pepper, finely diced	1

Wasabi Mayonnaise

2 tbsp	wasabi powder	30 mL
1 tbsp	hot water	15 mL
1/2 cup	mayonnaise	125 mL
2 tbsp	finely chopped green onion	30 mL
1	recipe Ahi Tuna Burgers (page 250)	1

1. *Asian Coleslaw:* In a large bowl, whisk together vinegar, vegetable oil, honey, sesame oil, salt and pepper. Add cabbage, carrot, bell pepper, red onion and cilantro. Taste and check for heat before adding serrano pepper to taste. Toss together and taste for seasoning and adjust with more vinegar, salt or pepper, if necessary. Refrigerate while cooking burgers.

2. *Wasabi Mayonnaise:* In a medium bowl, combine wasabi powder and water. Blend in mayonnaise and green onion. It may be hot enough for you at this point. If you want more heat, continue to add more wasabi powder 1/4 tsp (1 mL) at a time.

3. Assemble and cook tuna patties as directed in previous recipe.

4. Serve tuna cakes with a dollop of wasabi mayonnaise and Asian slaw on the side.

THE DISH **Dark Sesame Oil.** The darker (toasted) Asian sesame oil has a much more pronounced flavor than light sesame oil. Just 1 tsp (5 mL) or so is all it takes for this nutty oil to make its presence known. Look for it in the Asian foods aisle at the grocery store. Once opened, it will last longer if kept it in the refrigerator.

Fashion Plate

Begin this Asian-inspired meal with Spicy Thai Sweet Potato Soup with Lemongrass and Coconut Milk (page 126) and finish it with the simple but lovely Rustic Plum Tart (page 362).

Nothin'-But-Crab Cakes

A simple crab cake is a thing of beauty. The sweetness of crab needs little else to make us love it. That's why it's always so disappointing to order a crab cake in a restaurant, spend a fortune for it, and find it riddled with distractions like veggies and other fillers. "Leave the crab alone!" is our motto, so for our basic crab cake, that's exactly what we've done. With just enough seasoning and binder to keep everything together, our crab cake is the essence of freshness, simplicity and, for lack of a better word, crab.

Makes 8 cakes

Hands-on-time
30 minutes

Chilling time
2 hours

Start to finish
3 hours 30 minutes

Make Ahead

The crab cakes can be formed and kept, covered and refrigerated, for up to 8 hours.

1½ lbs	jumbo lump crabmeat, picked over (see The Dish, right)	750 g
⅓ cup	mayonnaise	75 mL
2	eggs	2
1 tbsp	Dijon or Creole mustard	15 mL
1 tsp	Chesapeake Bay or Old Bay seafood seasoning	5 mL
1½ tbsp	freshly squeezed lemon juice	22 mL
½ tsp	paprika	2 mL
¼ tsp	salt	1 mL
⅛ tsp	freshly ground black pepper	0.5 mL
2 cups	fresh bread crumbs, divided	500 mL
2 tbsp	olive oil	30 mL
2 tbsp	unsalted butter	30 mL
	Lemon wedges	

1. Pick through crabmeat and remove any stray bits of shell. In a bowl, whisk together mayonnaise, eggs, mustard, seafood seasoning, lemon juice, paprika, salt and pepper. Gently fold in ½ cup (125 mL) of the bread crumbs and all the crabmeat, taking care not to break the lumps. Cover and refrigerate for 2 hours or until chilled.

2. Place remaining bread crumbs in a shallow dish. Using a ½-cup (125 mL) measure, shape mixture into 8 crab cakes. Gently coat with bread crumbs. Place on a plate, covered, and refrigerate for 1 hour to firm.

3. In a large skillet, heat oil and butter over medium heat. Sauté cakes, in batches if necessary, for about 4 minutes per side until golden brown and crispy. Serve with lemon wedges on the side.

DOUBLE DISH

Quality Crab. Spending the time necessary to cook and pick the tender morsels out of the crab ourselves is not typically on our agenda, so we often rely on the pasteurized plastic tubs of crabmeat found refrigerated in the seafood department of good grocery stores. Although it can be expensive, we like to use as much jumbo lump crab as possible. We long to see the luxuriously big chunks of crab in our cakes, though you can certainly use other, less expensive types. Just make sure the crab smells fresh, with no off odors.

Seafood Seasoning. This go-to seasoning mix is made of mustard, paprika, celery seed, bay leaf, black pepper, cayenne pepper, cinnamon, cloves, allspice, nutmeg, cardamom, salt and ginger. In addition to flavoring seafood dishes, it can also be used as a condiment to top salads, eggs, corn on the cob, etc.

Fashion Plate

Love these with a side of Mango, Jicama and Pecan Slaw with Honey Lime Dressing (page 71).

Spicy Crab Cakes with Creole Rémoulade Sauce

While our Nothin'-But-Crab Cakes would be comfortable sitting next to fries and slaw, the addition of a creamy, New Orleans–style rémoulade sauce makes these slightly spicy, crispy cakes more sophisticated fare. The mayonnaise-based sauce is easy to prepare and a classic accompaniment to crab cakes. The mustard, lemon and horseradish help to cut through the richness of the cakes without overwhelming the delicate flavor of the crab.

Makes 8 cakes

Hands-on time
45 minutes

Start to finish
3 hours 15 minutes

Make Ahead

The crab cakes can be formed and kept, covered and refrigerated, for up to 8 hours. The remoulade sauce can be made a day ahead and kept covered and refrigerated.

- **Food processor**

Creole Rémoulade Sauce

¾ cup	mayonnaise	175 mL
2	green onions, green and white parts, chopped	2
2 tbsp	chopped flat-leaf parsley	30 mL
2 tbsp	Creole or whole-grain mustard	30 mL
1 tbsp	freshly squeezed lemon juice	15 mL
½ tsp	hot pepper sauce	2 mL
1 tbsp	each prepared horseradish and ketchup	15 mL
2 tsp	drained capers, rinsed	10 mL
	Salt and freshly ground black pepper	
1	recipe Nothin-But-Crab Cakes (page 254)	1
1 tsp	hot pepper sauce	5 mL
¼ tsp	cayenne pepper	1 mL

1. *Creole Rémoulade Sauce:* In a food processor, pulse mayonnaise, green onions, parsley, mustard, lemon juice, hot pepper sauce, horseradish, ketchup, capers and salt and pepper to taste until combined, but still slightly chunky. Keep covered in the refrigerator while preparing the crab cakes.

2. Follow directions for crab cakes in previous recipe, adding hot sauce and cayenne pepper to mayonnaise mixture in Step 1.

THE DISH **Mustard with a Kick.** We like Creole mustard because it knows what it wants to be — spicy but not too sharp. Creole mustard is typically a variation of whole-grain mustard in which the seeds are slightly crushed. For this recipe, you can use either Creole or whole-grain.

Pan-Fried Mahi-Mahi with Pineapple Salsa

Mahi-mahi is a buttery, firm-fleshed white fish perfect for grilling or a quick pan fry. When paired with a tart-sweet and spicy pineapple salsa, this dish brings back memories of Don Ho singing "Tiny Bubbles." Come to think of it, champagne would be an excellent accompaniment to this island classic.

Serves 6

Hands-on time
30 minutes

Start to finish
30 minutes

Make Ahead

The fish can sit in the lime juice no longer than 30 minutes or the acid will begin to cook the flesh. The salsa can be made and kept, covered and refrigerated, for up to 1 hour before serving.

¼ cup	freshly squeezed lime juice, divided	60 mL
4	mahi-mahi fillets (each about 6 oz/175 g)	4
1½ cups	diced fresh pineapple	375 mL
¼ cup	chopped red onion	60 mL
1 tbsp	chopped fresh cilantro	15 mL
1 tsp	minced jalapeño	5 mL
	Salt and freshly ground black pepper	
¼ cup	all-purpose flour	60 mL
2 tbsp	unsalted butter	30 mL

1. In a shallow dish, add 3 tbsp (45 mL) of the lime juice and dredge mahi-mahi fillets on both sides. Refrigerate while continuing with recipe. Do not let fish stand in lime juice for more than 30 minutes or the acid will begin to cook the fish.

2. In a medium bowl, combine remaining lime juice, pineapple, red onion, cilantro, jalapeño and ¼ tsp (1 mL) salt. Blend and taste for seasoning, adding more salt or jalapeño to taste. Set aside.

3. Remove fish from lime juice and pat dry. Season fish with salt and pepper.

4. Add flour to a shallow dish. Dredge seasoned fish in flour, shaking off excess.

5. Heat a large skillet over medium-high heat and add butter to pan. When butter is hot, add fish and cook for 4 minutes per side or until golden. Transfer fish to a serving platter and top with salsa.

A Really Hot Pan. One of the most common mistakes home cooks make is not getting a pan hot enough before adding ingredients. Heating a pan thoroughly before adding the butter or oil will help to keep food from sticking. When cooking fish, the best plan is to cook it quickly so that it browns on the outside with a golden crust and cooks through to a nice juicy firmness on the inside. Mahi-mahi, which is usually about 1 inch (2.5 cm) thick, is the perfect candidate for a hot, hot flash in the pan.

Choosing a Ripe Pineapple. An unripe pineapple is disappointing, to say the least. To ensure your fruit is at its peak of ripeness and flavor, look for a pineapple that is mostly golden in color and has a distinct pineapple aroma at the base.

Fashion Plate

Pair this duo with Roasted New Potatoes with Rosemary and Garlic (page 312). Finish with Vanilla Gelato with Summer Berries and Limoncello (page 350).

Macadamia-Crusted Mahi-Mahi with Caramelized Pineapple and Vanilla

The spirit of this dish just screams Hawaii, so dig out those aloha shirts and leis and tuck into the best fish dish this side of Lahaina. Crusting the mahi-mahi with macadamia nuts adds texture and flavor, while browning the pineapple with a touch of vanilla deepens and enriches its sweeter side. Best of all, this dish is so easy to bring together that you will be tempted to make it again and again.

Serves 6

Hands-on time
40 minutes

Start to finish
40 minutes

Make Ahead

The fish can be coated with the nut mixture, placed on a wire rack over a baking sheet and refrigerated for up to 4 hours before cooking.

• **Heated platter**

¼ cup	freshly squeezed lime juice, divided	60 mL
6	mahi-mahi fillets (each about 6 oz/175 g)	6
1½ cups	coarsely chopped macadamia nuts (see The Dish, right)	375 mL
¼ cup	all-purpose flour	60 mL
1	large egg, beaten	1
	Salt and freshly ground black pepper	
2 tbsp	vegetable oil	30 mL
2 tbsp	unsalted butter	30 mL
12	spears fresh pineapple	12
1	vanilla bean, split lengthwise	1
¼ cup	finely chopped red onion	60 mL
1 tbsp	chopped fresh cilantro	15 mL
1 tsp	minced jalapeño, optional	5 mL

1. In a shallow dish, add 3 tbsp (45 mL) of the lime juice and dredge mahi-mahi fillets on both sides. Refrigerate while continuing with recipe. Do not let fish stand in lime juice for more than 30 minutes or the acid will begin to cook the fish.

2. Place macadamia nuts in a shallow bowl or plate. Place flour in another plate. Set aside. In a shallow bowl, beat together egg and 1 tbsp (15 mL) water. Set aside.

3. Remove fish from lime juice and pat dry. Season fish with salt and pepper. Dredge in flour, shaking off excess. Dredge fish in egg wash. Then pat into nut mixture so that it adheres. Continue to coat remaining fish in the same way.

4. Heat a large skillet over medium-high heat and add oil. When oil is hot, add fish and cook for about 4 minutes or until nuts have browned. Turn fish and cook for 4 minutes or until browned and fish flakes easily when pierced with a fork. Transfer fish to a heated platter, tent with foil and set aside.

5. Add butter to pan along with pineapple spears. Scrape seeds from inside of vanilla bean and add to pineapple. Cook pineapple for about 3 minutes per side or until browned on both sides. Add remaining 1 tbsp (15 mL) of lime juice to pan and remove from heat.

6. Place 2 spears of pineapple on each plate and lean 1 fish fillet partially on top of one of the spears. Garnish plates with red onion, cilantro and jalapeño, if using.

THE DISH **Macadamia Nuts.** Buttery and rich, macadamia nuts have a high fat content, which makes them the perfect nutty crust for fish. We like to chop them in a food processor. Just pulse the nuts about 8 or 10 times. Don't overprocess or the nuts will become too finely ground and you will lose that lovely crunch.

Fashion Plate

For a nice contrast in flavor, serve this dish with Potato Galette with Celery Root (page 296).

Grilled Thai Shrimp

Thai flavors are nothing if not bold, and this dish is no exception. We've combined lime juice, chiles and garlic to make a vibrant marinade for these tart and spicy grilled shrimp. Don't let the fish sauce throw you off. It adds a certain complexity to a dish that's hard to describe, except to say that it tastes nothing like it smells. But if buying a bottle seems too much of a commitment, go ahead and substitute soy sauce. We won't tell.

Serves 6

Hands-on time
30 minutes

Start to finish
1 hour

Make Ahead
The marinade can be made 1 day ahead and kept covered and refrigerated.

- **Blender**

2	serrano chile peppers, coarsely chopped	2
2	cloves garlic	2
2 tbsp	Asian fish sauce (preferably Thai nam pla)	30 mL
¼ cup	freshly squeezed lime juice	60 mL
2 tbsp	brown sugar	30 mL
2 tbsp	vegetable oil	30 mL
24	large shrimp, peeled and deveined	24
2	green onions, white parts and half of greens, thinly sliced	2
2 tbsp	chopped fresh mint	30 mL
2 tbsp	chopped fresh cilantro	30 mL
	Boston lettuce leaves	

1. In a blender, combine chiles, garlic, fish sauce, lime juice and brown sugar and process for a few seconds. Transfer half of the marinade to a large bowl. Add oil and shrimp and toss to coat. Let shrimp marinate for up to 20 minutes while preheating the grill.

2. Preheat grill to medium-high heat or preheat broiler. Grill or broil shrimp for about 2 minutes per side or until pink and firm to the touch and opaque.

3. In a large bowl, toss shrimp with reserved marinade and stir in green onions, mint and cilantro.

4. Place lettuce leaves on serving plates or bowls and pile shrimp mixture on top.

THE DISH **Odd-Shaped Plates or Bowls.** The unexpected serving plate or bowl can add an element of sophistication with no real extra effort on your part. That's why we scour bargain bins for strangely shaped dinnerware. A square plate or asymmetrical bowl gives off a sense of whimsy and usually makes whatever you're serving look like it took you hours to make.

Vietnamese-Style Grilled Shrimp Summer Rolls with Peanut Dipping Sauce

Finger food that doesn't get your fingers messy is our favorite kind, and these fun but tidy summer rolls fit that category. Filled with citrusy noodles, crunchy vegetables and our spicy Grilled Thai Shrimp, these rolls are light, and when paired with our rich peanut sauce, they could be the centerpiece of a Thai-themed meal. Though they may look complex, the rolls come together much more quickly than you would think and would even make a fun project for guests who don't mind helping out in the kitchen.

Serves 4 to 6
Makes 10 summer rolls

Hands-on time
1 hour

Start to finish
1 hour

Make Ahead

Summer rolls can be made 4 hours ahead and refrigerated, covered with lightly dampened paper towels and then with plastic wrap. Let stand at room temperature for 30 minutes before serving.

• **Blender**

1	serrano chile pepper, coarsely chopped	1
2	cloves garlic	1
2 tbsp	Asian fish sauce (preferably Thai nam pla)	30 mL
¼ cup	freshly squeezed lime juice	60 mL
2 tbsp	brown sugar	30 mL
2 tbsp	vegetable oil	30 mL
15	large shrimp, peeled and deveined	15
3 oz	vermicelli rice-stick noodles	90 g
10	8-inch (20 cm) rice paper wrappers, plus additional in case some tear	10
60	fresh cilantro leaves (from about 1 bunch)	60
60	fresh mint leaves (from about 1 bunch)	60
1	medium seedless cucumber, peeled and cut into ⅛-inch (0.5 cm) thick matchsticks	1
3	green onions, cut into 3-inch (7.5 cm) julienne strips	3
	Peanut Dipping Sauce (page 74)	

1. In a blender, combine chile, garlic, fish sauce, lime juice and brown sugar and process for a few seconds. Reserve ¼ cup (60 mL) of the marinade and set aside. Add oil and shrimp to remaining marinade and toss to coat. Let shrimp marinate for 20 minutes while preheating grill and preparing noodles.

2. In a large bowl, cover noodles with hot water and soak for 15 minutes or until softened and pliable.

Continued on next page

3. Preheat grill to medium-high heat or preheat broiler. Grill or broil shrimp for about 2 minutes per side or until pink and opaque. Remove from grill and slice in half lengthwise.

4. Drain noodles in a colander, then rinse under cold running water and drain well again. Add $\frac{1}{4}$ cup (60 mL) of reserved marinade to noodles and toss to coat. Place a double thickness of paper towel on a work surface and fill a shallow baking pan with warm water. Check rice paper rounds and use only those that have no holes. Soak 1 round in warm water until pliable, 30 seconds to 1 minute. Carefully transfer to paper towels.

5. Arrange 3 cilantro leaves and 3 mint leaves across bottom third (part nearest you) of soaked rice paper. Top with 3 shrimp halves. Spread $\frac{1}{4}$ cup (60 mL) of noodles on top of shrimp and arrange 8 cucumber matchsticks and 6 green onion strips on top of noodles. Fold bottom of rice paper over filling and begin rolling up tightly, stopping at halfway point. Arrange 3 more mint leaves and 3 more cilantro leaves along crease, then fold in ends and continue rolling. Transfer summer roll, seam side down, to a plate and cover with dampened paper towels. Make 9 more rolls in same manner. Serve, whole or halved diagonally, with peanut dipping sauce.

THE DISH **Rice Paper Wrappers.** These fascinating rounds go by many names: rice paper, spring roll wrappers, Vietnamese rice paper, or banh trang, just to name a few. You'll know you've found the right wrapper by its clear, plastic-like appearance. These brittle rounds don't need to be cooked, but they do need to be moistened and pliable before rolling around a filling.

Fashion Plate

For a light but satisfying meal, pair this salad in a wrapper with the Spicy Thai Sweet Potato Soup with Lemongrass and Coconut Milk (page 126).

Roasted Salmon with Citrus Yogurt Sauce

The essence of simplicity, this salmon dish is fast, easy and a great excuse to open a bottle of Pinot Noir — especially on a Wednesday night when those "when will it ever be the weekend" doldrums set in. Just add a simple salad of baby greens with a light vinaigrette and call it dinner.

Serves 6

Hands-on time
15 minutes

Start to finish
20 minutes

Make Ahead

The Citrus Yogurt Sauce can be made up to 8 hours ahead of time and kept covered and refrigerated.

- **Preheat broiler**
- **Baking sheet, lined with foil**

6	wild salmon fillets with skin (each about 8 oz/250 g)	6
1/4 cup	olive oil, divided	60 mL
	Salt and freshly ground black pepper	

Citrus Yogurt Sauce

3/4 cup	thick or Greek yogurt	175 mL
1 tsp	grated orange zest	5 mL
3 tbsp	freshly squeezed orange juice	45 mL
1 tbsp	fresh dill, chopped (approx.)	15 mL
1 tsp	grated lemon zest	5 mL
1/2 tsp	salt	2 mL
1/4 tsp	freshly ground black pepper	1 mL
Pinch	cayenne pepper	Pinch

1. Place salmon on prepared baking sheet, about 2 inches (5 cm) apart. Drizzle salmon with 2 tbsp (30 mL) of the olive oil and season with salt and pepper to taste. Place baking sheet on second-highest rack in oven and broil for about 7 to 8 minutes or until fish flakes easily when pierced with a fork.

2. *Citrus Yogurt Sauce:* Meanwhile, in a medium bowl, combine yogurt, orange zest, orange juice, remaining olive oil, dill, lemon zest, salt, pepper and cayenne. Taste for seasoning and adjust with more salt, pepper or orange juice to taste, if necessary.

3. Serve salmon with a dollop of yogurt sauce drizzled to one side of each fillet. Garnish with extra dill, if desired.

Garam Masala

Garam masala is probably the best-known Indian spice blend outside of India. Though you may find this spice combination on a grocery shelf, toasting and grinding your own spice mixtures is so much more flavorful that it makes it worth the extra effort.

Makes about ¼ cup (60 mL)

Hands-on time
20 minutes

Start to finish
20 minutes

Make Ahead

Garam masala will keep for 3 or 4 months in a dark, dry place.

3	pieces (each 3 inches/7.5 cm) cinnamon sticks	3
2 tbsp	whole cloves	30 mL
2 tbsp	whole coriander seeds	30 mL
2 tbsp	whole black peppercorns	30 mL
2 tbsp	whole cumin seeds	30 mL
1 tbsp	cardamom seeds	15 mL

1. In a large skillet, heat cinnamon, cloves, coriander, peppercorns, cumin and cardamom over medium heat for about 2 minutes or until fragrant. Be careful not to let them color or burn. Let cool. Then grind in a spice mill. Store at room temperature in an airtight container.

Roasted Salmon with Indian Spices, Walnuts and Cranberries

We love the combination of warm spices, fatty, rich fish and cool yogurt spiked with cayenne. Don't let the garam masala scare you. You're going to love the coriander, cumin and cinnamon notes in this fragrant Indian spice blend. You may be tempted to dab a little behind your ears, which will make you good enough to eat as well!

Serves 6

Hands-on time
15 minutes

Start to finish
20 minutes

Make Ahead

The Citrus Yogurt Sauce can be made up to 8 hours ahead of time and kept covered and refrigerated.

- **Preheat broiler**
- **Baking sheet, lined with foil**

6	wild salmon fillets with skin (each about 8 oz/250 g)	6
¼ cup	olive oil, divided	60 mL
	Salt and freshly ground black pepper	
½ tsp	Garam Masala (see The Dish, right, and page 267) or store-bought	2 mL

Citrus Yogurt Sauce

¾ cup	thick or Greek yogurt	175 mL
1 tsp	grated orange zest	5 mL
3 tbsp	freshly squeezed orange juice	45 mL
2 tbsp	chopped fresh cilantro (approx.)	30 mL
1 tsp	grated lemon zest	5 mL
½ tsp	salt	2 mL
¼ tsp	freshly ground black pepper	1 mL
⅛ tsp	cayenne pepper	0.5 mL
¼ cup	chopped toasted walnuts	60 mL
¼ cup	dried cranberries	60 mL

1. Place salmon on prepared baking sheet, about 2 inches (5 cm) apart. Drizzle salmon with 2 tbsp (30 mL) of the olive oil and season with salt and pepper to taste. Sprinkle garam masala over fish. Place baking sheet on second-highest rack in oven and broil for about 7 to 8 minutes or until fish flakes easily when pierced with a fork.

2. *Citrus Yogurt Sauce:* Meanwhile, in a medium bowl, combine yogurt, orange zest, orange juice, remaining olive oil, cilantro, lemon zest, salt, pepper and cayenne. Taste for seasoning and adjust with more salt, pepper or orange juice to taste, if necessary.

3. Serve salmon with a dollop of yogurt sauce drizzled to one side of each fillet. Sprinkle over walnuts, cranberries and extra cilantro, if desired.

DOUBLE DISH

Fresh Salmon Fillets. Fresh fish doesn't always mean the fish on ice in the case. Ask your fishmonger how long the salmon has been sitting there. It could be that you can buy fresher fish — caught and frozen the same day — in the freezer case.

When it is cut into individual servings, frozen fish thaws very quickly in a sink of cool water. We especially love the flavor of wild salmon, such as Coho, Chinook or Copper River. It will cost more than farmed Atlantic salmon, but we think the taste and health benefits are worth it.

Garam Masala. The blend finds its way into many of India's subtly perfumed dishes as an ingredient and as a garnish. It can be found at Indian grocery stores or you can make it yourself (page 267). The fresher the better, so we encourage you to make your own, even if you can find it locally. There are many uses for it, as it is delicious sprinkled over chicken, lamb and even vegetables such as cauliflower and green beans.

Fashion Plate

Roasted New Potatoes with Rosemary and Garlic (page 312) pairs beautifully with the salmon and yogurt sauce.

Baja Grilled Fish Tacos

Your biggest concern with this recipe is going to be making sure you have enough, because these chile- and cumin-rubbed grilled white fish tacos can be addictive. Chunks of mild but well-seasoned fish are tucked into warm corn tortillas with crispy cabbage, drizzled with a lime and cilantro sour cream sauce and topped with a spoonful of fresh Pico de Gallo salsa. Arriba, arriba!

Serves 6

Hands-on time
40 minutes

Start to finish
1 hour 15 minutes

Make Ahead

The Sour Cream Sauce can be made and kept, covered and refrigerated, for up to 2 days.

1 tbsp	chile powder	15 mL
1 tsp	ground cumin	5 mL
4	cloves garlic, minced	4
¾ tsp	salt	3 mL
¼ tsp	freshly ground black pepper	1 mL
3 tbsp	olive oil	45 mL
2 lbs	tilapia fillets	1 kg

Sour Cream Sauce

1 cup	sour cream	250 mL
½ cup	mayonnaise	125 mL
¼ cup	chopped fresh cilantro	60 mL
	Zest of 1 lime	
1 tbsp	freshly squeezed lime juice	15 mL

18	6-inch (15 cm) corn tortillas	18
2 cups	shredded green cabbage	500 mL
2 cups	shredded red cabbage	500 mL
1	recipe Pico de Gallo (page 38)	1
	Lime quarters	

1. In a small bowl, combine chile powder, cumin, garlic, salt and pepper. Add oil and whisk until a loose paste is formed. Rub fish with spice paste and marinate for at least 30 minutes or for up to 4 hours in the refrigerator.

2. *Sour Cream Sauce:* In a bowl, whisk together sour cream, mayonnaise, cilantro, lime zest and lime juice. Set aside.

3. Preheat lightly greased barbecue grill to medium. Grill fish for 3 to 4 minutes per side or until fish flakes easily when tested with a sharp knife. Transfer fish to a cutting board and coarsely chop. Wrap 2 stacks of 9 tortillas in foil and place on grill for about 5 minutes or until heated through.

4. *To serve:* Top each tortilla with a few chunks of fish, green and red cabbage, Sour Cream Sauce and Pico de Gallo. Squeeze lime over filling. Fold each tortilla in half.

Grilled Tilapia with Lime Butter and Cilantro Slaw

Contrasting flavors and textures are often what make a dish great. Here, we have the soft but slightly spicy nature of the grilled fish playing against the limey, sweet crunchiness of the slaw. When the fish is topped with a small dollop of the rich lime butter, the whole thing amounts to one memorable meal.

Serves 4 to 6

Hands-on time
40 minutes

Start to finish
1 hour 20 minutes

1/3 cup	unsalted butter, at room temperature	75 mL
	Zest of 1 lime	
1 tbsp	chile powder	15 mL
1 tsp	ground cumin	5 mL
4	cloves garlic, minced	4
	Salt and freshly ground black pepper	
3 tbsp	olive oil	45 mL
2 lbs	tilapia fillets	1 kg
1/3 cup	freshly squeezed lime juice	75 mL
2 tbsp	rice vinegar	30 mL
2 tbsp	liquid honey	30 mL
1/3 cup	vegetable oil	75 mL
4 cups	shredded green cabbage	1 L
4 cups	shredded red cabbage	1 L
1/4 cup	chopped fresh cilantro	60 mL

1. In a small bowl, combine butter and lime zest. Keep covered in the refrigerator until ready to use.

2. In another bowl, combine chile powder, cumin, garlic, 3/4 tsp (3 mL) salt and 1/4 tsp (1 mL) pepper. Add olive oil and whisk until a loose paste is formed. Rub fish with spice paste and marinate for at least 30 minutes or for up to 4 hours in the refrigerator.

3. In a large bowl, whisk together lime juice, vinegar and honey. Slowly drizzle in vegetable oil, whisking continuously. Add green and red cabbage and cilantro and toss to coat.

4. Preheat lightly greased barbecue grill to medium. Grill fish for 3 to 4 minutes per side or until fish flakes easily when pierced with a sharp knife.

5. *To serve:* Place a fillet on each serving plate and top with a dollop of lime butter. Serve cilantro slaw on the side.

Prosciutto-Wrapped Salmon with Rosemary Butter

Yes, we enjoy a challenge, but what we love even more is something that's easy but looks like a challenge. This prosciutto-wrapped salmon certainly fits into that category. The simply seasoned seafood is encased in a paper-thin slice of prosciutto, baked, then topped with a dollop of rosemary-spiked butter. By the time the savory little package reaches the table, the hot salmon has melted the butter, creating the easiest sauce ever.

Serves 6

Hands-on time
10 minutes

Start to finish
25 minutes

Make Ahead

The salmon fillets can be seasoned and wrapped with the prosciutto up to 8 hours ahead and kept covered and refrigerated.

- **Preheat oven to 400°F (200°C)**
- **Baking sheet, lined with parchment paper**

Rosemary Butter

¼ cup	unsalted butter, at room temperature	60 mL
1½ tsp	minced fresh rosemary	7 mL
	Salt and freshly ground black pepper	
6	salmon fillets (each 6 oz/175 g), skin removed	6
6	paper-thin slices prosciutto	6

1. *Rosemary Butter:* In a small bowl, whisk together butter, rosemary, ¼ tsp (1 mL) salt and ¼ tsp (1 mL) pepper. Set aside.

2. Season salmon lightly with salt and pepper. Gently wrap one slice of prosciutto around each fillet. Place fillets on prepared baking sheet. Bake in preheated oven for 10 to 12 minutes or until salmon is just cooked through and flakes easily when tested with a sharp knife.

3. Place a dollop of Rosemary Butter atop each salmon fillet and serve.

THE DISH **Paper-Thin Slices of Prosciutto.**
Although you can buy prosciutto at almost any grocery store deli counter, you can't always find someone who knows how to slice it and package it. Prosciutto in most instances should be sliced nearly see-through thin. If the slicing is done correctly, stacking them together in the typical deli style will mean you'll have to tear them to shreds trying to get them apart. The solution: single layering in sets of two or three on pieces of wax paper (or whatever paper the deli uses).

EVERYDAY

Prosciutto-Wrapped Salmon with Roasted Corn, Peppers and Leeks

Salmon and corn go together like Fred and Ginger. The sweetness of the corn makes a perfect partner to the richness of the salmon. The cream-infused sauté of corn, peppers and leeks provide a bed, so to speak, for the salty prosciutto-wrapped salmon. Although we personally enjoy 600-thread count Egyptian cotton, we think the creamy corn mélange works better for the fish.

Serves 6

Hands-on time
30 minutes

Start to finish
45 minutes

Make Ahead

The recipe can be prepared through Step 3 and kept, covered and refrigerated, for up to 1 day ahead.

- **Preheat oven to 400°F (200°C)**
- **Food processor**

3 cups	fresh or frozen yellow corn kernels	750 mL
3 tbsp	olive oil, divided	45 mL
	Salt and freshly ground black pepper	
1 tbsp	unsalted butter	15 mL
2	leeks, white and pale green parts only, thinly sliced	2
2	red bell peppers, cut into small dice	2
1	recipe Prosciutto-Wrapped Salmon with Rosemary Butter (page 272)	1
½ cup	heavy or whipping (35%) cream	125 mL
1 tsp	freshly squeezed lemon juice	5 mL

1. Spread corn on a large baking sheet. Drizzle with 1½ tbsp (22 mL) of the olive oil and season with ½ tsp (2 mL) salt and ¼ tsp (1 mL) pepper. Toss to coat. Roast in preheated oven for 25 minutes or until some of the kernels begin to brown lightly. Do not overcook or the kernels will become too dried out. Set aside and let cool slightly. (Leave oven on to cook salmon.)

2. In a food processor, pulse half of the corn several times until creamy but still chunky. Set aside.

3. In a large skillet, heat remaining oil and butter over medium heat. Sauté leeks for 6 minutes or until softened. Add bell peppers and sauté for 3 to 5 minutes or until peppers are just tender-crisp. Remove from heat.

4. Prepare salmon and rosemary butter as instructed on page 272.

5. While salmon is roasting, add whole and puréed corn and cream to vegetables and sauté over medium heat for 3 minutes or until hot. Add lemon juice and season with salt and pepper to taste.

6. *To serve:* Divide vegetables between 6 serving plates. Place 1 salmon fillet on top and top with a slice of Rosemary Butter. Serve hot.

THE DISH **Chardonnay.** Not every dish has a clear wine match, but salmon and corn bring out the best in a buttery, slightly oaked Chardonnay. Look for a good California bottle. This dish is worth the price.

Fashion Plate

This summery meal is perfect during corn season when the roadside corn stands begin to pop up on every corner. We like to make this main course the star of the show by starting with a refreshing but simple appetizer like the Fresh Tomato and Basil Bruschettas (page 22) and ending with the lovely White Chocolate Soup with Chilled Berries (page 346).

Accessories
Sides

Everyday		to	Entertaining	
Spaetzle	278	▶	Herb Butter Fried Spaetzle	279
Basmati Rice Pilaf	280	▶	Turkish-Spiced Rice Pilaf	281
Buttermilk Mashed Potatoes	282	▶	Potato Haystacks with Gruyère	283
Green Beans with Lemon and Butter	286	▶	Green Beans with Bacon, Pecans and Pearl Onions	287
Maple-Glazed Carrots	288	▶	Gingered Carrot Purée	289
Roasted Asparagus	290	▶	Asparagus and Red Pepper Timbales	291
Pommes Anna	294	▶	Potato Galette with Celery Root	296
Corn Fritters	298	▶	Corn, Zucchini and Basil Fritters	299
Southern Corn Spoonbread	302	▶	Cheese, Chile and Cilantro Corn Spoonbread	303
Crispy Potato Cakes	304	▶	Crispy Potato Cakes with Pear Apple Salsa and Crème Fraîche	305
Wild Mushroom Risotto	306	▶	Crispy Wild Mushroom Risotto Cakes	307
Creamy Potato Gratin	308	▶	Creamy White Winter Gratin with Caramelized Onions	310
Roasted New Potatoes with Rosemary and Garlic	312	▶	Salt-Roasted New Potatoes with Rosemary Butter	313
Creamy Polenta	314	▶	Polenta with a Trio of Toppings	315
Roasted Butternut Squash with Goat Cheese and Pecans	316	▶	Butternut Squash Gratin with Caramelized Onions	318
Sugar Snap Pea and Sesame Stir-Fry	320	▶	Sugar Snap Peas with Carrots, Edamame and Mint	321

Spaetzle

Funny as it sounds, the word "spaetzle" (shpeht-sehl), translated from German, means "little sparrow." Although songbirds are not the first thing we think of when eating these adorable little noodles, their buttery, nutmeg-tinged flavor has us singing. Making this dish on a cold winter's night is about as close as you can come to saying "I love you" with food.

Serves 6

Hands-on time
20 minutes

Start to finish
30 minutes

Make Ahead

Spaetzle can be made 2 hours ahead. Toss with the butter in the skillet and let stand at room temperature. Reheat before serving.

- **Food processor**
- **Spaetzle maker, potato ricer or flat grater**

	Salt	
2¾ cups	unbleached all-purpose flour	675 mL
¾ cup	milk	175 mL
4	large eggs	4
Pinch	ground nutmeg	Pinch
Pinch	cayenne pepper	Pinch
¼ cup	unsalted butter	60 mL
	Freshly ground black pepper	

1. In a large pot, bring 5 quarts (5 L) water to a boil over high heat. Stir in 1 tbsp (15 mL) salt.

2. In a food processor, pulse flour and 1¼ tsp (6 mL) salt to blend. Add milk, eggs, nutmeg and cayenne. Process in pulses until a soft dough forms, about 8 pulses.

3. In a large skillet, heat butter over medium heat. Cook for about 4 minutes or until butter begins to brown. Set aside.

4. Working in batches, push batter through a spaetzle maker, a potato ricer or a flat grater held above the boiling water, pressing with spatula to form strands that fall into the boiling water. Stir gently to prevent sticking. Continue to cook until spaetzle float to surface, then continue cooking for 1 minute more. Using a slotted spoon, transfer spaetzle to large skillet containing butter. Continue to cook remaining spaetzle in the same manner. Toss over medium heat until coated with butter. Season with salt and pepper to taste.

THE DISH **Spaetzle Maker.** It consists of a flat grater with a lip on one end to fit over the edge of the pan of hot water, with a sliding hopper that you plop the batter into and then slide back and forth over the water. The noodles drop through the grater and into the water.

Herb Butter Fried Spaetzle

The addition of herbs and lemon zest make this dish a little more modern, colorful and lively. We can't resist adding these toothsome noodles to soups and stews, but we must admit there have been times when we've made a meal of spaetzle alone.

Serves 6

Hands-on time
20 minutes

Start to finish
30 minutes

Make Ahead

Spaetzle can be made 2 hours ahead. Toss with the butter in the skillet and let stand at room temperature. Reheat before serving.

- **Food processor**
- **Spaetzle maker, potato ricer or flat grater**

	Salt	
2¾ cups	unbleached all-purpose flour	675 mL
¾ cup	milk	175 mL
4	large eggs	4
Pinch	ground nutmeg	Pinch
Pinch	cayenne pepper	Pinch
¼ cup	minced flat-leaf parsley (approx.)	60 mL
2 tbsp	minced fresh thyme	30 mL
	Grated zest of 1 lemon	
¼ cup	unsalted butter	60 mL
	Freshly ground black pepper	

1. In a large pot, bring 5 quarts (5 L) water to a boil over high heat. Stir in 1 tbsp (15 mL) salt.

2. In a food processor, pulse flour and 1¼ tsp (6 mL) salt to blend. Add milk, eggs, nutmeg, cayenne, most of parsley, thyme and lemon zest. Process in pulses until a soft dough forms, about 8 pulses.

3. In a large skillet, heat butter over medium heat. Cook for about 4 minutes or until butter begins to brown. Set aside.

4. Working in batches, push the batter through a spaetzle maker, a potato ricer or a flat grater held above boiling water, pressing with spatula to form strands that fall into the boiling water. Stir gently to prevent sticking. Continue to cook until spaetzle float to surface, then continue cooking for 1 minute more. Using slotted spoon, transfer spaetzle to large skillet containing butter.

5. Heat over medium-high heat for about 4 minutes or until spaetzle starts to brown, scraping noodles from bottom of pan occasionally. Continue to cook, stirring occasionally, for 10 minutes more or until spaetzle are mostly browned and crispy. Season with salt and pepper to taste. Garnish with parsley.

Basmati Rice Pilaf

This delicious rice pilaf is a great accompaniment to any number of main course offerings. Using chicken or vegetable stock as the cooking liquid gives this dish a flavor boost, as does the fragrant basmati rice's brief sauté in butter and shallot. Though simple, a great pilaf is a thing of beauty and delicious to boot.

Serves 6

Hands-on time
15 minutes

Start to finish
35 minutes

Tip

The hallmark of a good pilaf is that it does not clump. The grains of rice should be easily separated. There are two conditions at work here for the best pilaf: (1) the rice must be rinsed before cooking to remove some of the starch coating the grain and (2) it mustn't be overcooked.

Make Ahead

The dish can be made up to 8 hours ahead and kept covered and refrigerated. Reheat in a microwave-safe bowl in 30-second spurts, stirring in between, until hot.

2 cups	basmati rice	500 mL
3 tbsp	unsalted butter	45 mL
2	shallots or 1 small onion, minced	2
3⅓ cups	reduced-sodium chicken or vegetable broth	825 mL
	Salt and freshly ground black pepper	

1. Place rice in a fine colander or sieve and wash, swishing with your hand, under cold running water until water no longer runs white. Drain and set aside.

2. In a medium saucepan, heat butter over medium heat. When butter sizzles, add minced shallots and sauté for 1 minute or until fragrant. Add rice and sauté for 3 to 4 minutes or until grains begin to look opaque. Add broth and bring to a simmer. Cover, reduce heat to low and simmer for 12 to 15 minutes or until most of the broth is absorbed by the rice.

3. Let stand, covered, for 5 minutes for rice to finish cooking. Remove lid and fluff rice with a fork. Season with salt and pepper to taste. Serve hot.

THE DISH **Basmati Rice.** A long-grain rice with a perfumed scent and flavor, basmati has been harvested for thousands of years. If you can't find it, substitute jasmine or regular long-grain rice, but steer clear of converted rices because they have variable cooking times and are easily overcooked.

Turkish-Spiced Rice Pilaf

Warm spices and sweet-tart fruit give this easy pilaf a unique spin. We used dried apricots in this recipe, but many other dried fruits, like dried cherries, cranberries or golden raisins, would work as well. With a dish as flavorful as this, it's simple to complete the plate by whipping up simply grilled or broiled fish, chicken or meat. We could make a meal of this pilaf alone, so be sure to make lots.

Serves 6

Hands-on time
15 minutes

Start to finish
35 minutes

Tip

The dried apricots are easily cut into quarters with a pair of kitchen shears. The almonds can be toasted by spreading them out on a plate and microwaving in 30-second intervals, stirring in between. They are toasted when fragrant, about 1½ minutes.

Make Ahead

The dish can be made up to 8 hours ahead and kept covered and refrigerated. Reheat in a microwave-safe bowl in 30-second spurts, stirring in between, until hot.

2 cups	basmati rice	500 mL
3 tbsp	unsalted butter	45 mL
1	onion, minced	1
1 cup	diced red bell pepper	250 mL
1 tsp	ground turmeric	5 mL
1 tsp	ground cumin	5 mL
½ cup	dried apricots, quartered	125 mL
¼ cup	dried currants	60 mL
3½ cups	reduced-sodium chicken or vegetable broth	875 mL
	Salt and freshly ground black pepper	
½ cup	slivered almonds, toasted	125 mL
¼ cup	minced fresh cilantro	60 mL

1. Place rice in a colander or sieve and wash, swishing with your hand, under cold running water until water no longer runs white. Drain and set aside.

2. In a medium saucepan, heat butter over medium heat. When butter sizzles, add onion and bell pepper and sauté for 3 minutes or until almost softened. Add rice, turmeric, cumin, apricots and currants and sauté for about 4 minutes or until grains begin to look opaque. Add broth and bring to a simmer. Cover, reduce heat to low and simmer for 12 to 15 minutes or until most of the broth is absorbed by the rice.

3. Let stand, covered, for 5 minutes for rice to finish cooking. Remove lid and fluff rice with a fork. Season with salt and pepper to taste. Transfer pilaf to a serving dish and top with almonds and a sprinkling of cilantro. Serve hot.

THE DISH **Turmeric and Cumin.** These spices are the dynamic duo used to make curries in Indian and Caribbean cooking. Turmeric's bright yellow-orange color adds oomph to any dish, and cumin's nutty flavor is a major ingredient in most blended chili powders.

Buttermilk Mashed Potatoes

Just like that old soft robe, mashed potatoes are everyone's idea of comfort — but some are thrown off by the indulgence factor. For these buttery, creamy spuds, we've kept the comfort but cut the calories by using Yukon gold potatoes, which naturally have a more buttery flavor and color than the usual russet or red-skinned varieties. Then, instead of whipping cream, we use buttermilk.

Serves 6 to 8

Hands-on time
5 minutes

Start to finish
40 minutes

Make Ahead

The potatoes can be made up to 20 minutes before serving, stirring occasionally, and kept warm, covered, over low heat.

2¼ lbs	Yukon gold potatoes (see The Dish, page 284)	1.125 kg
½ cup	buttermilk, warmed	125 mL
3 tbsp	unsalted butter, at room temperature	45 mL
1 tsp	salt	5 mL
¼ tsp	freshly ground black pepper	1 mL

1. Place potatoes in a large pot with lightly salted water to cover. Bring to a boil over high heat. Reduce heat and simmer for 35 to 40 minutes or until potatoes are tender. Drain potatoes.

2. Cut the potatoes in half and place them cut side down in a ricer. Push potato through ricer into a bowl and remove skin from ricer. Or peel potatoes and mash with a hand-held masher or mix in a stand mixer fitted with the paddle attachment.

3. With a wooden spoon, stir in ¼ cup (60 mL) of the buttermilk at a time, adding just enough to moisten and make potatoes fluffy and light. Stir in butter, salt and pepper, just until potatoes are blended and creamy. Do not overmix. Taste potatoes for seasoning and adjust with salt and pepper, if necessary. Return potatoes to hot pan they were cooked in and reheat, stirring occasionally, over low heat.

Fashion Plate

Serve these fluffy mounds of goodness with Guinness-Braised Short Ribs with Horseradish Cream (page 194).

Potato Haystacks with Gruyère

When looking for the perfect accompaniment to simply roasted or grilled meats, look no further than this recipe. This dish of beautifully piped mounds of fluffy potatoes drizzled with golden butter and cheese is one of those party maven sides that your guests will talk about for days. And only you will know how easy it is to make them.

Serves 6 to 8

Hands-on time
35 minutes

Start to finish
1 hour

Make Ahead

The potatoes can be piped onto a baking sheet and kept, covered lightly with plastic wrap, being careful not to smash, and refrigerated, for up to 1 day. Add a few minutes to the cooking time if baking them directly from the refrigerator.

- **Preheat oven to 400°F (200°C)**
- **Pastry bag with fluted tip**
- **Baking sheet, lined with parchment paper**

2¼ lbs	Yukon gold potatoes (see The Dish, page 284)	1.125 kg
½ cup	buttermilk, warmed	125 mL
6 tbsp	unsalted butter, at room temperature, divided	90 mL
1 tsp	salt	5 mL
¼ tsp	freshly ground black pepper	1 mL
2	large egg yolks	2
1 cup	shredded Gruyère or Swiss cheese, divided	250 mL

1. Place potatoes in a large pot with lightly salted water to cover. Bring to a boil over high heat. Reduce heat and simmer for 35 to 40 minutes or until potatoes are tender. Drain potatoes.

2. Cut potatoes in half and place cut side down in a ricer. Push potato through ricer into a bowl and remove skin from ricer. Or peel potatoes and mash with a hand-held masher or mix in a stand mixer fitted with paddle attachment.

3. With a wooden spoon, stir in ¼ cup (60 mL) of the buttermilk at a time, adding just enough to moisten and make potatoes fluffy and light. Stir in 3 tbsp (45 mL) of the butter, salt, pepper, egg yolks and ½ cup (125 mL) of the cheese, stirring occasionally, just until potatoes are blended and creamy. Do not overmix.

4. In a small saucepan, melt remaining butter over medium heat (or melt in a glass measuring cup in the microwave on medium-low (30%) power). Transfer potatoes to pastry bag with fluted tip. Pipe potatoes onto prepared baking sheet in 3-inch (7.5 cm) rounds, narrowing to top like a haystack. Drizzle potatoes with melted butter and sprinkle over remaining cheese. Bake in preheated oven for 12 to 15 minutes or until edges are golden and potatoes are heated through.

Continued on next page

DOUBLE DISH **Boiled Whole Unpeeled Potatoes.** We think this is important because (1) cooking the potatoes whole with their skins intact prevents them from absorbing cooking water, which (2) gives them a fluffier and less gluey texture and (3) results in a more pronounced potato flavor. If you have a ricer, by all means use it. But the old-fashioned masher, back of a fork or stand mixer fitted with the paddle attachment will get the job done as well. Just don't use a food processor.

Disposable Pastry Bag and Tip. Pick up disposable pastry bags at your nearest cookware store along with our favorite tip, Magic Tip 9FT, or any other fluted tip with at least a ¾-inch (2 cm) opening. You will use it for piping whipped cream and icing and many other decorative applications. The advantages of the disposable pastry bags speak for themselves. Buy large ones because in no time you will be a piping maniac.

Fashion Plate

These haystacks lend themselves to a more formal plate, so don't hesitate to serve them up with Pistachio-Crusted Rack of Lamb with Spiced Zinfandel Sauce (page 202) and Green Beans with Lemon and Butter (page 286).

Green Beans with Lemon and Butter

Green beans are always a welcome side dish, as they are a wonderful partner to almost any main course. They're also quite versatile and can be dressed up and down. Here, they are dressed simply with butter, a little lemon and some freshly chopped parsley. What could be easier or more elegant?

Serves 6

Hands-on time
15 minutes

Start to finish
20 minutes

Make Ahead

The green beans can be prepared through Step 1 and kept, covered and refrigerated, for up to 1 day.

- **Bowl of ice water**

	Salt	
1½ lbs	green beans, trimmed	750 g
3 tbsp	unsalted butter	45 mL
2 tsp	grated lemon zest	10 mL
¼ cup	finely chopped flat-leaf parsley	60 mL
	Freshly ground black pepper	

1. In a large pot, bring 6 quarts (6 L) water to a boil over high heat. Add 1 tbsp (15 mL) salt and green beans and cook for about 5 minutes or until just tender. Drain. Transfer to bowl of ice water and let cool. Drain and pat dry.

2. In a large deep skillet, melt butter over medium heat. Add beans and toss to heat through, about 5 minutes. Add lemon zest and toss to coat. Cook for 1 minute. Stir in parsley. Season with salt and pepper to taste. Transfer to a bowl.

THE DISH **Good Green Beans.** All right, stop snickering. It's not as easy as it seems to get a good green bean. You can't just plunge your hand into the green bean bin and pull out winners every time. You have to carefully pick and choose. Look for crisp, slender beans with no blemishes. If they are rubbery, or if the pod is bulging around the beans inside, or if they are marred with brown spots, they're rejects.

Fashion Plate

Serve this side with Butterflied Herb-Roasted Chicken (page 236) and Fudgy Brownie Cake (page 358).

Green Beans with Bacon, Pecans and Pearl Onions

We especially like to serve this dressed-up version of our Green Beans with Lemon Butter in the fall and winter, when heartier dishes are usually on the menu. Smoky bacon, toasted pecans and sweet, caramelized pearl onions make this side dish worthy of the most sophisticated meal.

Serves 6

Hands-on time
30 minutes

Start to finish
40 minutes

Make Ahead

The bacon and onions can be sautéed up to 1 day ahead and kept covered and refrigerated. The green beans can be prepared through Step 2 up to 1 day ahead and kept covered and refrigerated.

- **Bowl of ice water**

3	slices bacon, chopped	3
2 cups	frozen pearl onions (see The Dish, below)	500 mL
1 tsp	granulated sugar	5 mL
	Salt and freshly ground black pepper	
1½ lbs	green beans, trimmed	750 g
2 tbsp	unsalted butter	30 mL
½ cup	chopped toasted pecans	125 mL

1. In a large skillet over medium heat, sauté bacon for about 5 minutes or until crispy. Transfer bacon with a slotted spoon to drain on paper towels. Let cool and then crumble. Pour off all but 1 tbsp (15 mL) of fat and return skillet to medium-low heat. Add pearl onions and sugar and sauté for 15 to 20 minutes or until onions are deep brown and cooked through. Remove skillet from heat.

2. Meanwhile, in a large pot, bring 6 quarts (6 L) water to a boil over high heat. Add 1 tbsp (15 mL) salt and green beans and cook for about 5 minutes or until just tender. Drain. Transfer to bowl of ice water and let cool. Drain and pat dry.

3. Add butter to skillet with onions and place over medium heat. Add beans and toss to heat through, about 5 minutes. Add pecans and bacon. Season with salt and pepper to taste. Transfer to a warm serving bowl.

THE DISH **Frozen Pearl Onions.** Convenience products are not really our cup of tea, but legitimate food products that happen to be convenient are another thing altogether. Such is the case with frozen pearl onions. One only need spend the time it takes to peel a pint of fresh pearl onions to know what we're talking about.

Maple-Glazed Carrots

Carrots don't have to work too hard to liven up a plate. The pop of orange adds excitement to the plate in much the same way a cute colorful clutch complements a little black dress. You'll love the maple-flavored, buttery goodness of this basic yet fabulous carrot dish.

Serves 6

Hands-on time
10 minutes

Start to finish
25 minutes

Make Ahead

The carrots can be prepared up to 3 hours ahead and kept at room temperature. Reheat over medium heat until hot.

2 lbs	carrots, peeled and cut into ¼-inch (0.5 cm) thick slices	1 kg
1 tsp	salt	5 mL
¼ cup	pure maple syrup	60 mL
2 tbsp	unsalted butter	30 mL
	Salt and freshly ground black pepper	
2 tbsp	minced flat-leaf parsley	30 mL

1. In a large pot over medium-high heat, bring 3 cups (750 mL) water, carrots and salt to a boil. Cover, reduce heat and simmer carrots for about 10 minutes or until tender when pierced with a sharp knife.

2. Drain carrots and transfer to a large skillet over medium heat. Add maple syrup and butter and heat for about 5 minutes or until carrots have absorbed most of the liquid. Taste and adjust seasoning with salt and pepper. Garnish with parsley.

THE DISH **Real Maple Syrup.** There is simply no substitute for real maple syrup. The flavor is more complex than the pretenders, and it is also much better for you healthwise. The freshest maple syrup can be purchased in early spring, once the sap starts running in the maple trees. It takes about 40 gallons (40 L) of sap to boil down to 1 gallon (1 L) of syrup.

Fashion Plate

Pair this seductive side with Winter Salad with Orange Vinaigrette (page 98) and Pistachio-Crusted Rack of Lamb with Spiced Zinfandel Sauce (page 202).

Gingered Carrot Purée

The French are very big on purées, while Americans often relegate them to baby food. But there's something sexy about this silky smooth carrot purée flavored with fennel and ginger. And though we are grownups and capable of chewing our food, purées still have pride of place on our plates. Your guests will definitely be intrigued by this elusive dish.

Serves 6

Hands-on time
15 minutes

Start to finish
25 minutes

Make Ahead

The carrot purée can be prepared up to 3 hours ahead and kept at room temperature. Reheat over medium heat until hot.

- **Food processor**

1½ lbs	carrots, peeled and cut into ¼-inch (0.5 cm) thick slices	750 g
1	potato, peeled, quartered and cut into ¼-inch (0.5 cm) thick slices	1
1	head fennel, cut into ¼-inch (0.5 cm) thick slices	1
1 tsp	salt	5 mL
¼ cup	heavy or whipping (35%) cream	60 mL
¼ cup	pure maple syrup	60 mL
¼ cup	unsalted butter	60 mL
2 tbsp	grated fresh gingerroot	30 mL
	Salt and freshly ground black pepper	
2 tbsp	minced flat-leaf parsley	30 mL

1. In a large pot over medium-high heat, bring 4 cups (1 L) water, carrots, potato, fennel and salt to a boil. Cover, reduce heat and simmer for about 10 minutes or until vegetables are tender when pierced with a sharp knife.

2. Drain vegetables and transfer to a food processor. Add cream in 2 batches and purée until smooth. Scrape down sides of bowl occasionally for a smoother purée.

3. Transfer purée to a large skillet and heat over medium heat for about 10 minutes or until thickened slightly. Add maple syrup, butter and ginger. Taste for seasoning and adjust with salt and pepper. Garnish with parsley.

THE DISH **Food Processor.** A food processor makes this dish a cinch to pull together. We really don't know what we would do without one. Go ahead and process the carrots for a minute or more. While you could certainly achieve the wonderful flavor of this dish by using a potato masher, the texture of the purée will be silkier if done in a food processor.

Roasted Asparagus

Not only is this asparagus dish delicious but it's beautiful as well, which is always a good combination. Roasting helps concentrate the flavor while avoiding the dreaded mushy spear syndrome. Say good-bye to limp and waterlogged boiled asparagus and say hello to spring's trumpet — tender-crisp stalks of green and purple.

Serves 4

Hands-on time
5 minutes

Start to finish
25 minutes

Make Ahead

This is really a last-minute kind of side dish. Reheated, it just doesn't have the texture and flavor of the just-cooked dish.

- **Preheat oven to 400°F (200°C)**

1 lb	asparagus, trimmed	500 g
1 tbsp	olive oil	15 mL
	Salt and freshly ground black pepper	
1 tsp	grated lemon zest	5 mL
	Lemon oil	

1. Spread asparagus on a baking sheet and drizzle with olive oil. Sprinkle with salt and pepper and roll asparagus to coat evenly. Roast asparagus for 20 minutes or until tender.

2. Transfer asparagus to serving plates. Sprinkle with lemon zest and drizzle with lemon oil.

THE DISH **Lemon Oil.** Lemon oil is pretty much what it sounds like. But because it is lemon flavor trapped in a fat, the flavor is much more pronounced than even lemon zest's and it won't fade the vibrant green color of the asparagus like lemon juice does. Lemon oil can be found in many cookware stores or online. We use it on all vegetables, but 1/2 tsp (2 mL) or so is also a welcome addition to baked goods such as blueberry muffins or lemon cream pie. Lemon oil is definitely a fun flavoring to have in your pantry, so buy a little bottle and start experimenting today.

Asparagus and Red Pepper Timbales

Asparagus loves to get dressed up in sinfully rich and silky herbed custard. Flecked with red pepper and green chives and topped with nutty Gruyère cheese, this is as tasty as asparagus gets. This mouth-watering version of roasted asparagus is ready for the catwalk and rave reviews; just follow the recipe . . . to Nirvana.

Serves 6

Hands-on time
15 minutes

Start to finish
50 minutes

Make Ahead

The timbales can be assembled up to 8 hours ahead of time and kept covered and refrigerated. Add 5 minutes to the cooking time if baking them directly from the refrigerator.

- **Preheat oven to 400°F (200°C)**
- **Six 4-oz (125 mL) ramekins, buttered**
- **13- by 9-inch (33 by 23 cm) baking dish, lined with dish towel**

1	recipe Roasted Asparagus (page 290)	1
1 cup	heavy or whipping (35%) cream	250 mL
3	large eggs	3
2 tbsp	minced chives	30 mL
½ tsp	salt	2 mL
Pinch	freshly grated nutmeg	Pinch
Pinch	cayenne pepper	Pinch
¼ cup	minced roasted red pepper	60 mL
1 cup	shredded Gruyère cheese	250 mL

1. Make Roasted Asparagus as in the previous recipe, omitting the lemon oil. Let stand until cool enough to handle. Cut asparagus into 1-inch (2.5 cm) pieces.

2. In a bowl, whisk together cream, eggs, chives, salt, nutmeg and cayenne. Stir in red pepper.

3. Arrange ramekins in prepared baking dish so they don't touch. Bring a kettle of water to a boil.

4. Pour custard into a 2-cup (500 mL) measuring cup. Divide mixture equally among ramekins and divide asparagus among them. Sprinkle cheese over top.

5. Pull out middle rack of oven and set dish on rack. Carefully pour boiling water into dish until halfway up the sides of the ramekins. Gently push rack back into oven, close door and reduce oven temperature to 350°F (180°C). Bake timbales for about 30 minutes or until custard is set. Remove dish from oven and let custards stand in hot water for 5 minutes. Remove from water and let cool for 5 minutes more before unmolding.

Continued on next page

6. Run a knife around outside edge of ramekin. Lay upside down on a serving plate and with both hands holding the plate unmold the timbale with a quick downward jerk. If timbale doesn't unmold, repeat the motion. Serve hot.

DOUBLE DISH

Four-oz (125 mL) Ramekins. Believe us when we say that you will use them over and over again. It is convenient to have 6, but more is always better. The white, glazed ceramic is our ramekin of choice as it goes with just about everyone's china or everyday dishes.

Chives. Chives give this vegetable timbale a little oniony zing that we find irresistible. If you don't have a chive patch growing in your back yard, try adding 1 to 2 tsp (5 to 10 mL) fresh thyme and parsley chopped up together. Whatever you do, don't use dried herbs. In a pinch, use just the fresh parsley if that's all you have.

Fashion Plate

Highlight this showy side with a simple main dish like Butterflied Herb-Roasted Chicken (page 236). Finish with the Almond Cornmeal Cake with Balsamic Strawberries (page 332).

Pommes Anna

Pommes Anna is a classic French dish composed of little more than potatoes, butter and a little salt and pepper. Crispy on the outside but meltingly tender on the inside, this dish is the perfect accompaniment to roasted or grilled meats. Pommes Anna crisping up on the stovetop definitely makes life more delicious.

Serves 6

Hands-on time
30 minutes

Start to finish
1 hour

Tip

If you have a food processor with a thin slicing blade, you can use it to slice the potato for this recipe. A Benriner, or Japanese mandoline, is a less expensive option than the French versions and will work beautifully too. Of course, a sharp knife will also do the job, although with considerably more work and less consistent results. The slices should be cut into $\frac{1}{8}$- to $\frac{1}{4}$-inch (3 mm to 0.5 cm) slices.

Make Ahead

Pommes Anna can be made up to 4 hours ahead and kept at room temperature. Just before serving, transfer the skillet to a preheated 375°F (190°C) oven and bake for 10 to 15 minutes or until reheated.

- **8-inch (20 cm) nonstick skillet with lid**

6 tbsp	unsalted butter	90 mL
2 lbs	red-skinned or Yukon gold potatoes, peeled and sliced very thin (see Tip, left)	1 kg
	Salt and freshly ground black pepper	
2 tbsp	minced flat-leaf parsley	30 mL

1. In a small skillet, heat butter over medium heat until sizzling. Continue to cook butter for about 4 minutes, until water has cooked off (it will stop spitting) and bottom of pan has browned lightly. You now have clarified butter, which will help prevent the bottom of your dish from becoming overbrowned.

2. Brush bottom of nonstick skillet with some of clarified butter and place over medium heat. Arrange enough of potato slices to cover bottom of skillet, overlapping edges until entire bottom is covered. Very lightly (you will be salting and peppering with each layer) salt and pepper potatoes in pan and drizzle with some of the butter.

3. Lay a second layer of potatoes in pan in opposite direction, overlapping edges, seasoning with salt and pepper and drizzling with the butter. Continue to make layers in the same manner until you have used up all the potatoes. You should have about 8 layers. The bottom of the pan should be sizzling. Cover skillet and reduce heat to low. Cook for about 20 minutes, checking every now and then to make sure the bottom of pan isn't browning too quickly.

4. Check for doneness by removing lid and sticking a pointed knife into middle of the potato pie. If there is no resistance, the potatoes have cooked through. Increase heat to medium-high and crisp bottom of potatoes, lifting up the side with a spatula to check bottom for browning. It should be brown and crispy on the bottom.

5. Invert a serving platter on top of skillet, flip skillet and serving platter over and turn out Pommes Anna. Cut into 6 wedges and serve garnished with parsley.

THE DISH **Clarified Butter.** The milk solids in butter are the first to brown and burn, so removing them from the butter allows a dish to cook for a longer period of time or with higher heat without overbrowning or burning. There are a few ways to clarify butter. The first is to melt it and then scoop off the white milk solids as they rise to the top. The second, explained in Step 1, is our preferred method because browning the butter gives it a more pronounced flavor.

Fashion Plate

Serve this versatile side dish with the Pistachio-Crusted Rack of Lamb with Spiced Zinfandel Sauce (page 202) and Green Beans with Lemon and Butter (page 286). End with the elegant White Chocolate Terrine with Dark Chocolate Biscotti (page 348).

Potato Galette with Celery Root

Celery root and potatoes is a to-die-for combination that changes classic Pommes Anna to an au courant potato galette. Let's face it, the previous recipe is just about perfect, but by adding Parmesan cheese and fresh thyme, we've managed to add a subtly different flavor profile to this enticing potato pie.

Serves 6

Hands-on time
30 minutes

Start to finish
1 hour

Make Ahead

The galette can be made up to 4 hours ahead and kept at room temperature. Just before serving, transfer the skillet to a preheated 375°F (190°C) oven and bake for 10 to 15 minutes or until reheated.

- **8-inch (20 cm) nonstick skillet with lid**

6 tbsp	unsalted butter	90 mL
2 lbs	red-skinned or Yukon gold potatoes, peeled and sliced very thin (see Tip, page 294)	1 kg
	Salt and freshly ground black pepper	
2	heads celery root (about 8 oz/250 g), peeled and very thinly sliced (see Tip, page 294)	2
2 tsp	minced fresh thyme	10 mL
⅓ cup	finely grated Parmesan cheese	75 mL
2 tbsp	minced flat-leaf parsley	30 mL

1. In a small skillet, heat butter over medium heat until sizzling. Continue to cook butter for about 4 minutes, until water has cooked off (it will stop spitting) and bottom of pan has browned lightly. You now have clarified butter, which will help prevent the bottom of your dish from becoming overbrowned.

2. Brush bottom of nonstick skillet with some of clarified butter and place over medium heat. Arrange enough of potato slices to cover bottom of skillet, overlapping edges until entire bottom is covered. Very lightly (you will be salting and peppering with each layer) salt and pepper potatoes in pan and drizzle with some of the butter.

3. Place a layer of celery root with a sprinkling of thyme, Parmesan, salt and pepper. Then continue with another potato layer. Continue to create layers until all potatoes and celery root are used. You should have about 8 to 10 layers.

4. The bottom of the pan should be sizzling. Cover skillet and reduce heat to low. Cook for about 20 minutes, checking every now and then to make sure the bottom of pan isn't browning too quickly by lifting the edge with a spatula.

5. Check for doneness by removing lid and sticking a pointed knife into middle of the potato pie. If there is no resistance, the potatoes have cooked through. Increase heat to medium-high and crisp bottom of potatoes, lifting up the side with a spatula to check bottom for browning. It should be brown and crispy on the bottom.

6. Invert a serving platter on top of skillet, flip skillet and serving platter over and turn out Potato Galette. Serve in wedges, garnished with parsley.

THE DISH **Celery Root.** An underused vegetable in North America, celery root is very popular in Europe. Knobby, round and dirty, with little fibrous roots, it must be peeled and washed before cutting. We love it on its own, but it really shines as a partner to potatoes because it lightens the starch content just a bit and adds an herbal, celery-like note. We like to think that, just like peas and carrots, the pairing of celery root and potatoes will never go out of style.

Fashion Plate

Serve with Roasted Beet Salad on Endive Spears (page 90), Prosciutto-Wrapped Salmon with Rosemary Butter (page 272) and Chocolate Mousse (page 338).

Corn Fritters

Who knows how the fritter got its name? The word "fritter" conjures images of n'er-do-wells and wastefulness. Who hasn't frittered an afternoon away or heard of someone who frittered away his inheritance? But you won't be wasting your time or money making these divine little corn pancakes. They are definitely more savory than sweet, but we promise not to tell if you pour on a bit of maple syrup in a weak moment — really, we won't.

Makes 6 to 8 fritters

Hands-on time
30 minutes

Start to finish
30 minutes

Make Ahead

The fritters can be made up to 1 hour ahead and kept in a warm (200°F/100°C) oven.

- Preheat oven to 200°F (100°C)
- Baking sheet, lined with parchment paper

1 cup	frozen corn kernels, thawed	250 mL
1/2 cup	yellow cornmeal, preferably stone-ground	125 mL
1/2 cup	minced onion	125 mL
1/4 cup	minced red bell pepper	60 mL
3 tbsp	all-purpose flour	45 mL
1 tsp	granulated sugar	5 mL
1 tsp	grated lemon zest	5 mL
1/4 tsp	baking soda	1 mL
1/4 tsp	salt	1 mL
Pinch	freshly ground black pepper	Pinch
Pinch	cayenne pepper	Pinch
1	large egg, beaten	1
1/4 cup	milk	60 mL
1/4 cup	sour cream	60 mL
3 tbsp	vegetable oil, divided	45 mL
	Sour cream	

1. In a large bowl, combine corn, cornmeal, onion, bell pepper, flour, sugar, lemon zest, baking soda, salt, black pepper and cayenne.

2. In a small bowl, combine egg, milk and sour cream. Add to dry ingredients and stir just until combined. Be careful not to overmix.

3. In a large skillet, heat 1 tbsp (15 mL) of the oil over medium-high heat. When hot, add scant 1/4 cup (60 mL) of the batter for each fritter. Flatten with tines of a fork and tidy up the edges. Fry for about 2 minutes, flip and cook other side for 2 minutes more or until browned and cooked through. Transfer fritters as they are cooked to prepared baking sheet and keep warm in preheated oven. Continue to cook remaining batter in the same manner, adding more oil and adjusting heat between batches as necessary.

4. Serve fritters warm, garnished with sour cream.

Corn, Zucchini and Basil Fritters

Adding zucchini to these corn fritters takes them to the next taste level. And it gives you another use for the proliferation of zucchini that land on your porch, aka the surplus from ardent neighborhood gardeners. Thank heavens for the many uses the zucchini inspires, from sweet zucchini bread to these toothsome hotcakes.

Makes 10 fritters

Hands-on time
35 minutes

Start to finish
35 minutes

Make Ahead

The fritters can be made up to 1 hour ahead and kept in a warm (200°F/100°C) oven.

- **Preheat oven to 200°F (100°C)**
- **Baking sheet, lined with parchment paper**

1 cup	frozen corn kernels, thawed	250 mL
1/2 cup	yellow cornmeal, preferably stone-ground	125 mL
1/2 cup	minced onion	125 mL
1/4 cup	minced red bell pepper	60 mL
1/4 cup	all-purpose flour	60 mL
1 tsp	granulated sugar	5 mL
1 tsp	grated lemon zest	5 mL
1/4 tsp	baking soda	1 mL
1/4 tsp	salt	1 mL
Pinch	freshly ground black pepper	Pinch
Pinch	cayenne pepper	Pinch
1	large zucchini (about 6 oz/175 g), grated	1
2 tbsp	coarsely sliced fresh basil	30 mL
2 tbsp	minced flat-leaf parsley	30 mL
1	large egg, beaten	1
1/4 cup	milk	60 mL
1/4 cup	sour cream	60 mL
3 tbsp	vegetable oil, divided	45 mL
	Sour cream, optional	

1. In a large bowl, combine corn, cornmeal, onion, bell pepper, flour, sugar, lemon zest, baking soda, salt, black pepper and cayenne. Add grated zucchini, basil and parsley.

2. In a small bowl, combine egg, milk and sour cream. Add to dry ingredients and stir just until combined. Be careful not to overmix.

Continued on next page

3. In a large skillet, heat 1 tbsp (15 mL) of the oil over medium-high heat. When hot, add scant ¼ cup (60 mL) of the batter per fritter. Flatten with tines of a fork and tidy up the edges. Fry for about 2 minutes, flip and cook other side for 2 minutes more or until browned and cooked through. (The fritters will be a little more fragile to turn than the previous recipe, but they will also be more vegetal and less bready as a result of the added zucchini.) Transfer fritters as they are cooked to prepared baking sheet and keep warm in preheated oven. Continue to cook remaining batter in the same manner, adding more oil and adjusting heat between batches as necessary.

4. Garnish with sour cream, if desired.

DOUBLE DISH

Cornmeal. All cornmeal is not created equal. Though any cornmeal will do, searching out fresh stone-ground cornmeal will reap tantalizing rewards. The coarse texture and enhanced flavor of a locally grown and ground product will add pizzazz to everything that you make with it.

A Thin Spatula. There is very little binder in these fritters, so they will be fragile to turn. A thin spatula slides easily under the fritter without tearing it. One of our favorites is a thin metal spatula that narrows to the handle, with perforations that allow the food to be flipped without sticking.

Fashion Plate

This fritter is more like a corn and zucchini pancake and serves as a delicious base for roasted fish or meats. Place a fritter on a plate and top with a serving of Grilled Herbed Pork Tenderloin (page 212).

Southern Corn Spoonbread

Sort of a corn soufflé without the "will it or won't it fall" stress, this light but satisfying side dish could easily stand in as a vegetarian main dish, making it a nice, diplomatic choice for a mixed crowd. Corn kernels and green onions give this spoonbread nice texture and flavor.

Serves 4 to 6

Hands-on time
15 minutes

Start to finish
45 minutes

- **Preheat oven to 375°F (190°C)**
- **Soufflé dish or 8-inch (2 L) square glass baking dish, greased**

2 cups	milk	500 mL
½ cup	heavy or whipping (35%) cream	125 mL
1 cup	cornmeal	250 mL
¾ tsp	salt	3 mL
¼ tsp	freshly ground black pepper	1 mL
3	large eggs, separated	3
1 tbsp	Dijon mustard	15 mL
2 cups	fresh or frozen corn kernels	500 mL
½ cup	thinly sliced green onions	125 mL

1. In a medium saucepan, heat milk and cream over medium heat until just boiling. Slowly add cornmeal, whisking constantly, and continue to cook for about 1 minute or until thick and smooth. Transfer to a bowl and season with salt and pepper. Let cool slightly. Stir in egg yolks and mustard and combine well. Stir in corn and green onions.

2. In a bowl, using an electric mixer, beat egg whites until just stiff. Gently fold into corn batter. Pour batter into prepared dish and bake in middle of preheated oven for about 30 minutes or until just puffed and lightly golden.

THE DISH **A Watchful Eye.** As is true in much of life, timing is everything. This dish is easy to make, but real success comes in not overcooking it, which makes it dry. Keep an eye out, and when you see it's puffed but still slightly jiggly in the middle, pull it out. Don't worry if it falls. It most likely will, but the good news is that it tastes just as good inflated or deflated.

Cheese, Chile and Cilantro Corn Spoonbread

Southern Corn Spoonbread makes a wonderful canvas for the home cook to use as the basis for their own culinary creation. We have applied cilantro, Cheddar and chiles to create a slightly Southwest vibe. You could just as easily add bacon, ham, Gruyère or even chopped cooked spinach (thoroughly dried, of course). Whatever inspires you at the moment (or whatever is on hand at the time).

Serves 6

Hands-on time
20 minutes

Start to finish
50 minutes

- **Preheat oven to 375°F (190°C)**
- **Soufflé dish or 8-inch (2 L) square glass baking dish, greased**

2 cups	milk	500 mL
½ cup	heavy or whipping (35%) cream	125 mL
1 cup	cornmeal	250 mL
¾ tsp	salt	3 mL
¼ tsp	freshly ground black pepper	1 mL
3	large eggs, separated	3
1 tbsp	Dijon mustard	15 mL
2 cups	fresh or frozen corn kernels	500 mL
½ cup	chopped fresh cilantro	125 mL
1 cup	sharp (aged) Cheddar cheese	250 mL
1	can (6 oz/175 g) green chiles	1

1. In a medium saucepan, heat milk and cream over medium heat until just boiling. Slowly add cornmeal, whisking constantly, and continue to cook for about 1 minute or until thick and smooth. Transfer to a bowl and season with salt and pepper. Let cool slightly. Stir in egg yolks and mustard and combine well. Stir in corn, cilantro, cheese and chiles.

2. In a bowl, using an electric mixer, beat egg whites until just stiff. Gently fold into corn batter. Pour batter into prepared dish and bake in middle of preheated oven for about 30 minutes or until just puffed and lightly golden.

Fashion Plate

Serve with Lime and Tequila–Marinated Flank Steak with Sweet-and-Sour Chipotle Sauce (page 198) and Roasted Asparagus (page 290). Finish with Tres Leches Cake (page 342).

Crispy Potato Cakes

There are two kinds of potato cakes: the ones made from mashed potatoes, which are crispy on the outside but soft on the inside, and the ones that remind us more of hash browns and are made from grated potatoes and onions, which become deliciously browned and crispy throughout. This dish is decidedly the latter, and while any potato cake is a good thing, if you pushed us, we'd have to admit this is our favorite.

Makes about 20 to 22 cakes

Hands-on time
40 minutes

Start to finish
40 minutes

Make Ahead

Cooked potato cakes can be place on a baking sheet and kept warm for up to 30 minutes until ready to serve.

- Preheat oven to 200°F (100°C)
- Sieve, lined with cheesecloth
- Baking sheet, lined with paper towels

2 lbs	russet potatoes, peeled and grated	1 kg
1	medium onion, grated	1
1	large egg, lightly beaten	1
¼ cup	all-purpose flour	60 mL
1¼ tsp	salt	6 mL
½ tsp	freshly ground black pepper	2 mL
	Vegetable oil for frying	

1. Transfer potatoes to prepared sieve. Set over a large bowl and twist cheesecloth tightly into a pouch. Continue twisting in order to squeeze as much moisture out of the potatoes as possible. Pour the liquid out of the bowl and add potatoes, onion, egg, flour, salt and pepper. Toss to combine.

2. In a large skillet, heat ¼ inch (0.5 cm) of oil over medium-high heat until hot. Drop heaping tablespoons of potato mixture and flatten to about a 3-inch (7.5 cm) diameter. Fry for 3 to 4 minutes per side or until golden brown. Transfer to prepared baking sheet as completed.

THE DISH   **Sides.** There's a reason that side dishes are called sides. They are usually served to the side of the main event on the plate. Upscale restaurants have changed the character of many sides by using them as a base, stacking broiled fish or grilled steak directly on top, whether the side is a potato cake or mashed potatoes. It's kind of fun to arrange a plate architecturally, so don't be afraid to tap into your inner Frank Lloyd Wright. He's in there somewhere — really!

Crispy Potato Cakes with Pear Apple Salsa and Crème Fraîche

We admit it, we're suckers for the savory-sweet combo. That little tango that happens in your mouth is just plain fun. These crispy, salty little potato cakes are paired with the sweet fall flavors of the Pear Apple Salsa. Then we've tied everything together with a dollop of rich crème fraîche. Move over, apple sauce and sour cream, there's a new twist in town.

Makes about 20 to 22 cakes

Hands-on time
55 minutes

Start to finish
55 minutes

Make Ahead

Cooked potato cakes can be placed on a baking sheet and kept warm for up to 30 minutes until ready to serve. Salsa can be made up to 4 hours ahead and kept covered and refrigerated.

- **Preheat oven to 200°F (100°C)**
- **Baking sheet, lined with paper towels**

1	recipe Crispy Potato Cakes (page 304)	1
2	large ripe but firm pears, chopped	2
1	small Granny Smith apple, peeled, cored, chopped	1
¼ cup	chopped green onion	60 mL
2 tbsp	liquid honey	30 mL
1½ tbsp	freshly squeezed lime juice	22 mL
¼ tsp	ground allspice	1 mL
¼ tsp	ground cinnamon	1 mL
	Pinch salt	Pinch
½ cup	crème fraîche	125 mL

1. Place cooked potato cakes on prepared baking sheet and keep warm in preheated oven for up to 30 minutes until ready to serve.

2. Meanwhile, in a bowl, combine pears, apple, green onion, honey, lime juice, allspice, cinnamon and salt. Set salsa aside for 10 minutes to allow flavors to blend.

3. Top each serving of potato cakes with a large spoonful of salsa and a dollop of crème fraîche.

THE DISH **Crème Fraîche.** We like anything rich and sexy, which is probably the reason why we're attracted to crème fraîche. This cultured cream product has its roots in France but can often be found in North American grocery stores, sometimes in the cheese section. If you can't find it in your local market, feel free to substitute sour cream.

Wild Mushroom Risotto

Once you understand how to make this creamy, luxurious risotto, you can pretty much make any kind of risotto you like. For this recipe, we're adding earthy sautéed wild mushrooms, but we could just as easily add in small diced butternut squash or throw in peas and prosciutto toward the end.

Serves 6

Hands-on time
30 minutes

Start to finish
30 minutes

Make Ahead

Risotto cannot be successfully finished ahead. It will continue to cook and become mushy. You can, however, cook the risotto about three-quarters of the way through and transfer it to a large baking sheet, spreading it out in a thin layer. It can then be covered and kept in the refrigerator for up to 1 day. When ready to serve, heat the risotto in a saucepan and continue with the recipe, adding warm stock until done.

2 tbsp	unsalted butter	30 mL
1 tbsp	olive oil	15 mL
2	medium shallots, finely chopped	2
8 oz	cremini or other wild mushrooms, sliced	250 g
4 cups	Brown or Quick Chicken Stock (pages 110 and 119) or ready-to-use chicken broth	1 L
1½ cups	Arborio rice	375 mL
½ cup	dry white wine	125 mL
3 tbsp	unsalted butter	45 mL
½ cup	freshly grated Parmesan cheese	125 mL
	Salt and freshly ground black pepper	

1. In a large heavy-bottomed pot, heat butter and oil over medium-high heat. Sauté shallots for about 6 minutes or until softened.

2. Add mushrooms and sauté for 5 minutes or until they soften and give off their juices. Reduce the heat to medium. Continue to sauté until juices have evaporated. While the mushrooms sauté, add stock to a saucepan and heat over medium-high. When hot, turn heat down to low. Keep hot.

3. Add rice to mushrooms and stir for 3 to 4 minutes or until rice begins to look opaque. Add wine and sauté for about 3 minutes or until wine has evaporated. Reduce heat to low and ladle about ½ cup (125 mL) of the hot broth into rice and stir for about 2 minutes. When liquid is absorbed, add another ½ cup (125 mL) of broth, stirring for 2 to 3 minutes, until liquid is again absorbed. Continue adding broth, stirring occasionally, for 15 to 20 minutes or until rice is tender. Taste the rice; it should be slightly al dente. Add cheese and salt and pepper to taste.

Crispy Wild Mushroom Risotto Cakes

Risotto cakes, crispy on the outside and creamy on the inside, make an unexpectedly wonderful side dish to almost any meal. The problem is that they're so good they tend to steal the show (much like babies and puppies and . . . Jimmy Choos). For this reason, they are perfect to serve with simpler main dishes or even as the center of a vegetarian meal.

Makes 10 cakes

Hands-on time
45 minutes

Start to finish
2 hours 45 minutes

Make Ahead

The risotto cakes can be held in a 200°F (100°C) oven for up to 1 hour before serving.

1	recipe Wild Mushroom Risotto (page 306)	1
2 cups	panko bread crumbs	500 mL
¼ cup	olive oil	60 mL

1. Place cooked risotto on a baking sheet and spread into a thin layer. This allows the rice to cool quickly. Once cooled, the risotto can be transferred to a bowl and chilled in the refrigerator.

2. To make risotto cakes, shape a scant ½ cup (125 mL) of the chilled risotto into patties 1 inch (2.5 cm) thick. Dredge patties in bread crumbs.

3. In a large skillet, heat oil over medium-high heat. When oil is hot, add patties, 2 or 3 at a time, and cook about 3 minutes per side, until browned and crispy. Transfer patties to a baking sheet and keep warm. Cook remaining patties in the same way.

THE DISH **Panko Bread Crumbs.** A Japanese variety of bread crumbs, panko is typically made from white bread with the crusts cut off and tends to make a much lighter, crispier coating than ordinary crumbs. Look for it in the Asian foods section of your local grocery store.

Fashion Plate

Serve with Pistachio-Crusted Rack of Lamb with Spiced Zinfandel Sauce (page 202) and Roasted Pear Salad with Gorgonzola Rounds (page 95).

Creamy Potato Gratin

Potatoes and cream . . . hmmm, need we say more? No, but we will anyway. This simple but delightfully decadent dish finds its way onto our dinner tables more often than we'd like to admit. That's probably because, in addition to being fabulous on its own, it's also a wonderful plate partner for any number of meat dishes. The neutral nature of cream and potatoes makes them the perfect accompaniment to anything from meat loaf to filet mignon.

Serves 8

Hands-on time
30 minutes

Start to finish
1 hour 45 minutes

Make Ahead

The gratin can be made up to 1 hour ahead and kept, covered with foil, in a 200°F (100°C) oven.

- **Preheat oven to 375°F (190°C)**
- **Wide shallow 2-quart (2 L) baking dish, greased**

1⅔ cups	heavy or whipping (35%) cream	400 mL
1⅔ cups	whole milk	400 mL
4	cloves garlic, thinly sliced	4
3 lbs	baking potatoes, peeled and cut into ¼-inch (0.5 cm) slices (see The Dish, below)	1.5 kg
2 tsp	salt	10 mL
½ tsp	freshly ground black pepper	2 mL
2 tbsp	unsalted butter, at room temperature	30 mL

1. In a medium saucepan over medium heat, combine cream, milk and garlic. Bring to a simmer and remove from heat. Let steep for 10 minutes.

2. Meanwhile, arrange one-third of potato slices in bottom of prepared dish. Sprinkle lightly with salt and pepper. Pour one-third of the cream mixture over potatoes. Repeat layers two more times, dotting the top with butter. Place gratin dish on rimmed baking sheet.

3. Bake gratin in preheated oven for 45 minutes to 1 hour or until top is brown and sauce is bubbling at edges. Let gratin stand for 15 minutes before serving.

THE DISH **Baking Potatoes.** Russets, Idahoes, whatever you want to call them, baking potatoes are what you want to use in this dish. They contain a higher starch content and will absorb the liquid better during the baking process. Lower-starch potatoes, such as new potatoes or red-skinned potatoes, will hold their shape better during the cooking process but won't take in the liquid as well. This results in potatoes that are literally floating in the cream at the end of their baking time, making them difficult and messy to serve and not nearly as pleasant to eat.

Creamy White Winter Gratin with Caramelized Onions

Root vegetables are the perfect vehicle for a gratin, which is essentially a casserole of sliced vegetables covered in a creamy sauce and baked. We often use potatoes alone, but when the mood strikes us — and let's face it, some kind of mood is always striking us — we like to mix it up with other types of vegetables. Here, we're combining potatoes with the sweetness of parsnips and the subtle but sophisticated flavor of celery root. Then (just when you thought it couldn't get any better, right?), we layer on deeply caramelized onions, which gives the entire dish a new and welcome twist.

Serves 8

Hands-on time
50 minutes

Start to finish
2 hours 5 minutes

Make Ahead

The gratin can be made up to 1 hour ahead and kept, covered with foil, in a 200°F (100°C) oven.

- **Preheat oven to 375°F (190°C)**
- **Wide shallow 2-quart (2 L) baking dish, greased**

5 tbsp	unsalted butter, at room temperature, divided	75 mL
2 lbs	onions, trimmed and thinly sliced	1 kg
2 tsp	salt, divided	10 mL
1 tsp	granulated sugar	5 mL
1 tbsp	chopped fresh sage	15 mL
1½ cups	heavy or whipping (35%) cream	375 mL
1½ cups	whole milk	375 mL
2	cloves garlic, thinly sliced	2
1 lb	russet potatoes, peeled and cut into ¼-inch (0.5 cm) slices	500 g
1 lb	parsnip, peeled and cut into ¼-inch (0.5 cm) slices	500 g
1 lb	celery root, peeled and cut into ¼-inch (0.5 cm) slices	500 g
½ tsp	freshly ground black pepper	2 mL

1. In a large skillet, melt 3 tbsp (45 mL) of the butter over medium heat. Add onions, ½ tsp (2 mL) of the salt and sugar and sauté for 20 minutes or until onions are deep walnut brown. Add sage and continue to sauté for 1 minute more.

2. In a medium saucepan over medium heat, combine cream, milk and garlic. Bring to a simmer and remove from heat. Let steep for 10 minutes.

3. Meanwhile, arrange one-third of potato, parsnip and celery root slices in bottom of prepared dish. Sprinkle lightly with salt and pepper. Spread one-third of onions over vegetables. Pour one-third of cream mixture over onions. Repeat layers two more times, dotting top with remaining butter. Place gratin dish on rimmed baking sheet.

4. Bake gratin in preheated oven for 45 minutes to 1 hour or until top is brown and sauce is bubbling at edges. Let gratin stand for 15 minutes before serving.

THE DISH | **A Good Gratin Dish.** Can you make this dish in a pie tin? Yes. Will it be as good as it would if you made it in a lovely gratin dish? No. We hate to be equipment snobs, but a nice oval gratin dish should be part of anyone's kitchen arsenal. These shallow ceramic oven-to-table casseroles are useful for a million different things, and they add a certain elegance to whatever is being served from them.

Fashion Plate

Serve with Baby Greens Salad with Goat Cheese and Balsamic Vinaigrette (page 62) and Fig and Escarole–Stuffed Chicken Thighs with Sherry Cream Sauce (page 220).

Roasted New Potatoes with Rosemary and Garlic

Roasted new potatoes are one of life's simple pleasures. Slightly crisp on the outside and creamy on the inside, these potatoes once again harken back to the message "Keep it simple, stupid." When new potatoes are in season, they don't need much to shine. Here, we roast the potatoes in rosemary butter along with whole cloves of garlic. The garlic comes out golden and soft and just the thing to slather on a slice of French bread.

Serves 6 to 8

Hands-on time
15 minutes

Start to finish
50 minutes

- **Preheat oven to 400°F (200°C)**
- **2 baking sheets**

¼ cup	unsalted butter	60 mL
2 tbsp	finely chopped fresh rosemary	30 mL
3 lbs	small red-skinned potatoes	1.5 kg
1 tsp	salt	5 mL
½ tsp	freshly ground black pepper	2 mL
16	whole cloves garlic, peeled	16

1. In a small saucepan, melt butter over medium heat. Stir in rosemary and remove from heat.

2. Toss potatoes with 2 tbsp (30 mL) of the rosemary butter. Season with salt and pepper. Transfer potatoes to 2 baking sheets and bake in preheated oven for 20 minutes. Add garlic cloves and toss lightly to coat with butter. Bake for 20 minutes more or until potatoes and garlic are golden brown.

3. Transfer potatoes and garlic to a large bowl. Add remaining rosemary butter and toss. Season with salt and pepper to taste.

THE DISH **New Potatoes.** New potatoes are thin-skinned, small potatoes that begin to arrive in the markets in May or June. They're creamier and sweeter than their baking potato counterparts, such as Idahoes or russets. Although small potatoes (such as baby red potatoes) can be found in markets year-round, they are never as good as those enjoyed in late spring or early summer.

Salt-Roasted New Potatoes with Rosemary Butter

Roasting potatoes in salt may seem like an odd technique, but this technique is often used in professional kitchens to cook everything from meat to fish to vegetables. The salt around the food forms a seal and roasts whatever is inside without letting any of the flavor or moisture escape. Don't worry. For the most part, the salt falls away from the potatoes after cooking and any excess can easily be brushed aside.

Serves 6 to 8

Hands-on time
15 minutes

Start to finish
50 minutes

Make Ahead

The potatoes can be roasted, removed from the oven and kept submerged, covered in the salt, for up to 30 minutes.

- **Preheat oven to 400°F (200°C)**

¼ cup	unsalted butter, at room temperature	60 mL
2 tbsp	finely chopped fresh rosemary	30 mL
Pinch	salt	Pinch
3 lbs	small new potatoes	1.5 kg
4 cups	kosher salt	1 L

1. In a small bowl, combine rosemary, butter and salt. Set aside.
2. Place potatoes on a large baking sheet. Pour salt over potatoes. (There should be enough salt so that only the very tops of the potatoes peek through.)
3. Roast potatoes in preheated oven for about 45 minutes or until tender. Brush salt off potatoes before serving. Serve hot with a dollop of rosemary butter on top.

THE DISH **Kosher Salt.** While some rarer (or trendier) salts can be quite expensive, kosher salt remains a bargain, making this incredibly easy cooking technique a guilt-free one. To make it even more cost-effective, after it's cooled we always save our salt in a plastic bag for the next time, but not if it's been used with meats. We tend to use kosher salt for most of our everyday cooking. The flavor is clean and not overwhelmingly salty.

Fashion Plate

Serve with Steak with Red Wine Sauce and Mushrooms (page 183) for a wonderful fireside meal.

Creamy Polenta

If you cook Italian as much as we do, it pays to know how to make polenta. Actually, it pays to know how to cook polenta whether you cook Italian or not, because this cheesy, buttery side dish, much like mashed potatoes, makes the perfect partner for almost any main course. Basic polenta is nothing more than water and cornmeal with the addition of a healthy dose of cheese and butter.

Serves 6

Hands-on time
15 minutes

Start to finish
55 minutes

Make Ahead

Polenta can be made 20 minutes ahead and kept, covered, at room temperature (do not let stand longer or it will solidify).

1½ tsp	salt	7 mL
1½ cups	polenta (not quick-cooking) or yellow cornmeal	375 mL
3 tbsp	unsalted butter	45 mL
½ cup	freshly grated Parmesan cheese	125 mL

1. In a large heavy pot, bring 6 cups (1.5 L) water and salt to a boil. Add polenta in a thin stream, whisking constantly. Cook over medium heat, whisking, for 2 minutes. Cover, reduce heat to low and simmer polenta, stirring for 1 minute after every 10 minutes of cooking, 45 minutes total. Remove from heat and stir in butter and cheese. Serve warm.

THE DISH **A Heavy Saucepan.** Polenta is easy, but only if you have the right pan. An inexpensive, thin-bottomed saucepan will almost ensure burnt polenta. The lower the quality of pan, the less control you have of the heat. This means your food will tend to burn where the flame or electric burner is making contact with the pan and will not cook completely in the places where it's not.

Fashion Plate

We like to serve this dish as a vegetarian entrée. Serve with Arugula Salad with Grape Tomatoes and Shallot Vinaigrette (page 86).

Polenta with a Trio of Toppings

Polenta makes an appetizing foundation for this trio of tastes. Sautéed peppers and onions in a hearty tomato sauce, vibrant basil pesto along with Gorgonzola and toasty walnuts are arranged (like the Italian flag) in strips down the center of creamy polenta. This allows your guests to choose their own toppings and for you to make a big impression.

Serves 6

Hands-on time
45 minutes

Start to finish
55 minutes

Make Ahead

The pepper and onion topping can be made the day before and kept covered and refrigerated.

- **Large warmed serving platter**

2 tbsp	olive oil	30 mL
2	medium yellow onions, cut into ¼-inch (0.5 cm) slices	2
1	red bell pepper, julienned	1
1	yellow bell pepper, julienned	1
2	cloves garlic, minced	2
1	can (14 oz/398 mL) crushed tomatoes	1
2 tbsp	balsamic vinegar	30 mL
¼ tsp	hot pepper flakes	1 mL
½ tsp	salt	2 mL
½ tsp	freshly ground black pepper	2 mL
1	recipe Creamy Polenta (page 314)	1
1 cup	crumbled Gorgonzola cheese	250 mL
1 cup	chopped toasted walnuts	250 mL
1	recipe Pesto (page 25) or store-bought	1

1. In a large sauté pan, heat oil over medium heat. Add onions and sauté for 15 to 20 minutes or until softened and browned. Add red and yellow bell peppers, garlic, tomatoes, balsamic vinegar, hot pepper flakes, salt and pepper and continue sautéing for 10 minutes more. Set aside.

2. To serve, pour polenta onto a large warm serving platter. Arrange toppings on polenta in three strips (to resemble the Italian flag), with pepper/tomato mixture on the right, Gorgonzola and toasted walnuts in center and pesto on the left. Serve warm.

THE DISH **A Rustic Platter.** Polenta is nothing if not rustic. It would seem completely out of place to serve this dish on fine china. So this is the time to bring out your inner Martha Stewart and use your imagination. We have been known to serve polenta on a clean wooden cutting board. Hey, sometimes you have to go with what you've got!

Roasted Butternut Squash with Goat Cheese and Pecans

Under the assumption that everything is better with a little goat cheese, we had to include this easy-to-make casserole. Constructed of only three main ingredients — squash, goat cheese and pecans — the flavors play off each other beautifully. Roasting the squash makes it easier to peel and also renders the juicy flesh sweet and tender. The addition of tangy goat cheese and earthy pecans make this dish a match made in heaven.

Serves 6 to 8

Hands-on time
20 minutes

Start to finish
1 hour 20 minutes

Make Ahead

The casserole can be assembled 1 day in advance and kept covered and refrigerated. If baking from the refrigerator, add a few minutes to the cooking time. It can be kept warm in a 200°F (100°C) oven for up to 1 hour.

- **Preheat oven to 375°F (190°C)**
- **Baking sheet, lined with parchment paper**
- **8-cup (2 L) casserole dish, buttered**

2 lbs	butternut squash, halved, seeds scooped	1 kg
2 tsp	olive oil	10 mL
½ tsp	salt, divided	2 mL
	Freshly ground black pepper	
1 tsp	unsalted butter	5 mL
5 oz	cold goat cheese	150 g
½ cup	finely chopped pecans	125 mL

1. Place butternut squash on prepared baking sheet, cut side up. Drizzle olive oil over cut surface and sprinkle with some salt and pepper. Turn over, cut side down, and roast in preheated oven for 45 minutes to 1 hour or until tender. Set aside. When cool enough to handle, peel and cut into 1-inch (2.5 cm) thick slices. Leave oven on.

2. Place squash in prepared casserole dish. Sprinkle with remaining salt and pepper to taste. Cut goat cheese into thin slices and cover top of squash with cheese. Sprinkle pecans over top.

3. Bake in preheated oven for 20 minutes or until heated through and cheese is melted.

Fashion Plate

Serve this casserole with simply grilled or broiled meats or chicken or with Maple-Brined Pork Chops with Mustard Sauce and Sweet Potato–Apple Gratins (page 206).

Butternut Squash Gratin with Caramelized Onions

Rich and creamy custard holds together sweet, tender squash and browned onions and goat cheese with just a hint of nutmeg and cayenne. This pièce de résistance deserves center-of-the-plate status, but a few slices of roasted leg of lamb or pork tenderloin would be a tantalizing addition.

Serves 6 to 8

Hands-on time
30 minutes

Start to finish
2 hours

Make Ahead

The casserole can be assembled 1 day in advance and kept covered and refrigerated. If baking from the refrigerator, add a few minutes to the cooking time. It can be kept warm in a 200°F (100°C) oven for up to 1 hour.

- **Preheat oven to 375°F (190°C)**
- **8-cup (2 L) casserole dish, buttered**

2 lbs	butternut squash, halved, seeds scooped	1 kg
2 tsp	olive oil	10 mL
2 tbsp	unsalted butter	30 mL
1	large onion, thinly sliced	1
	Salt and freshly ground black pepper	
2 cups	heavy or whipping (35%) cream	500 mL
3	cloves garlic, smashed	3
5 oz	cold goat cheese	150 g
½ cup	finely chopped pecans	125 mL
Pinch	ground nutmeg	Pinch
Pinch	cayenne pepper	Pinch
2	large eggs	2
1	large yolk	1

1. Place butternut squash on prepared baking sheet, cut side up. Drizzle olive oil over cut surface and sprinkle with some salt and pepper. Turn over, cut side down, and roast in preheated oven for 45 minute to 1 hour or until tender. Set aside. When cool enough to handle, peel and cut into 1-inch (2.5 cm) thick slices. Leave oven on.

2. In a large skillet, heat butter over medium-high heat. When butter sizzles, add onion and a sprinkle of salt and pepper. When onions begin to brown, about 3 minutes, reduce heat to medium-low and continue to cook, stirring occasionally, for about 25 minutes or until onions are soft and golden.

3. In a small saucepan, heat cream and garlic over medium heat until steaming. Remove from heat, cover and let stand for 15 to 20 minutes so garlic can flavor cream.

4. Place squash in prepared casserole dish. Cut goat cheese into thin slices and cover top of squash with cheese. Sprinkle pecans over top. Scatter onions over top.

5. In a medium bowl, whisk together nutmeg, cayenne, eggs and yolk. Slowly whisk in heated cream. Remove garlic with a slotted spoon. Pour egg mixture over squash. Bake in preheated oven for 35 to 40 minutes or until custard is set. Let stand for at least 10 minutes before cutting into squares.

DOUBLE DISH

Pecans. Pecans give this dish more than nutty crunch. They also offset the richness of the squash and goat cheese. If you don't have pecans, don't worry. Walnuts or hazelnuts will do the trick as well.

Caramelized Onion. There are few things more irresistible than browned onions. When colored over a medium heat, the sugars brown and make the onions sweet with an unctuous, jammy quality. Make lots and keep them in the refrigerator. You'll use them up in omelets, casseroles, soups or as a simple garnish to roasted or grilled meats.

Fashion Plate

Mustard and Garlic–Roasted Pork Loin (page 208) would accompany this dish beautifully.

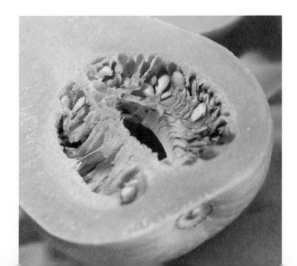

Sugar Snap Pea and Sesame Stir-Fry

Any hot dish that can be cooked and on the table in 15 minutes makes us happy, but when it's sugar snap peas infused with the Asian flavors of ginger, garlic and sesame, well, we're downright thrilled.

Serves 4

Hands-on time
15 minutes

Start to finish
15 minutes

1 tbsp	vegetable oil	15 mL
1 tbsp	minced fresh gingerroot	15 mL
1	clove garlic, minced	1
1 lb	sugar snap peas, trimmed	500 g
1 tbsp	sesame seeds	15 mL
1 tsp	toasted sesame oil	5 mL
¼ tsp	salt	1 mL

1. In a large nonstick skillet or wok, heat oil over medium-high heat. Sauté ginger, garlic and sugar snap peas for 4 to 5 minutes or until peas are just tender-crisp. Add sesame seeds, sesame oil and salt and sauté for 30 seconds more.

THE DISH **Stringless Sugar Snap Peas.** Sugar snap peas sometimes come with a woody stem and strings that run down the side. The unpleasantness of trying to chew a pod with the string still attached can't be measured. OK, it's not the worst thing that will ever happen to you, but it's not the best either. To remove the stem and string, hold the stem between your thumb and index finger, snap and pull down. Or buy snap peas labeled "stringless" and save yourself the trouble.

Sugar Snap Peas with Carrots, Edamame and Mint

If you believe the age-old adage "You eat with your eyes first," you know how appetizing a colorful dish can be. This side dish could win a beauty pageant with its bright green snap peas and intensely colored carrots. Add to that the additional sensations of crunchy, toasty and minty and you have a carnival of color and flavor.

Serves 4

Hands-on time
20 minutes

Start to finish
20 minutes

1 tbsp	vegetable oil	15 mL
1 cup	thinly sliced peeled carrots	250 mL
1 tbsp	minced fresh gingerroot	15 mL
1	clove garlic, minced	1
1 lb	sugar snap peas, trimmed	500 g
½ cup	shelled edamame	125 mL
1 tsp	toasted sesame oil	5 mL
¼ tsp	salt	1 mL
2 tbsp	finely chopped fresh mint	30 mL

1. In a large nonstick skillet or wok, heat oil over medium-high heat. Sauté carrots, ginger and garlic for 2 minutes. Add sugar peas and sauté for 3 to 4 minutes or until peas are just tender-crisp. Add edamame, sesame oil and salt and sauté for 1 minute more. Transfer to a serving platter and garnish with fresh mint.

THE DISH **Edamame.** Edamame are fresh soybeans that are most often boiled in their shell and eaten out of hand with salt. It's essentially the Asian equivalent of potato chips, in that they're often eaten as a snack and you can't eat just one. Of course, they're way better for you than chips, and we're beginning to see them more and more often served out of their shell as an ingredient in a variety of dishes.

Fashion Plate

Serve this great side with Grilled Thai Shrimp (page 262) and Navel Oranges with Caramel (page 372).

Finishing Touches
Desserts

White Wine Poached Pears with Rosemary Syrup and Triple Crème Cheese

Poached pears are always a welcome sight when dessert draws near. Meltingly tender pears pick up the flavor of the wine and citrus, along with the surprising scent of savory rosemary, vanilla and pepper. You'll be surprised how appealing the scent and taste of rosemary is in this dish. We can't resist it.

Serves 6

Hands-on time
20 minutes

Start to finish
1 hour

Make Ahead

The pears can be poached and syrup reduced up to 2 days before using and kept stored in syrup, covered and refrigerated. Let come to room temperature before serving. The syrup will thicken after refrigeration, so warm up it up in the microwave so that it drizzles nicely.

- **Parchment paper**

1	bottle (750 mL) dry white wine, such as Sauvignon Blanc or Pinot Grigio	1
¾ cup	granulated sugar	175 mL
2	fresh rosemary branches, about 4-inches (10 cm) long, bruised (see Tip, right)	2
	Grated zest of 1 orange	
¼ cup	freshly squeezed orange juice	60 mL
1	vanilla bean, split lengthwise	1
½ tsp	whole black peppercorns or Szechwan peppercorns	2 mL
1	piece (5 inches/12.5 cm) cinnamon stick	1
3	firm ripe Anjou or Bartlett pears	3
6 oz	triple crème cheese, cut into 6 wedges	175 g
⅓ cup	toasted walnuts, coarsely chopped	75 mL

1. In a large saucepan, combine wine, sugar, rosemary, orange zest, orange juice, vanilla bean, peppercorns and cinnamon stick. Bring to a simmer over medium-high heat.

2. Meanwhile, peel pears and cut in half lengthwise. Scoop out cores, leaving stems on. Add pears to wine mixture and top with a piece of parchment paper. Place a heatproof plate that fits on the inside of the saucepan on top of the paper. (This will keep the pears submerged in the liquid.) Reduce heat to low and simmer pears for about 30 minutes or until tender when pierced with a sharp knife. Remove from heat and let pears cool in the liquid for 15 minutes. Remove pears from liquid with a slotted spoon. Strain poaching liquid and return to saucepan. Increase heat to medium-high and boil syrup for about 20 minutes or until reduced to about ¾ cup (175 mL). Let cool. Discard cinnamon stick.

3. Make about 6 lengthwise slices almost to the stem in each pear and fan them out.

4. *To serve:* Center pears and a wedge of cheese on dessert plates. Drizzle with some of the reduced syrup and sprinkle with walnuts.

DOUBLE DISH

Fresh Rosemary. You are probably familiar with rosemary as a savory herb, but it goes surprisingly well with fruit. Besides, it's fun to inject a surprise element into a dish. Make rosemary the theme of the evening by arranging small potted rosemary plants in front of each place setting. Your guests will have a ball touching them and smelling their piney scent throughout the meal. Later they can take the spikey little plants home to continue their own experiments with this sun-kissed herb.

Toasted Walnuts. Walnuts are at their peak of freshness in the fall, so stock up and keep some in the freezer for later use. Toasting the walnuts makes a huge difference in the taste. Just place on a baking sheet and in a toast in a 350°F (180°C) oven for 5 to 8 minutes or until lightly browned (see Tip, page 358).

Tips

To bruise rosemary, lightly smash it with the flat side of a knife blade.

Triple crème cheese is just what it sounds like — rich and sensuous. These extravagant cheeses have a mild and often buttery texture. Look for Explorateur, Boursault or St. André. If you can't find these cheeses, just use the readily available Brie. Everyone will love it.

Fashion Plate

This dessert begs to be served after Grilled Veal Rolls with Arugula, Currants and Pine Nuts (page 190) and Creamy Potato Gratin (page 308).

Zinfandel Poached Pear Galettes with Almonds and Red Wine Raspberry Syrup

Whether you're using Sauvignon Blanc or Zinfandel, poaching pears is a wonderful technique for creating a light but sophisticated dessert. In this recipe, we love how the pears pick up a deep blush color from their bath in spicy red wine along with the herbal notes from the rosemary and the heat from the peppercorns. It isn't too sugary, and some of the flavors point more toward a savory dish than a sweet, but that is the charm of this little herbal pear tart. When a dessert looks this good and tastes this good — it must be really good!

Serves 6

Hands-on time
30 minutes

Start to finish
1 hour 10 minutes

Make Ahead

The pears can be poached and syrup reduced up to 2 days before using. The pastry can be cut out 1 hour before serving and kept in the refrigerator. Assemble just before baking. The tarts can be baked up to 6 hours before serving and kept at room temperature. The sauce will thicken after refrigeration, so warm it up in the microwave so that it drizzles nicely.

- **Baking sheet, lined with parchment paper**

1	bottle (750 mL) Zinfandel wine	1
¾ cup	granulated sugar	175 mL
2	fresh rosemary branches, about 4-inches (10 cm) long, bruised (see Tip, page 325)	2
	Grated zest of 1 orange	
¼ cup	freshly squeezed orange juice	60 mL
1	vanilla bean, split lengthwise	1
½ tsp	whole black peppercorns or Szechwan peppercorns	2 mL
1	piece (5 inches/12.5 cm) cinnamon stick	1
3	firm ripe Anjou or Bartlett pears	3
1	box (18 oz/540 g) frozen puff pastry (2 sheets dough), thawed (see Tip, right)	1
¼ cup	seedless raspberry jam	60 mL
⅓ cup	toasted sliced almonds	75 mL
	Ice cream or sweetened whipped cream, optional	

1. In a large saucepan, combine wine, sugar, rosemary, orange zest, orange juice, vanilla bean, peppercorns and cinnamon stick. Bring to a simmer over medium-high heat.

2. Meanwhile, peel pears and cut in half lengthwise. Scoop out cores, leaving stems on. Add pears to wine mixture and top with a piece of parchment paper. Place a heatproof plate that fits on the inside of the saucepan on top of the paper. (This will keep the pears submerged in the liquid.) Reduce heat to low and simmer pears for about 30 minutes or until tender when pierced with a sharp knife. Removed from heat and let pears cool in the liquid for about 15 minutes. Remove pears from liquid with a slotted spoon. Strain poaching liquid and return to saucepan.

3. Increase heat to medium-high and boil syrup for about 20 minutes or until reduced to about ¾ cup (175 mL). Strain syrup through a fine-mesh sieve, pressing to remove solids. Discard solids. Let cool.

4. Slice pear halves lengthwise, almost to the stem, and fan out. Preheat oven to 425°F (230°C).

5. Place puff pastry on a lightly floured work surface. If necessary, roll out to ⅛-inch (3 mm) thickness. Place one of the pears on a corner of the pastry, and using the pear as a template, cut with a sharp knife around the outside perimeter of the fanned-out pear, leaving a ¼-inch (0.5 cm) border beyond the perimeter of the pear. Transfer the pear-topped pastry to prepared baking sheet. Repeat with remaining pears.

6. Bake in preheated oven for about 20 minutes or until pastry is browned and crispy on bottom.

7. In a small saucepan, heat jam over medium heat. Brush pears with jam and sprinkle with almonds. Serve with a scoop of ice cream, if desired.

THE DISH **Zinfandel.** Zinfandel wine is renowned for its spicy, raspberry-like flavors, which makes it a great wine to use for poaching fruits. And while we would never encourage you to buy cheap wine, there's no need to break the bank on a bottle for this dish. There are many bottles in the $10 to $15 range that will cajole the best flavors from your pears and reduce into the most delectable sauce that ever graced a plate.

Tip
Packages of puff pastry vary in size between brands. You can use any package from 14 to 18 oz (400 to 540 g) for this recipe. If using a smaller package, the pastry will be a little thinner, but the recipe will still work.

Chocolate Chip Bread Pudding

Bread pudding is comfort food at its best. Our version is rich, gooey, chocolaty and nutty, just like your favorite chocolate chip cookie. It's the dessert to turn to when consoling a broken heart or celebrating the end of your mother-in-law's long, long, long visit. Whenever you're in desperate need of a food friend, bread pudding will always be there for you.

Serves 8

Hands-on time
20 minutes

Start to finish
1 hour 50 minutes

Make Ahead

The bread pudding can be assembled and kept, covered and refrigerated, for up to 4 hours ahead. You may need to add an extra 10 minutes to the bake time.

- **Preheat oven to 325°F (160°C)**
- **8-cup (2 L) baking dish, greased**
- **Large baking pan or roasting pan**

1⅓ cups	granulated sugar	325 mL
4	large eggs	4
2 cups	whole milk	500 mL
½ cup	heavy or whipping (35%) cream	125 mL
1 tsp	vanilla extract	5 mL
¼ tsp	salt	1 mL
6 cups	cubed country-style white bread	1.5 L
1⅓ cups	semisweet chocolate chips (about 8 oz/250 g)	325 mL
¾ cup	chopped toasted walnuts	175 mL
	Boiling water	
	Good-quality vanilla ice cream	

1. In a large bowl, whisk together sugar and eggs. Whisk in milk, cream, vanilla and salt.

2. Place bread cubes in prepared baking dish. Add chocolate chips and walnuts. Toss to combine. Pour custard mixture over bread cubes and let stand for 30 minutes to allow bread to absorb some of the liquid. Set the baking dish in a larger baking pan or roasting pan. Place pan on middle rack of preheated oven.

3. Pour boiling water into roasting pan to reach halfway up side of dish. Bake for about 50 minutes or until custard is slightly jiggly in the middle. Use a knife to peak inside the center of pudding. If it is still liquidy at the bottom, it's not done. Return to oven and check every 5 minutes until it is ready. Dish into bowls and serve with a scoop of vanilla ice cream.

Individual Chocolate and Almond Bread Puddings

While bread pudding is often thought of as comfort food, this sophisticated version will make you swoon with its silky, light texture and elegant flavors. For this swanky take on our more rustic but oh-so-good Chocolate Chip Bread Pudding, we've created individual servings infused with almond paste, dotted with deep, dark bittersweet chocolate and topped with a satisfying dollop of our luscious Amaretto Cream. Trust us, this one is a dessert that will impress the boss or the boy.

Serves 8

Hands-on time
30 minutes

Start to finish
1 hour 40 minutes

Make Ahead

The bread puddings can be assembled and kept, covered and refrigerated, for up to 4 hours. You may need to add an additional 10 minutes to the cooking time.

- **Preheat oven to 325°F (190°C)**
- **Food processor**
- **Eight 6-oz (175 mL) custard cups or ramekins, buttered**

5 oz	almond paste	150 g
1 cup	granulated sugar	250 mL
4	large eggs	4
2 cups	whole milk	500 mL
½ cup	heavy or whipping (35%) cream	125 mL
1 tsp	vanilla extract	5 mL
¼ tsp	salt	1 mL
6 cups	cubed (¼-inch/0.5 cm) day-old home-style white bread	1.5 L
6 oz	bittersweet (dark) chocolate, cut into small chunks	175 g
	Boiling water	

Amaretto Cream

1 cup	heavy or whipping (35%) cream	250 mL
1 tbsp	confectioner's (icing) sugar	15 mL
1 tbsp	almond liqueur, such as Amaretto	15 mL

1. In a food processor, pulse almond paste and sugar several times until finely crumbled. While food processor is running, add eggs, one at a time, through feed tube. Pour mixture into a large bowl. Stir in milk, cream, vanilla and salt.

Continued on next page

2. Divide bread cubes equally among prepared custard cups. Divide chopped chocolate among cups and toss slightly to distribute chocolate evenly throughout the bread. Fill half-full with custard and set in a large roasting pan. Fill molds to top with custard. Let puddings stand at room temperature for 30 minutes. (If you find you have leftover custard when you have filled the cups, wait until after they've set for 30 minutes. The bread absorbs some of the liquid and there is usually enough room for you to pour a bit more custard in each cup.)

3. Pour boiling water into roasting pan to reach halfway up sides of custard cups. Bake in preheated oven for about 30 minutes or until custard is slightly jiggly in middle. Use a knife to peak inside center of puddings. If there is any liquid left, it's not done. Return to oven and check every 5 minutes until it is ready.

4. *Amaretto Cream:* While puddings are baking, in a medium chilled bowl, using a whisk or electric mixer, whip cream to soft peaks. Add confectioner's sugar and almond liqueur and whip to combine.

5. Let baked custards stand for at least 10 minutes or for up to 30 minutes. Then run a knife along edge of each custard cup, turn over onto a serving plate and remove cup. Serve bread puddings warm with a dollop of Amaretto Cream on top.

THE DISH **Good-Quality Dark Chocolate.** The best ingredients, left largely to their own devices, can transform a dish from decent to divine. In this recipe, chunks of dark chocolate float in the pillowy bread pudding, and when the chocolate is topnotch (we like Scharffen Berger or Valrhona), every piece is like finding a little treasure.

Fashion Plate

Let this be the topper to an elegant affair. We like to serve this after a meal of Glazed Pork Loin Stuffed with Apricots and Figs (page 210) and Green Beans with Lemon and Butter (page 286).

Almond Cornmeal Cake with Balsamic Strawberries

We call this a "dump" recipe — an admittedly unlovely term used for recipes that only require you to toss (or dump) all the ingredients into a bowl or food processor at once, and with a few strokes or pulses you're done.

Serves 8 to 10
Makes one 10-inch (25 cm) cake

Hands-on time
15 minutes

Start to finish
1 hour 30 minutes

Make Ahead

The cake can be made 1 day ahead and kept, covered, at room temperature.

- Preheat oven to 325°F (160°C)
- 10-inch (25 cm) springform pan, greased and floured
- Food processor

½ cup	each all-purpose flour and cornmeal	125 mL
1½ tsp	baking powder	7 mL
1 tsp	grated orange zest	5 mL
¼ tsp	salt	1 mL
1½ cups	granulated sugar	375 mL
8 oz	almond paste	250 g
1 cup	unsalted butter, at room temperature	250 mL
1 tsp	vanilla extract	5 mL
5	large eggs	5
4 cups	sliced strawberries	1 L
1 tbsp	balsamic vinegar	15 mL
2 tbsp	confectioner's (icing) sugar	30 mL
	Sweetened Whipped Cream (page 333)	

1. In a food processor, pulse flour, cornmeal, baking powder, orange zest and salt just until blended. Add sugar and almond paste and pulse until finely ground. Toss in butter and vanilla and pulse again for a few seconds until fine crumbs start to form. Add eggs, one at a time, pulsing after each addition, until incorporated.

2. Pour batter into prepared pan. Bake in preheated oven for 1 to 1¼ hours or until a toothpick comes out clean. Let cool completely in pan on a wire rack.

3. Meanwhile, in a large bowl, combine strawberries, vinegar and icing sugar. Refrigerate for 15 minutes or for up to 2 hours.

4. When cake is cool, run a small thin knife around pan sides to loosen cake. Release sides and either run a thin spatula under bottom of cake and move to a platter or serve off the base.

5. *To serve:* Cut cake into wedges and place on dessert plate. Garnish with strawberry mixture and a dollop of whipped cream.

Sweetened Whipped Cream

There is no substitute for freshly whipped real cream. The whipped "cream" you buy in tubs at the grocery store has a strange flavor and waxy texture that will do nothing good for your delicious homemade dessert.

1 cup	heavy or whipping (35%) cream, well chilled	250 mL
2 tbsp	confectioner's (icing) sugar	30 mL
½ tsp	vanilla extract	2 mL

1. Freeze mixer bowl and whisk attachment or beaters for 5 minutes.

2. Pour cream into chilled bowl. Using electric mixer, beat on medium speed until starting to thicken. Add confectioner's sugar and vanilla. Increase speed to medium-high and whip cream to desired texture — softly billowing or firm enough to pipe in a pastry bag.

Makes 2 cups (500 mL)

Hands-on time
2 minutes

Start to finish
7 minutes

Tip

If you're using a powerful stand mixer, it only takes about 20 seconds to move from soft to firm, so watch carefully. With a hand-held mixer, it doesn't happen as quickly, but it's still good to pay attention.

Make Ahead

Whipped cream will keep for hours in the refrigerator, so go ahead and whip it up before company arrives. It will be ready and waiting for you when it's time for dessert.

Almond Cake with Apricot Filling and Whipped Cream

We're not pastry chefs by any stretch of the imagination, but this cake makes us look like we could be. By substituting flour for the cornmeal in our Almond Cornmeal Cake, we've created a more delicate texture. But it's the addition of an easy apricot filling, a piped topping of whipped cream and a coating of toasted almonds that makes this dessert the star of the show and you the star of the meal.

Serves 8 to 10

Hands-on time
45 minutes

Start to finish
2 hours

Make Ahead

The cake can be made 1 day ahead (assembled without the whipped cream) and kept covered and refrigerated. Pipe on the cream no more than 4 hours ahead of time and keep refrigerated.

- **Preheat oven to 325°F (160°C)**
- **10-inch (25 cm) springform pan, greased and floured**
- **Food processor**
- **Piping bag with large star tip**

1 cup	all-purpose flour	250 mL
1½ tsp	baking powder	7 mL
¼ tsp	salt	1 mL
1½ cups	granulated sugar	375 mL
8 oz	almond paste	250 g
1 cup	unsalted butter, at room temperature	250 mL
1 tsp	vanilla extract	5 mL
5	large eggs	5
1¼ cups	apricot jam	300 mL
2 tbsp	brandy	30 mL
½ cup	sliced almonds, toasted	125 mL
	Sweetened Whipped Cream (page 333)	

1. In a food processor, pulse flour, baking powder and salt, just until blended. Add sugar and almond paste and pulse until finely ground. Toss in butter and vanilla and pulse again for a few seconds until fine crumbs start to form. Add eggs, one at a time, pulsing after each addition, until incorporated.

2. Pour batter into prepared pan. Bake in preheated oven for 1 to 1¼ hours or until a toothpick comes out clean. Let cool completely in pan on a wire rack.

3. When cake is cool, run a small thin knife around pan sides to loosen cake. Release sides and either run a thin spatula under bottom of cake and move to a serving platter, or easier yet, serve it off the base.

4. In food processor, pulse apricot jam and brandy until smooth.

5. Using a long serrated knife, gently slice cake in half crosswise creating two layers. Place bottom layer onto a cake platter and spread with three-quarters of the apricot mixture. Top with remaining layer. Brush remaining apricot mixture on top and sides of cake. Lightly press toasted almonds onto side of cake. Place whipped cream into a piping bag with a large star tip and pipe decoratively onto top of cake.

DOUBLE DISH

Room Temperature Ingredients. For reasons best explained by a food scientist, baking ingredients work better when they're at room temperature. It's especially important for eggs and butter because they will incorporate more easily and thoroughly with other ingredients when they're not too cold. This will help give your cake an even texture and lift.

A Food Processor. Yes, you can make this recipe using a mixer or, God forbid, with a wooden spoon and a serious application of elbow grease, but why, when a food processor is soooo easy? We are always shocked at how many home cooks don't own one. If you belong to this group, it's time to rethink your kitchen equipment. A good food processor can save you precious time in the kitchen and is definitely worth the investment.

Fashion Plate

This dessert is rich and filling and works best at the end of a light meal. We find it's the perfect finish to a soup and salad combo like Roasted Vegetable Soup with Harissa (page 141) and Lentil Salad with Dried Cranberries and Pistachios (page 85).

Hazelnut Biscotti

Whether you dunk it in an espresso or a glass of Muscato, this easy but impressive cookie ends any meal on a high note.

Makes 40 biscotti

Hands-on time
25 minutes

Start to finish
1 hour 25 minutes

Make Ahead

Biscotti can be made up to 2 days ahead and kept in an airtight container at room temperature.

- **Preheat to 350°F (180°C)**
- **2 baking sheets, lined with parchment paper**

2¾ cups	all-purpose flour	675 mL
1½ cups	granulated sugar	375 mL
½ cup	unsalted butter, cut into small pieces	125 mL
1½ tsp	baking powder	7 mL
¾ tsp	salt	3 mL
2	eggs	2
¼ cup	brandy	60 mL
½ tsp	almond extract	2 mL
1⅔ cups	hazelnuts, toasted, skinned and coarsely chopped (see The Dish, below)	400 mL

1. In a bowl, using an electric mixer, combine flour, sugar, butter, baking powder and salt and mix until coarse crumbs form.

2. In a small bowl, whisk together eggs, brandy and almond extract. Add to flour mixture. Add hazelnuts and continue to mix on low speed until dough is moist. Divide dough into thirds and shape into three logs, each 12 by 2 inches (30 by 5 cm), and place on prepared baking sheet.

3. Bake in preheated oven for 30 minutes until firm. Let logs cool on pan on a wire rack. Transfer cookie logs to a cutting board and cut crosswise into ¾-inch (2 cm) slices. Reduce temperature to 300°F (150°C). Place biscotti back on baking sheets and bake for 10 minutes. Turn biscotti over and bake for 15 minutes more, until lightly browned.

THE DISH **Toasted Skinned Hazelnuts.** Hazelnuts have a unique flavor that lends itself perfectly to desserts. But they typically come with a dark bitter skin that needs to be removed, so they do need to be toasted and skinned to be appreciated. To do this, roast on a baking sheet in a 400°F (200°C) oven for 7 to 10 minutes or until lightly toasted. Place in a clean kitchen towel, cover and let steam inside the towel for a few minutes, then rub with the towel to remove the skins. Of course, if you can find them already toasted and skinned, all the better.

Dark Chocolate Hazelnut Biscotti with Mexican Coffee

This kick-ass coffee is worth making whether or not you like to dunk the cookie in it. The choice is yours. But seriously, we love the combination of the dark chocolate–drizzled biscotti and the Kahlúa and Grand Marnier scented coffee.

Makes 40 cookies
and 6 cups of coffee

Hands-on time
25 minutes

Start to finish
1 hour 25 minutes

- **Cooling rack set over parchment paper**

1	recipe Hazelnut Biscotti (page 336)	1
8 oz	bittersweet (dark) chocolate, melted	250 g
½ cup	heavy or whipping (35%) cream	125 mL
2 tbsp	confectioner's (icing) sugar	30 mL
½ tsp	ground cinnamon (approx.)	2 mL
6 oz	coffee liqueur (such as Kahlúa)	175 mL
3 oz	cognac	90 mL
3 oz	Grand Marnier	90 mL
6 cups	freshly brewed strong coffee	1.5 L

1. Place biscotti on prepared cooling rack or a large baking sheet. Drizzle melted chocolate decoratively over cookies. Let cookies set for at least 30 minutes to allow chocolate to harden.

2. In a chilled bowl, using an electric mixer whip cream on low speed for about 2 minutes or until slightly thickened. Add confectioner's sugar and cinnamon and whip to fluffy peaks, about 2 minutes. Keep chilled until ready to serve, for up to 4 hours.

3. Warm 6 coffee mugs or cups. Pour 1 oz (30 mL) of coffee liqueur and ½ oz (15 mL) each of cognac and Grand Marnier in the bottom of each. Pour in a serving of coffee. Top off the mug with a generous swirl of the cinnamon whipped cream and garnish with another sprinkle of cinnamon. Serve with biscotti on the side. Extra biscotti can be enjoyed another time.

THE DISH — **A Well-Stocked Liquor Cabinet.** For obvious reasons.

Chocolate Mousse

Luscious, decadent and done in a flash — we're already in love, and we haven't even got to the chocolate part yet. Our version of chocolate mousse is as simple as it gets. All we do is melt a generous amount of good-quality chocolate with a splash of coffee and fold it into a billowing cloud of whipped cream. How easy is that?

Serves 6 to 8

Hands-on time
20 minutes

Start to finish
20 minutes

Tip
A higher percentage of cocoa makes for a more intense and less sweet chocolate flavor.

Make Ahead
Chocolate Mousse can be made 1 day ahead and kept covered and refrigerated.

- **Large pastry bag and tip, optional**

8 oz	semisweet chocolate, chopped	250 g
4 oz	bittersweet (dark) chocolate, chopped (see Tip, left)	125 g
¼ cup	strong brewed coffee	60 mL
1 tsp	vanilla extract	5 mL
Pinch	salt	Pinch
3 cups	heavy or whipping (35%) cream	750 mL

1. In a heatproof bowl set over a saucepan of simmering water, combine semisweet and bittersweet chocolates and coffee. Stir until melted and smooth. Remove bowl from simmering water and whisk in vanilla and salt. Set aside and let cool to room temperature.

2. In a chilled bowl, using an electric mixer, whip cream until soft peaks form. Fold about one-quarter of the whipped cream into the melted chocolate to lighten. Add chocolate mixture to remaining whipped cream and fold gently to combine. Transfer mousse to pastry bag and pipe or simply spoon into chilled serving cups or bowls.

THE DISH **Stainless Steel Mixing Bowls.** When a double boiler is not in your kitchen cabinet, a stainless steel bowl comes to the rescue and does double duty as a mixing bowl and an efficient heatproof container to set on a pan of simmering water.

Fashion Plate

Begin this French-inspired meal with Winter Salad with Orange Vinaigrette (page 98), Roasted Rack of Lamb (page 200), Roasted Butternut Squash with Goat Cheese and Pecans (page 316) and follow with this decadent chocolaty dessert.

Chocolate Mousse–Filled Profiteroles

Pâte à choux (pronounced paht ah shoo) is not only fun to say, but also fun to make. Really, all it adds up to is a cream puff. But don't you feel sexier saying pâte à choux? We like to throw around French terms that no one else understands whenever we can. It makes us feel superior. Trust us, it'll work for you too. Here, we're using it to contain our delectable and delicious Chocolate Mousse, and just to gild the lily, we drizzle a smidgeon of our divine hot chocolate sauce on top. If there's a more seductive dessert out there, let us know.

Serves 6

Hands on
45 minutes

Start to finish
1 hour 10 minutes

Make Ahead

The profiteroles can be made up to 1 hour before serving.

- Preheat oven to 425°F (220°C)
- Food processor
- Pastry bag
- Large baking sheet, lined with parchment paper

6 tbsp	unsalted butter, cut into pieces	90 mL
1 tbsp	granulated sugar	15 mL
¼ tsp	salt	1 mL
¾ cup	all-purpose flour	175 mL
4	eggs	4

Chocolate Sauce

4 oz	semisweet chocolate, finely chopped	125 g
2 oz	bittersweet (dark) chocolate, finely chopped	60 g
½ cup	heavy or whipping (35%) cream	125 mL
2 tbsp	light (white) corn syrup	30 mL
1 tsp	vanilla extract	5 mL
1	recipe Chocolate Mousse (page 338)	1

1. In a heavy saucepan over high heat, bring butter, ¾ cup (175 mL) water, sugar and salt to a boil, stirring, until butter is melted. Reduce heat to medium. Add flour all at once, stirring. Cook, beating with a wooden spoon, for about 1 minute or until mixture pulls away from side of pan, forming a ball. Let cool for 2 to 3 minutes. Transfer mixture to a food processor. Add eggs through feed tube, one at a time, pulsing to combine well after each addition.

2. Transfer mixture to pastry bag and pipe 18 mounds (about 1¼ inches/3 cm in diameter), about 1 inch (2.5 cm) apart on prepared baking sheet.

3. Bake profiteroles in preheated oven for 10 minutes. Reduce heat to 350°F (180°C) and continue to bake for 15 minutes more or until puffed and golden brown and they sound hollow when tapped. Transfer to a wire rack to cool completely.

4. *Chocolate Sauce:* In a medium heatproof bowl, combine semisweet and bittersweet chocolates. In a small saucepan, combine cream and corn syrup and bring to a simmer over medium heat. Pour liquid over chocolate and let stand for 3 to 4 minutes or until chocolate has melted. Add vanilla and whisk until smooth.

5. *To serve:* Cut profiteroles in half horizontally, then pipe or spoon chocolate mousse into bottom half of each profiterole. Place tops on top of mousse. Put 3 profiteroles on each plate and drizzle generously with warm chocolate sauce.

THE DISH   **A Good Wooden Spoon.** Every cook needs a heavy-duty wooden spoon dedicated solely to kitchen tasks. Look for spoons made of olive wood. They have good heft and last forever.

Fashion Plate

A pretty dessert like this deserves an equally attractive entrée. That's why we'd pair this confection with Roasted Beet Salad on Endive Spears (page 90) and Sautéed Chicken with Lemon Beurre Blanc and Liquid Rubies (page 228).

Tres Leches Cake

Tres Leches Cake is not only easy but delicious and slightly exotic all at the same time, and frankly, isn't that how we'd all like to be thought of? Tres leches means "three milks" in Spanish, strange name for a cake, we know, but it comes from the mixture of condensed and evaporated milk and half-and-half cream that is soaked into a layer of eggy yellow cake. The result is a moist, sweet cake that in South America is often served on special occasions. It's so easy, though, that you can serve it anytime.

Serves 12

Hands-on time
30 minutes

Refrigeration time
Overnight

Start to finish
1 day

- **Preheat oven to 350°F (180°C)**
- **13- by 9-inch (33 by 23 cm) metal baking pan, greased**

1½ cups	all-purpose flour	375 mL
1 tsp	baking powder	5 mL
½ tsp	salt	2 mL
½ cup	unsalted butter, at room temperature	125 mL
1¾ cups	granulated sugar, divided	425 mL
5	large eggs	5
2 tsp	vanilla extract, divided	10 mL
1 cup	half-and-half (10%) cream	250 mL
1	can (14 oz or 300 mL) sweetened condensed milk	1
1	can (12 oz/370 mL) evaporated milk	1
2 cups	heavy or whipping (35%) cream	500 mL

1. In a medium bowl, whisk together flour, baking powder and salt. Set aside.

2. In a stand mixer or using an electric mixer on medium speed, cream together butter and 1 cup (250 mL) of the sugar until fluffy. Beat in eggs, one at a time, and 1 tsp (5 mL) of the vanilla until well blended. Gradually beat in flour mixture on low speed until blended.

3. Pour batter into prepared pan. Bake in preheated oven for 20 to 30 minutes or until a toothpick inserted into the center comes out clean.

4. Immediately pierce cake all over with a fork or skewer and let cool in pan on a wire rack for 30 minutes.

5. In a large bowl, combine half-and-half cream, condensed milk and evaporated milk. Pour over top of cooled cake. Refrigerate overnight.

6. In a chilled bowl, combine whipping cream and remaining sugar and vanilla. Using an electric mixer, beat on medium speed until stiff peaks form. Spread topping over cake and refrigerate until ready to serve, for no more than 4 hours.

THE DISH **Time.** We're all about quick and easy, but for this cake you have to plan ahead. It needs an overnight stay in the fridge to be all it can be. Otherwise, the milk mixture won't have the time to thoroughly soak into the cake and you'll have excess liquid sitting on the bottom of your cake pan and a cake that's not as moist as it should be.

Fashion Plate

A rich dessert like Tres Leches Cake begs for a lighter main course offering such as Tequila-Marinated Chicken Breasts with Mango Citrus Salsa (page 234).

Caribbean Coconut Rum Cake with White Chocolate Whipped Cream and Tropical Fruit

Not that we think we're clever or anything — OK, we think we're a little clever, although we may stand alone on that point — but this turn on the already delicious Tres Leches Cake is pretty cool. Here, we've used coconut milk and rum to give the cake a decidedly Caribbean flavor and added white chocolate and toasted coconut to the topping for an extra flourish. The result is a dreamy dessert. We like to serve it with fresh papaya, mango and pineapple just to drive the island theme home.

Serves 12

Hands-on time
45 minutes

Refrigeration time
Overnight

Start to finish
1 day

Tip

Unsweetened coconut milk often separates in the can into a thick, creamy layer and thin, more watery layer. This is natural and not a problem. Sometimes the top creamy layer will actually harden a bit and can be difficult to whisk smoothly with the other milks. For this reason, we strain this milk mixture before pouring it over the top of the cooled cake.

- **Preheat oven to 350°F (180°C)**
- **13- by 9-inch (33 by 23 cm) metal baking pan, greased**

1 cup	sweetened flaked coconut	250 mL
1½ cups	all-purpose flour	375 mL
1 tsp	baking powder	5 mL
½ tsp	salt	2 mL
½ cup	unsalted butter, at room temperature	125 mL
1⅓ cups	granulated sugar, divided	325 mL
5	large eggs	5
2 tsp	vanilla extract, divided	10 mL
½ cup	half-and-half (10%) cream	125 mL
1	can (14 oz or 300 mL) sweetened condensed milk	1
1	can (14 oz/400 mL) unsweetened coconut milk (see Tip, left)	1
⅓ cup	dark rum	75 mL
4 oz	white chocolate, chopped	125 g
½ cup	sweetened cream of coconut (such as Coco Lopez)	125 mL
2 cups	heavy or whipping (35%) cream	500 mL
2 cups	cubes (½ inch/1 cm) pineapple	500 mL
1 cup	cubes (½ inch/1 cm) papaya (about 1 large)	250 mL
1 cup	cubes (½ inch/1 cm) mango (about 1 large)	250 mL

1. Spread coconut in a shallow baking pan and toast in preheated oven, stirring occasionally and watching carefully to avoid burning, until golden, 10 to 12 minutes. Transfer to a bowl and let cool.

2. In a medium bowl, whisk together flour, baking powder and salt. Set aside

3. In a stand mixer on medium speed, cream together butter and 1 cup (250 mL) of the sugar until fluffy. Beat in eggs, one at a time, and 1 tsp (5 mL) of the vanilla until well blended. Gradually beat in flour mixture on low speed until well blended.

4. Pour batter into prepared pan. Bake in preheated oven for 20 to 30 minutes or until tester inserted into center comes out clean.

5. Immediately pierce cake all over with a fork or skewer. Let cool for 30 minutes. In a bowl, combine half-and-half cream, condensed milk, coconut milk and rum. Strain though a fine-mesh sieve and pour over top of cooled cake. Refrigerate overnight.

6. Meanwhile, in a heatproof bowl set over a saucepan of simmering water, melt white chocolate. Whisk in cream of coconut until smooth. Set aside and let cool completely.

7. In a chilled bowl, combine whipping cream and remaining sugar and vanilla. Using an electric mixer on medium speed, beat until stiff peaks form. Fold whipped cream into cooled white chocolate mixture. Spread white chocolate whipped cream over top of cake. Sprinkle top with toasted coconut. Refrigerate for at least 1 hour or for up to 4 hours. Serve with pineapple, papaya and mango.

THE DISH **Dark Rum.** We like our rum like we like our men: dark and intoxicating. We find the dark rums have a fuller body and richer flavor, and always prefer to use a dark rum in desserts.

Fashion Plate

We can't think of anything we'd rather pair up with this summery dessert than Lime and Tequila–Marinated Flank Steak with Sweet-and-Sour Chipotle Sauce (page 198) and Cheese, Chile and Cilantro Corn Spoonbread (page 303).

White Chocolate Soup with Chilled Berries

This dessert should be served with some kind of warning to protect the innocent. A rich custard soup flavored with vanilla and white chocolate, this dish has frequently been referred to as "sex on a spoon."

Now that we have your attention, you really must make this dessert when berries (preferably organic) are fresh. Not only are they beautiful, but they offer a bit of acid that balances the richness of this mouth-watering soup. And remember, serving desserts like this could give you a reputation — as a kitchen goddess.

Serves 10

Hands-on time
30 minutes

Start to finish
1 hour

Variation

Drizzle a little Grand Marnier over the chilled berries after ladling in the soup. The warm orange of the liqueur creates a harmonious tingle as you swallow. Serve decaf coffee with maybe a little Grand Marnier in that as well and linger at the table enjoying your guests. You deserve it, you seductress, you.

Make Ahead

The soup will keep, covered and refrigerated, for up to 3 days. Reheat gently in a metal or heat-resistant bowl over simmering water, stirring constantly. Be careful not to let it get too hot or the eggs will scramble.

White Chocolate Soup

2 cups	whole milk	500 mL
2 cups	heavy or whipping (35%) cream, divided	500 mL
¾ cup	granulated sugar	175 mL
Pinch	salt	Pinch
6	large egg yolks	6
8 oz	white chocolate, chopped	250 g
1 tsp	vanilla extract	5 mL

Chilled Berries

2 cups	blueberries, chilled	500 mL
2 cups	raspberries, chilled	500 mL
2 cups	blackberries, chilled	500 mL
4 cups	strawberries, hulled and halved if large, chilled	1 L
	Fresh mint leaves	

1. *White Chocolate Soup:* In a large saucepan, heat milk and 1 cup (250 mL) of the cream over medium heat until steaming.

2. In a large bowl, whisk together sugar, salt and egg yolks. Gradually whisk hot milk mixture into egg mixture. Return mixture to saucepan and cook over medium heat, stirring constantly with a wooden spoon or a silicone spatula, for about 4 minutes or until beginning to thicken slightly and look velvety. Remove from heat. Immediately add chocolate, vanilla and remaining cream and stir until melted.

3. Divide berries equally among shallow serving bowls. Pour about ½ cup (125 mL) of warm soup over berries. Garnish with mint leaves.

White Chocolate Terrine with Dark Chocolate Biscotti

White chocolate soup is just a heartbeat away from becoming white chocolate ice cream in this molded and frozen confection. When sliced, the luscious ice cream layered with crunchy chocolate biscotti looks as good as it tastes. As a bonus, this dish can sit in your freezer for weeks, just waiting to be sliced and enjoyed. With a dessert like this in your freezer, you can entertain at a moment's notice and leap tall buildings in a single bound.

Serves 8

Hands-on time
30 minutes

Freezing time
3 hours

Start to finish
3 hours 30 minutes

Tip

This is one of those desserts that screams to be garnished creatively. Add the coulis to a squeeze bottle with a narrow tip. Squeeze some out on a plate to check that the hole is the right size. You might need to cut the tip a bit larger with scissors. Squeeze the coulis onto the plates with a creative flourish and carefully lay the terrine down on top.

Make Ahead

Can be assembled and kept, frozen, for up to 2 weeks.

- **Ice cream maker**
- **9- by 5-inch (23 by 12.5 cm) loaf pan, lined with plastic wrap, leaving a wide overhang**
- **Frozen serving plate**

1	recipe White Chocolate Soup (page 346), chilled	1
5	store-bought dark chocolate biscotti, crumbled	5
1	recipe Raspberry Coulis (page 349) Fresh raspberries for garnish, optional	1

1. Make ice cream from white chocolate soup base following the manufacturer's directions on your ice cream maker.

2. Spread one-third of the ice cream in bottom of prepared pan. Sprinkle half of the biscotti over top. Spread another layer of ice cream over biscotti and top with remaining biscotti, followed by a layer of ice cream. You may have some ice cream left over, depending on how much air your machine added during the churn (go ahead and gobble it up. No one will know). Smooth top and fold overhanging plastic wrap over to cover ice cream. Freeze for at least 3 hours or until firm.

3. Moments before serving, unwrap ice cream terrine and remove from mold by pulling on the sides of plastic. Place terrine on a frozen plate and cut into 1-inch (2.5 cm) thick slices. Garnish each dessert plate with a drizzle of raspberry coulis and top with a slice of terrine. Scatter over raspberries, if using, and serve immediately.

THE DISH **White Chocolate.** Try to find a good imported white chocolate such as Lindt, Callebaut or Valrhona. They melt smoothly on the tongue with no waxy taste and have a superior flavor.

Raspberry Coulis

Pronounced koo-lee, this sprightly purée of raspberry will brighten almost any dessert plate. We especially love it paired with anything chocolate.

Makes about 1 cup (250 mL)

Hands-on time
5 minutes

Start to finish
5 minutes

Make Ahead

The coulis can be made up to 2 days ahead and kept covered and refrigerated.

• **Food processor**

1	package (12 oz/375 g) frozen raspberries in syrup, thawed	1
1 tbsp	freshly squeezed lemon juice	15 mL

1. In a food processor, purée raspberries with syrup for 30 seconds or until puréed smooth.

2. Strain sauce through a fine-mesh sieve, pressing on berries and discarding seeds. Stir in lemon juice.

3. Pour coulis and into a squeeze bottle with a narrow tip for easy garnishing or drizzle over dish as directed in the recipe.

Vanilla Gelato with Summer Berries and Limoncello

Gelato is one of the best things among many (Prada, Armani, Gucci) to come from Italy. It contains less fat than most premium ice creams, but because it also has less air pumped into it, it is at once light on the tongue but still dense and rich. The vanilla bean provides powerful vanilla flavor, and those little flecks of vanilla seeds guarantee that what you see is what you get. Even if you've never been to Tuscany, we'd like to help you taste a little bit of Italia in your own back yard.

Makes 1 quart (1 L) gelato

Hands-on time
30 minutes

Chilling time
overnight

Start to finish
24 hours

Tip

Because of its alcohol content, limoncello will not freeze solid but will be a little syrupy when you pour it.

Make Ahead

The gelato will be best if served a few hours after churning. After a night in the freezer, it will become hard to scoop. Let stand on the counter for a few minutes to soften up.

- **Ice cream maker**

2 cups	milk	500 mL
1	vanilla bean, split lengthwise	1
Pinch	salt	Pinch
1 cup	granulated sugar	250 mL
8	egg yolks	8
2 cups	half-and-half (10%) cream	500 mL
1 cup	blueberries	250 mL
1 cup	sliced strawberries	250 mL
1 cup	blackberries	250 mL
6 oz	limoncello liqueur, frozen for at least 4 hours (see Tip, left)	175 mL

1. In a large saucepan, combine milk, vanilla bean and salt and heat over medium-high heat until steaming. Remove pan from heat, cover and let stand for about 15 minutes to infuse flavor.

2. Remove bean from milk and scrape seeds from pod with back of a knife. Scrape seeds back into milk and stir to combine. Discard pod.

3. In a large bowl, whisk together sugar and egg yolks. Gradually whisk hot milk mixture into yolks. Return mixture to saucepan and cook over medium heat, stirring, for about 4 minutes or until custard thickens and coats back of a spoon. Remove pan from heat and quickly stir in cream to cool it down. Place plastic wrap directly on the surface. Refrigerate the mixture overnight.

4. Freeze in an ice cream maker according to manufacturer's directions. Transfer gelato to a chilled container and freeze for 2 hours or until set and can be scooped.

5. In a large bowl, combine blueberries, strawberries and blackberries. Scoop gelato into chilled bowls and top each serving with spoonfuls of fruit and 1 oz (30 mL) of limoncello.

DOUBLE DISH

Limoncello. Did we just say that gelato was one of the best things to come from Italy? Well, let's add limoncello to that list as well. It's an intensely lemon-flavored liquor often served at the end of a meal. But this versatile lemon bomb is a hip addition to many desserts as well. It combines well with berries or stone fruits of any kind, but don't forget its simplest function — served in a little shot glass as a digestif after the meal.

Ice Cream Maker. With models available for as little as $50, you too can live the dream of eating better-tasting ice cream than you can buy. We also like the fact that you can make your ice cream as fat or as lean as you choose. But best of all, you'll have ice cream with no emulsifiers, guar gum thickeners and corn syrup sweeteners. It tastes cleaner and fresher. Dare we say you will never buy ice cream again?

Fashion Plate

Serve this summery dessert with Smoked Salmon on Toast Points (page 18) and Gazpacho (page 104).

Limoncello Shortcakes with Berries and Vanilla Gelato

We're unabashed lemon lovers. We think everything tastes better with limoncello, so we decided to use it two ways in this recipe: as an ingredient in the shortcakes and a delectable drizzle on top of the fruit. Grandma's shortcakes were good, but these light and lemony rounds will be sure to delight the grownup kid in you.

Serves 6

Hands-on time
1 hour

Chilling time
2 hours

Start to finish
24 hours

Make Ahead

The gelato will be best if served a few hours after churning. After a night in the freezer, it will become hard to scoop. Let stand on the counter for a few minutes to soften up. The shortcakes can be made 4 hours in advance and kept, covered, at room temperature. The berries can be prepared up to 4 hours ahead and kept, covered, in the refrigerator.

- **Preheat oven to 350°F (180°C)**
- **3-inch (7.5 cm) round cutter**
- **Baking sheet, lined with parchment paper**

1	recipe Vanilla Gelato (page 350)	1
2 cups	all-purpose flour (see Tip, page 368)	500 mL
²⁄₃ cup	granulated sugar, divided	150 mL
1 tbsp	baking powder	15 mL
½ tsp	salt	2 mL
½ cup	unsalted butter, at room temperature	125 mL
	Grated zest of 1 lemon	
½ cup	heavy or whipping (35%) cream (approx.)	125 mL
¼ cup	limoncello liqueur (approx.), frozen for at least 4 hours	60 mL
2 tbsp	coarse sugar, optional	30 mL
3 cups	sliced strawberries	750 mL
2½ cups	blackberries or blueberries	625 mL

1. Make gelato in previous recipe and freeze for at least 2 hours to firm up.

2. In a large bowl, whisk together flour, ⅓ cup (75 mL) of the granulated sugar, baking powder and salt. Add butter and lemon zest and, with your fingers, crumble butter into flour until combined. Add cream and limoncello and stir just until combined.

3. Turn dough out onto a floured surface and pat or roll out until 1 inch (2.5 cm) thick. Cut out 6 biscuits with round cutter, rerolling scraps as necessary. Place rounds on prepared baking sheet, about 2 inches (5 cm) apart. Brush rounds with additional cream and sprinkle with coarse sugar, if desired.

4. Bake in preheated oven for 25 minutes or until golden. Let cool on pan on a wire rack.

5. Meanwhile, in a large bowl, combine strawberries, blackberries and remaining ⅓ cup (75 mL) of the sugar and toss to coat. Refrigerate until serving.

6. Split shortbreads and fill with a scoop of gelato. Place mixed berries on top. Drizzle a little of the limoncello over top of berries, if desired.

DOUBLE DISH

Round Cutter. A 3-inch (7.5 cm) round metal cutter will make short work of these little cakes. If you really want to make them especially pretty, purchase a cutter with a fluted edge. The shortcakes will look a little more "dressed up," and you can use it to cut out cookies, biscuits and pastry as well.

Parchment Paper. We really can't bake without it. Not only does it keep the cleanup to a minimum, but it actually helps prevent sticking and then ripping and tearing as the food is removed.

Fashion Plate

For a light dinner, serve Potato Salad à la Niçoise (page 101) and Tuscan Bean and Barley Soup with Crispy Pancetta (page 135) along with this dessert.

Baked Pears with Mascarpone Cream

We just love pears. Maybe it's because we relate to the way they're shaped. Or maybe it's because they're delicious eaten out of hand and are even more so when baked. In this recipe, we let the oven do all the work. The heat concentrates the sugar and tenderizes the sometimes tough specimens to an al dente–like texture. Add rich and creamy mascarpone cheese, and you have a classic yet easy dessert on your hands. We think that's the best kind!

Serves 6

Hands-on time
15 minutes

Start to finish
50 minutes

Tip

Not only are pears available year-round, but they ripen after being picked. As long as you buy them a few days before you need to use them, they will be ready when you are. For a lark, try to locate the most beautiful pears in the bin, take them home and line them up on your kitchen counter to ripen for a few days. That way, they can serve as your own private art installation before they become dessert.

Make Ahead

The pears can be roasted 1 day in advance and kept, covered and refrigerated, along with the mascarpone cream. Bring the pears and cream to room temperature before serving.

- **Preheat oven to 375°F (190°C)**
- **Melon baller**
- **8-cup (2 L) baking dish, buttered**

3	large ripe Bartlett or Anjou pears	3
2 tbsp	unsalted butter	30 mL
⅓ cup	packed brown sugar	75 mL
3 tbsp	freshly squeezed lemon juice	45 mL
Pinch	salt	Pinch
⅔ cup	mascarpone cheese	150 mL
¼ tsp	vanilla extract	1 mL
	Confectioner's (icing) sugar	

1. Peel pears and cut in half lengthwise. Scoop out cores with a melon baller, leaving stems intact. Arrange pears in prepared dish, cut side up, in one layer. Divide butter over top. Sprinkle brown sugar over pears. Drizzle lemon juice and salt over all.

2. Bake pears in preheated oven for about 20 minutes or until they begin to soften. Turn pears over and bake for 15 minutes more or until tip of a knife easily penetrates pear. Transfer pears to a plate, reserving juices, and cover to keep warm.

3. In a medium bowl, combine mascarpone cheese and pear cooking juices. Mix well and taste. Add more brown sugar or lemon juice to taste, if necessary.

4. Arrange warm pears on serving plates with a dollop of mascarpone cream. Using a small sieve, sift confectioner's (icing) sugar over pears.

EVERYDAY

Pear Jalousie with Marsala Mascarpone Cream

You will be amazed at the simplicity and taste of this fresh fruit tart. Instead of roasting pears on their own, as we did in Baked Pears with Mascarpone Cream, here we are framing the pears in delicious apricot and buttery puff pastry. Baking the pears concentrates their flavor and the easy-as-pie filling comes straight from a jar of apricot preserves. Don't resist the urge to cut and serve this magnificent tart at the table, the better to bask in the glow of your admiring tablemates.

Serves 8

Hands-on time
35 minutes

Start to finish
1 hour

Tip

A jalousie is a tart with slashes cut into the top pastry so the filling can be seen. This type of tart gets its name from the jalousie windows with the panes of glass that roll open and closed in warmer climes.

Make Ahead

The tart can be assembled and kept, covered and refrigerated, for up to 4 hours. It can be baked and kept at room temperature for up to 8 hours. The cream can be made up to 1 day ahead and kept covered and refrigerated.

- **Preheat oven to 425°F (220°C)**
- **Melon baller**
- **2 baking sheets, lined with parchment paper**

2	Bartlett or Anjou pears	2
1/4 cup	granulated sugar, divided	60 mL
Pinch	salt	Pinch
1	package (18 oz/540 g) frozen puff pastry (see Tip, page 58)	1
1/2 cup	apricot preserves or jam	125 mL
1 tbsp	milk	15 mL
2/3 cup	mascarpone cheese	150 mL
2 tbsp	packed brown sugar	30 mL
2 tbsp	Marsala wine	30 mL
1/4 tsp	vanilla extract	1 mL
	Confectioner's (icing) sugar, optional	

1. Peel pears and cut in half lengthwise. Scoop out cores with a melon baller and trim out stems. Slice lengthwise into thin slices, about 1/8 inch (3 mm). Arrange on prepared baking sheet in one layer. Sprinkle 3 tbsp (45 mL) of the sugar over top along with salt. Bake pears in preheated oven for about 20 minutes or until tender and slightly dried out. Let cool.

2. Roll out one half of the pastry to a 12- by 9-inch (30 by 23 cm) rectangle. Transfer pastry to second prepared baking sheet. Spread preserves over pastry leaving a 1-inch (2.5 cm) border around edges. Arrange baked pears on top of preserves leaving an edge to seal. Refrigerate while rolling out top.

3. Roll out remaining puff pastry to a 14- by 11-inch (35 by 28 cm) rectangle. Fold one long side in so outside edge is in center of pastry. With a sharp knife make 2-inch (5 cm) cuts on folded side, about 2 inches (5 cm) apart. Open pastry out and do same thing to other side. Fold pastry in half so it doesn't tear and transfer to top of tart. Fold top edges under bottom crust and press tines of a fork along edge to seal it.

4. Brush top of pastry with milk. Sprinkle remaining sugar over top. Bake in lower third of preheated oven for 25 minutes or until tart is browned on top and bottom is crispy. Let cool for at least 5 minutes.

5. In a small bowl, combine mascarpone, brown sugar, Marsala and vanilla.

6. Serve warm tart with a dollop of mascarpone cream. Using a small sieve, sift confectioner's sugar over pears as garnish, if desired.

THE DISH **Mascarpone.** Mascarpone is cream cheese's sexy, rich Italian cousin. This Italian triple crème cheese could make a dessert out of an old shoe, not that we recommend you try it. But, really, mascarpone makes anything more delicious, especially pears. For even more deliciousness, we've directed you to add the pear's cooking juices to the mascarpone in the previous recipe. It really is just too good to describe.

Fashion Plate

Begin the meal with Steak with Red Wine Sauce and Mushrooms (page 183) paired with Salt-Roasted New Potatoes with Rosemary Butter (page 313) and Gingered Carrot Purée (page 289). Gild the lily with Pear Jalousie with Marsala Mascarpone Cream.

Fudgy Brownie Cake

It's safe to say that almost everyone likes brownies. You can put just about anything into them and they still taste great. This is a theory we spent many of our formative years studying. And the theory continues to hold true in this combination of fudgy chocolate and crispy nuts drizzled with . . . you guessed it, even more chocolate.

Makes 9 large squares

Hands-on time
30 minutes

Start to finish
1 hour 15 minutes

Tips

Did you know that you can toast nuts in the microwave? Just spread them out on a microwave-safe plate and microwave on High for 30 seconds. Give them a little stir and microwave again for 30 seconds. Repeat one or two more times. When they're fragrant, they're done.

If you want to make a statement, serve brownie squares on a pool of Crème Anglaise (page 359) and garnish with raspberries. Or just serve as is with ice cream.

Make Ahead

The brownie cake can be made 1 day in advance and kept, covered, at room temperature.

- **Preheat oven to 350°F (180°C)**
- **8-inch (20 cm) square metal baking pan, greased then lined with parchment paper, paper greased and floured**

3 oz	unsweetened chocolate, chopped	90 g
5 oz	bittersweet (dark) chocolate, chopped	150 g
1/2 cup	unsalted butter, at room temperature	125 mL
1 cup plus 2 tbsp	granulated sugar	280 mL
3	large eggs	3
1 tsp	vanilla extract	5 mL
1 cup	all-purpose flour (see Tip, page 368)	250 mL
1/2 tsp	salt	2 mL
1/2 cup	toasted chopped walnuts	125 mL
3 oz	white chocolate, chopped	90 g

1. In a medium heatproof bowl set over a saucepan of simmering water, melt unsweetened and bittersweet chocolates. Or in a microwave-safe bowl, microwave on Medium (50%). Let cool.

2. In a bowl, using an electric mixer, cream together butter and sugar on medium speed for about 2 minutes or until light and fluffy. Beat in eggs, one at a time, beating well after each egg. Beat in vanilla and cooled melted chocolate until smooth. Scrape down bowl. On low speed, beat in flour, salt and walnuts just until combined.

3. Spread batter into prepared pan. Bake for 35 to 40 minutes or until firm. Let brownies cool in pan on a wire rack.

4. In a medium heatproof bowl set over a saucepan of simmering water, melt white chocolate. (Or microwave in a microwave-safe bowl on Medium (50%).) Drizzle chocolate over top of brownie cake. Refrigerate for about 20 minutes for chocolate to set. Cut into squares.

Crème Anglaise

This custard sauce can be poured over a brownie, drizzled over a slice of apple pie or just slurped out of the bowl with a big spoon. Any leftovers will be dispatched tout de suite.

Makes about 2 cups (500 mL)

Hands-on time
30 minutes

Hands on time
15 minutes

¾ cup	milk	175 mL
¾ cup	heavy or whipping (35%) cream	175 mL
1	vanilla bean, split lengthwise	1
⅓ cup	granulated sugar	75 mL
Pinch	salt	Pinch
5	large egg yolks	5
	Ice	

1. In a large saucepan, combine milk, cream, vanilla bean and sugar. Heat over medium heat until steaming. Turn off heat, cover saucepan and let stand for 15 minutes to infuse flavor of vanilla bean.

2. Remove bean from liquid and scrape seeds from pod with back of a knife. Scrape beans from knife into pan, return pod and stir to combine.

3. Place a heatproof bowl in a larger bowl filled with ice. Set aside. In another large heatproof bowl, whisk egg yolks until blended. Gradually pour in hot milk mixture in a steady stream, whisking constantly. Return to pan and return to medium heat. Cook, stirring constantly with a wooden spoon, for about 4 minutes or until mixture begins to thicken slightly and look velvety. Cook, stirring, for 1 minute more. Remove from heat and pour through a medium strainer into prepared bowl set over ice to speed cooling. Stir custard until cool. Remove pod and discard. Cover and refrigerate until ready to serve.

Tip

To be clear, crème Anglaise is very easy to prepare, but you do have to watch so that it doesn't curdle. It demands your total attention for the 5 minutes that you are actually cooking it. We like to stir it constantly in a figure 8, scraping the bottom of the pan. You will know when the custard is beginning to thicken by the slippery feel of the spoon scraping the bottom of the pan. Then you will notice that the mixture has become velvety. At that point, cook for another minute, remove from the heat, strain and let cool. Easy.

Make Ahead

The custard keeps for up to 3 days, covered and refrigerated.

Fudgy Chocolate Babycakes with Peanut Buttercream

Cupcakes are just so haute and these audacious fudgy sweets are sure to beguile even the strictest dieters. Just wait until you bite into one of these chocolate bombs dressed in peanut buttercream icing and itty-bitty chocolate chips. These tantalizing babycakes will become your go-to dish when you need a pick-em-up-and-go dessert. As far as we're concerned, chocolate is the new black.

<table>
<tr><td>Makes 8 to 10 babycakes</td></tr>
<tr><td>Hands-on time
50 minutes</td></tr>
<tr><td>Start to finish
1 hour 15 minutes</td></tr>
</table>

Tip

Don't let these divine cupcakes become a fashion victim! The ubiquitous yellow, pink, green and blue paper muffin cups from the grocery store make even the most fabulous cupcakes look common and trite. Hunt down plain white paper or the beautiful brown and gold paper cups for these cupcakes so that they look as good as they taste.

Make Ahead

The cakes can be made 1 day in advance and kept covered and refrigerated. Bring to room temperature before serving.

- **Preheat oven to 350°F (180°C)**
- **12-cup muffin pan, 8 to 10 cups lined with paper liners**

3 oz	unsweetened chocolate, chopped	90 g
5 oz	bittersweet (dark) chocolate, chopped	150 g
½ cup	unsalted butter, at room temperature	125 mL
1 cup plus 2 tbsp	granulated sugar	280 mL
3	large eggs	3
1 tsp	vanilla extract	5 mL
1 cup	all-purpose flour (see Tip, page 368)	250 mL
½ tsp	salt	2 mL

Peanut Buttercream

½ cup	smooth peanut butter (not old-fashioned or freshly ground)	125 mL
¼ cup	unsalted butter, at room temperature	60 mL
2 tbsp	milk	30 mL
1 tsp	vanilla extract	5 mL
Pinch	salt	Pinch
3 cups	confectioner's (icing) sugar	750 mL
¾ cups	miniature chocolate chips	175 mL

1. In a medium heatproof bowl set over a saucepan of simmering water, melt unsweetened and bittersweet chocolate. (Or microwave in a microwave-safe bowl on Medium.) Let cool.

2. In a large bowl, using an electric mixer, cream together butter and sugar for about 2 minutes or until light and fluffy. Beat in eggs, one at a time, beating well after each egg. Beat in vanilla and cooled melted chocolate until smooth. Scrape down bowl. On low speed, beat in flour and salt until just combined.

3. Using an ice cream scoop, fill 8 to 10 prepared muffin cups with batter. Bake in preheated oven for 30 to 35 minutes or until a tester comes out with moist sticky crumbs clinging to it. Let brownies cool in pan on a wire rack.

4. *Peanut Buttercream:* In a large bowl, using an electric mixer, beat peanut butter, butter, milk, vanilla and salt. Gradually add confectioner's sugar until combined and smooth. If too thick to spread, add 1 tsp (5 mL) or so of water to thin icing.

5. Frost brownies with peanut buttercream and top with a sprinkling of tiny chocolate chips.

THE DISH **Good-Quality Bittersweet Chocolate.**
Try brands such as Callebaut, Ghirardelli, Scharffen Berger or Valrhona. The taste of bittersweet chocolate is denser and not as sweet as semisweet, so the chocolate flavor is more pronounced. If you buy it in a block, be sure to break it down into small pieces so it melts evenly.

Fashion Plate

These luscious cakes get our vote paired with a finger-friendly meal of Wild Mushroom Turnovers (page 58) and Thai Chicken Lettuce Wraps with Two Dipping Sauces (page 74).

Rustic Plum Tart

Plums are a refreshing option when pondering what's for dessert. They become soft and rich with a nice touch of tart when baked in a pastry crust.

Here, we offer you our time-tested, tried and true best pastry recipe ever (page 366) in hopes that you will try it and enjoy making pastry as much as we do. If you follow our advice and make up a few batches to store in your freezer, you'll be able to pull together this rustic but tantalizing tart in a jiffy.

This tart is so pretty, you'll want to take a picture of the juicy purple sweet-tart fruit against the sandy, golden-flecked, tender pastry.

Serves 6 to 8

Hands-on time
30 minutes

Start to finish
1 hour

Variation

If plums don't look good, try making this tart with nectarines.

Make Ahead

The tart can be made up to 8 hours ahead and kept at room temperature. If serving warm, reheat in a 350°F (180°C) oven for about 15 minutes.

- **Preheat oven to 425°F (220°C)**
- **Baking sheet, lined with parchment paper**

1	recipe Flaky Pastry (page 366)	1
1½ lbs	plums (about 6 small or 3 large), each cut into 8 sections	750 g
⅓ cup	granulated sugar (approx.)	75 mL
2 tbsp	all-purpose flour	30 mL
1 tbsp	freshly squeezed lemon juice	15 mL
Pinch	salt	Pinch
Pinch	freshly grated nutmeg	Pinch
1	egg, beaten with 1 tbsp (15 mL) water	1
	Vanilla ice cream	

1. Roll out pastry into a circle about 16 inches (40 cm) in diameter and place on prepared baking sheet. Refrigerate pastry while continuing with the recipe.

2. In a large bowl, toss together plums, sugar, flour, lemon juice, salt and nutmeg. Taste and adjust flavor with more sugar, if necessary.

3. Pour fruit into center of pastry and arrange so fruit spreads into a circle about 8 inches (20 cm) in diameter. Flip an edge of the pastry over top of fruit and continue to pleat pastry over fruit so that about a 4-inch (10 cm) circle of fruit remains in center of tart. Brush pastry with egg wash and sprinkle extra sugar over all. If pastry has become warm, pop tart in refrigerator for about 20 minutes to firm up.

4. Bake on the lower rack of preheated oven for about 35 minutes or until tart is browned on top and crispy on bottom. Let tart cool on pan on a wire rack. Serve warm or at room temperature with vanilla ice cream.

Individual Plum Tartlets with Frangipane and Plum Brandy

The trend to individual desserts has been motoring along for the last 50 years for a very good reason: the hostess doesn't need to leave her guests to cut and plate what can sometimes be a messy dish. For these diminutive tarts, we've paired plums with frangipane, a mixture of almond paste, eggs and sugar, accompanied by little shots of plum brandy on the side. The mix of tastes is fun and sure to end your evening on a high note — pun intended.

Serves 6

Hands-on time
40 minutes

Start to finish
1 hour 5 minutes

Variation

Blend 3 tbsp (45 mL) brown sugar and 1 cup (250 mL) sour cream with 1 tsp (5 mL) vanilla. Top the tartlets with the sweetened sour cream instead of the ice cream.

Make Ahead

The tartlets can be made up to 8 hours ahead and kept at room temperature. Reheat in a 350°F (180°C) oven for about 15 minutes.

- **Preheat oven to 425°F (220°C)**
- **Baking sheet, lined with parchment paper**
- **Food processor**

1	recipe Rustic Plum Tart (page 362), unassembled	1
¾ cup	blanched almonds	175 mL
¼ cup	granulated sugar	60 mL
3 tbsp	unsalted butter, at room temperature	45 mL
2 tsp	all-purpose flour	10 mL
1	large egg	1
½ tsp	almond extract	2 mL
Pinch	salt	Pinch
1	egg, beaten	1
	Granulated sugar	
	Vanilla ice cream	
	Plum brandy	

1. Roll out pastry into a rectangle, about 15 by 10 inches (38 by 25 cm). Cut pastry into 6 squares and arrange on prepared baking sheet, at least 3 inches (7.5 cm) apart. Return pastry to refrigerator while continuing with the recipe.

2. Assemble filling from previous recipe and set aside.

3. In a food processor, process almonds and sugar until almonds are finely ground. Add butter, flour, egg, almond extract and salt and pulse until well mixed. The frangipane should be thick.

4. Add a large spoonful of frangipane onto center of each pastry square and spread out evenly into a 4-inch (10 cm) circle. (You may have some left over.) Divide plum mixture among the squares. (You may have some left over. Be careful not to overfill. You will need to pull the pastry up and over the tops a bit.) Once they are all filled, bring tips of corners of pastry up and over top of tartlets. Pinch open corners so it forms a cup so the filling doesn't escape. Brush tartlets with egg wash and sprinkle with sugar. Bake on lower rack in preheated oven for 25 minutes or until golden and crisp on bottom. Let cool on a wire rack.

5. To serve, place a warm tartlet on each plate along with a scoop of ice cream and a shot glass of plum brandy.

THE DISH **Frangipane.** A mixture of blanched ground almonds, butter, eggs and sugar, frangipane is a welcome addition to fruit tarts. There are a number of fruits that go well with frangipane. We think that plums are the tastiest, but pears and apples come a close second and third.

Fashion Plate

Begin a meal with Frisée Salad with Warm Bacon and Balsamic Vinaigrette (page 63), Braised Short Ribs (page 192) and end with Individual Plum Tartlets with Frangipane and Plum Brandy.

Flaky Pastry

Ahh . . . pastry. Once you know how to make it, this buttery dough opens the door to countless desserts and crusty-topped savories. The ingredients are as basic as it gets, but the path to superlative pastry lies, literally, in the tips of your fingers. Cold hands are a bonus when working with pastry because your fingers won't heat up the dough as fast. Finally, a plus for all you cold-handed warm hearts out there.

Makes one 14-inch (35 cm) shell

Hands-on time
10 minutes

Start to finish
1 hour 10 minutes

Tip

The taste and texture of homemade pastry is always preferable to store-bought — especially when you know how to make an all-butter pastry devoid of those nasty-tasting and bad-for-you manufactured trans fats found in hydrogenated oils.

- **Food processor**

1½ cups	all-purpose flour, chilled in refrigerator for 30 minutes (see Tip, page 367)	375 mL
10 tbsp	cold unsalted butter, cut into ½-inch (1 cm) cubes	150 mL
¼ tsp	salt	1 mL
⅓ cup	ice water	75 mL

1. *Food processor method:* In a food processor, pulse chilled flour, cold butter and salt with 10 short bursts or until butter is the size of small peas.

2. Through the feed tube, with motor running, quickly add ice water while pulsing dough. When dough almost comes together, stop the machine. To make tender, flaky pastry, it is important not to overprocess at this point. Remove pastry from bowl and compress with your hands into a disk. Wrap in plastic wrap and refrigerate for about 30 minutes to chill and make easier to roll out.

3. *Hand method:* In a medium bowl, combine chilled flour, butter and salt and mix flour and butter together by rubbing between your fingertips. When mixture looks like cornmeal with small pea-size lumps of butter, sprinkle water over mixture and continue to work with your fingertips until it begins to come together. Turn mixture out onto a work surface and compress with your hands until it comes together and forms a disk. Refrigerate as directed above.

How to Roll Pastry

When you are ready to roll out the dough, lightly flour a work surface. Place chilled disk of dough on top of flour and lightly dust top of the disk with flour. Roll dough gently but firmly, picking up after each roll and rotating from 12 o'clock to 3 o'clock. This rotation keeps dough from sticking and also helps dough to keep its round shape. Add a dusting of additional flour to the work surface under the pastry, if necessary.

When you have rolled dough to its desired thickness (typically about $\frac{1}{8}$ inch/3 mm thick), fold dough in half and then into a quarter to prevent dough from tearing while in transit from work surface to pie plate. If dough warms up appreciably, refrigerate for about 10 minutes before proceeding with recipe.

Freezing Rolled Dough

Wrap circle of dough between sheets of parchment paper on a baking sheet, wrap the sheet in plastic wrap and freeze for up to 6 weeks. To thaw, simply remove rolled pastry sheet on the parchment from freezer and let stand on the counter for about 30 minutes. It is ready to use when it becomes pliable and easily fits into your baking pan. Do not let it warm up too much; it should remain chilled.

If you don't have space in your freezer for rolled-out dough, freeze the unrolled disk wrapped in plastic wrap and then sealed in a resealable bag. To thaw, transfer the disk from the freezer to the refrigerator and let thaw overnight. It might still be too firm to roll out. In that case, allow the pastry disk to stand at room temperature for about 10 minutes. It should roll out nicely at that point.

Tip

Making pastry is really pretty simple. The trick is in keeping the ingredients cold and working quickly. Our recommendation is to make two or more batches whenever the spirit strikes you, since they freeze beautifully and are the key to quick and easy pies, tarts or pot pies on the fly.

Chocolate Chip and Ice Cream Cookie-Wiches

In memory of delightful days gone by, how about serving a grownup ice cream sandwich at your next soiree? Chewy and chock full of chips, these cookies are just the ticket to envelope your favorite ice cream, allowing you and your friends to once again eat ice cream with your fingers.

Makes about 13 cookie-wiches

Hands-on time
30 minutes

Start to finish
1 hour

Tip

We think it's always a good idea to go the less processed route with food products. They are generally healthier, with more of their nutrition intact. That's why we use unbleached flour when baking or cooking. There can be a slightly higher gluten content, so it takes a bit more water to moisten than bleached flour. If you use bleached flour, hold back a teaspoon or so of the liquid to be sure that the dough doesn't become too wet. If you need more moisture, just go ahead and add the remaining water. Better safe than sorry.

- **Preheat the oven to 350°F (180°C)**
- **2-tbsp (30 mL) ice cream scoop**
- **Baking sheets, lined with parchment paper**

2½ cups	all-purpose flour (see Tip, left)	625 mL
1 tsp	baking soda	5 mL
1 tsp	salt	5 mL
1 cup	unsalted butter, at room temperature	250 mL
¾ cup	lightly packed light brown sugar	175 mL
½ cup	granulated sugar	125 mL
2 tsp	vanilla extract	10 mL
2	large eggs	2
2 cups	semisweet chocolate chips	500 mL
2 quarts	your favorite ice cream or gelato	2 L
1 cup	miniature chocolate chips	250 mL

1. In a medium bowl, sift together flour, baking soda and salt. Set aside.

2. In a large bowl, using an electric mixture, cream together butter, brown sugar and granulated sugar until light and fluffy. Scrape down sides of bowl with a rubber spatula. Beat in vanilla and eggs. On low speed, gradually beat in dry ingredients, beating until a smooth batter forms. Using rubber spatula, stir in semisweet chocolate chips.

3. Using ice cream scoop, drop dough onto prepared baking sheets, about 2 inches (5 cm) apart. Bake, one sheet at a time, in preheated oven for about 15 minutes or until cookies are light brown for chewy cookies.

4. Let cookies cool on baking sheets for 1 minute before transferring to a wire rack to cool completely. Repeat with remaining dough.

5. Soften ice cream so that it is easy to scoop. (Leave at room temperature for about 10 minutes to soften.) Place a dollop of ice cream (about ¼ cup/60 mL) on the bottom of 1 cookie and top it, bottom side down, with another cookie. Squeeze cookies together so that the ice cream spreads to the edges of the cookie. (Be careful not to let the cookie crumble.) Do the same with the remaining cookies and ice cream, returning the cookie-wiches as they are made to the freezer. Ideally the cookie-wiches should freeze for at least 2 hours. You will want the ice cream to be firm so that it doesn't spread out from the sides when you bite into it.

6. Just before serving, dump miniature chocolate chips into a wide bowl or plate. Garnish ice cream edges with chips by lightly dipping the sandwich into chips all around outside edge. Serve immediately.

THE DISH **Small Ice Cream Scoop.** A petite scoop (2 tbsp/30 mL size) will come in handy anytime you make cookies. For one thing, it keeps the cookies a uniform size. But the real reason we love scooping cookies onto a baking sheet is because it saves time. Look for a variety of scoops at kitchenware stores or some supermarkets. You will use them more often than you think.

Make Ahead

The cookies can be made and frozen for up to 2 weeks. The assembled cookie-wiches can be frozen for up to 1 week. Thaw for 45 minutes in the refrigerator before serving to soften them up a bit.

Fashion Plate

These little ice cream sandwiches would be fun to serve after a night of nibbling appetizers. Three of our favorites are Bruschetta with Tuscan White Beans, Kalamata Olives and Roasted Red Peppers (page 50), Grilled Prosciutto-Wrapped Scallop Skewers (page 26) and Mini Grilled Caramelized Onion and Brie Sandwiches (page 34).

Coffee Cookie Tower with Espresso Hot Fudge Sauce

If the previous recipe gets in touch with your inner child, this grownup version can be said to leave even the most jaded sweet tooth hungry for more. If you love coffee, this impressive ode to the bean blends the flavors of chocolate chip cookies, coffee ice cream and espresso hot fudge sauce. If you enjoy a cup of joe as a pick-me-up, this dessert will blast you into the stratosphere.

Serves 6

Hands-on time
30 minutes

Freezing time
2 hours

Start to finish
2 hours 30 minutes

Tip

If you want to save the remaining cookie dough for another time, freeze the uncooked balls of dough on a sheet pan. Once frozen, transfer them to a resealable freezer bag and save in the freezer to bake off at another time. When ready to bake, just set them out on a parchment-lined baking sheet and let stand while the oven preheats. Bake as directed.

- **Six 8-oz (227 g) cans, with both ends cut out (see The Dish, right)**
- **Baking sheet, lined with parchment paper**

1	recipe Chocolate Chip Ice Cream Cookie-Wiches (page 368)	1
2 quarts	coffee ice cream or gelato	2 L
1 cup	miniature chocolate chips	250 mL
½ cup	heavy or whipping (35%) cream	125 mL
⅓ cup	light corn syrup	75 mL
¼ cup	packed dark brown sugar	60 mL
¼ cup	unsweetened cocoa powder	60 mL
1 tbsp	espresso powder, dissolved in 2 tbsp (30 mL) hot water	15 mL
¼ tsp	salt	1 mL
	Grated zest of 1 orange	
6 oz	bittersweet (dark) chocolate, finely chopped	175 g
2 tbsp	unsalted butter	30 mL
1 tsp	vanilla extract	5 mL
	Chocolate-covered coffee beans, optional	

1. Complete previous recipe through Step 4, baking only 12 cookies (see Tip, left).

2. Soften ice cream so that it is easy to scoop. Arrange 6 empty cans on prepared baking sheet. Drop one cookie down into each. If cookies are a little large, just press can down onto them to cut away some of the overlapping edges. Drop in a scoop of ice cream (about ¼ cup/60 mL). Working quickly, smooth and spread ice cream to edges of can (a fork works well) and top ice cream with one of the cookies, bottom side down. Add another layer of ice cream and smooth top again. Sprinkle evenly with chocolate chips. Freeze tray of molds for at least 2 hours for ice cream to firm up.

3. Meanwhile, make hot fudge sauce. In a medium saucepan, combine cream, corn syrup, brown sugar, cocoa powder, espresso, salt and orange zest. Bring mixture to a boil over medium-high heat, stirring to dissolve sugar. Reduce heat to medium and boil, stirring occasionally, for about 5 minutes, until thickened. Remove pan from heat and add chocolate, butter and vanilla. Stir to melt chocolate. Set aside.

4. To unmold towers, run a sharp knife around perimeter of mold. Push down on center of tower while lifting can up. Drizzle warm sauce over top of the tower and around the perimeter of the plate. Garnish with a few chocolate-covered coffee beans, if desired.

THE DISH **Leftover 8-oz (227 g) Cans.** We like the ones that are 3 inches (7.5 cm) in diameter that bamboo shoots and canned tuna (thoroughly washed, of course) come in. The cans will serve as a mold for each individual cookie tower. You can also use the cans to mold hot couscous or pilaf, roasted vegetables, potato salad, coleslaw, etc., on a plate.

Make Ahead

The towers can be assembled, covered and frozen 2 weeks before serving. The fudge sauce can be made up to 4 days in advance and kept covered and refrigerated. Reheat the sauce in a heatproof bowl set over simmering water.

Fashion Plate

We like to pair this impressive dessert with a meal beginning with Whole-Leaf Caesar Salad with Parmesan Fricos (page 66), Grilled Pork Tenderloin with Berry Sauce (page 214) and Roasted Butternut Squash with Goat Cheese and Pecans (page 316).

Navel Oranges with Caramel

Oranges and caramel are a classic duo, much like coffee and chocolate. Both are great alone but are really good paired.

You won't believe how easy it is to pull this bright orange and crispy caramel-flecked dish together. We find ourselves craving it every few weeks or so, even for breakfast, so stock up on the citrus. It's good for you. Really!

Serves 4

Hands-on time
30 minutes

Start to finish
30 minutes

Make Ahead

The hard caramel will melt into a delicious syrup if the oranges are held, covered and refrigerated, for more than 4 hours. (We like it both ways.)

- **Heatproof serving plate**

4	navel oranges, peeled and sliced into rounds	4
⅔ cup	granulated sugar	150 mL

1. Arrange oranges on heatproof serving plate.

2. In a small saucepan, heat sugar and ¼ cup (60 mL) water over medium-high heat, without stirring, until sugar is melted. (Swirl pan to wet down sugar and a few times more to melt sugar evenly.) Boil, without swirling, until syrup begins to turn amber. At this point watch the syrup carefully as it will brown quickly. Boil until syrup is a dark, caramelized amber color. Immediately remove from heat and drizzle over oranges.

3. Serve warm or refrigerate for up to 8 hours.

THE DISH   **The Winter Blues.** This is the perfect remedy, because at no time of the year can you enjoy naval oranges more than in the dead of winter. When all our other fruit and veggie friends lie dormant, citrus fruits come to life.

Fashion Plate

This light and refreshing dish would be the perfect ending after a meal of Pear Salad with Hazelnuts and Gorgonzola (page 94) and Roasted Vegetable Soup with Harissa (page 141).

Oranges and Pink Grapefruit with Cardamom and Ginger

If you ever wondered what dessert they eat at the Kasbah, now you know. The flavors of cardamom and ginger epitomize Middle Eastern cooking. Here, the fragrant cardamom gives a touch of sophistication to this dish of succulent citrus and toasty-sweet caramel. Then we've topped it off with candied ginger for just a hint of sweet heat. It's so good even Bogie would ask you to "Play it again, Mam."

Serves 4

Hands-on time
30 minutes

Start to finish
30 minutes

Tip

Cardamom seeds often come in a pale-colored pod that can be crushed to free the seeds (the pod is edible, but it may not look very nice in your caramel). Just dump the crushed pods through a fine-mesh sieve and collect the seeds. Or they can be purchased already free of the pods (desiccated). The way that we don't want you to buy them is ground, because the cardamom seeds begin to lose essential oils as soon as they're ground, thereby diminishing in flavor and aroma. They're expensive little babies, but the good news is that a little cardamom goes a long way. Grind them up fresh in a mortar and pestle for the best flavor.

- **Heatproof serving platter**

2	navel oranges, peeled and sliced into rounds	2
2	pink grapefruit, peeled, seeded and sliced into half rounds	2
Pinch	cardamom seeds (see Tip, left)	Pinch
⅔ cup	granulated sugar	150 mL
2 tbsp	chopped candied ginger	30 mL

1. Arrange oranges and grapefruit on a heatproof serving plate. Crack cardamom seeds or grind in a mortar and pestle.

2. In a small saucepan, heat sugar, ¼ cup (60 mL) water and cardamom seeds over medium-high heat, without stirring, until sugar is melted. (Swirl pan to wet down sugar and a few times more to melt sugar evenly.) Boil, without swirling, until syrup begins to turn amber. At this point watch the syrup carefully as it will brown quickly. Boil until syrup is a dark, caramelized amber color. Immediately remove from heat and drizzle over oranges and grapefruit. Scatter candied ginger over all.

3. Serve warm or refrigerate for up to 8 hours.

THE DISH **Cardamom Seeds.** Cardamom is a fragrant spice with a warm, spicy-sweet flavor. It is one of the key spices in Indian curries and many Middle Eastern dishes. Its unique taste makes it an absolute The Dish for this dish and many others, as there is no real substitute for its distinctive flavor.

Index

C

D

Library and Archives Canada Cataloguing in Publication

Deeds, Meredith
Everyday to entertaining : 200 sensational recipes that transform from casual to elegant / Meredith Deeds, Carla Snyder.

Includes index.
ISBN 978-0-7788-0271-6

1. Entertaining. 2. Cooking. I. Snyder, Carla II. Title.

TX714.D434 2011   642'.4   C2010-907389-4